GEND

Series editors:
Lynn Abrams, Cordelia Beattie, Pam Sharpe and Penny Summerfield

The expansion of research into the history of women and gender since the 1970s has changed the face of history. Using the insights of feminist theory and of historians of women, gender historians have explored the configuration in the past of gender identities and relations between the sexes. They have also investigated the history of sexuality and family relations, and analysed ideas and ideals of masculinity and femininity. Yet gender history has not abandoned the original, inspirational project of women's history: to recover and reveal the lived experience of women in the past and the present.

The series Gender in History provides a forum for these developments. Its historical coverage extends from the medieval to the modern periods, and its geographical scope encompasses not only Europe and North America but all corners of the globe. The series aims to investigate the social and cultural constructions of gender in historical sources, as well as the gendering of historical discourse itself. It embraces both detailed case studies of specific regions or periods, and broader treatments of major themes. Gender in History titles are designed to meet the needs of both scholars and students working in this dynamic area of historical research.

The 'perpetual fair'

Manchester University Press

THE 'PERPETUAL FAIR'
GENDER, DISORDER, AND URBAN AMUSEMENT IN EIGHTEENTH-CENTURY LONDON

―― Anne Wohlcke ――

Manchester University Press

Published by Manchester University Press
Altrincham Street, Manchester M1 7JA, UK
www.manchesteruniversitypress.co.uk

British Library Cataloguing-in-Publication Data is available

Library of Congress Cataloging-in-Publication Data is available

ISBN 978 1 7849 9287 3 *paperback*

First published by Manchester University Press in hardback 2014

This edition first published 2016

Printed by Lightning Source

For David

Contents

Figures

Abbreviations

BL	British Library
LMA	London Metropolitan Archives
NA	National Archives
OBP	Proceedings of the Old Bailey
Rep	Repertories of the Court of Aldermen

Acknowledgements

I am grateful for the guidance of many individuals who provided direction and encouragement throughout the research and writing process. My project has benefited from conversations with historians I admire greatly, including Lamar Hill, Ulrike Strasser, Tim Tackett, Bob Moeller, Lynn Mally, Mark Poster, Marjorie Beale, Heidi Tinsman, Amy Nelson, Kathy Jones, and Roger Ekirch. I appreciate, also, the camaraderie of colleagues in graduate seminars at UC Irvine, who helped shape this project at its earliest stages. I am grateful especially to Sharlene Sayegh and Birte Pfleger for their support and friendship. My work has profited from professional advice and input received from numerous scholars more recently, including Philippa Levine, Elise Wirtschafter, Miles Ogborn, Erika Rappaport, Chris Taylor, Brad Wood, Eileen Wallis, Amanda Podany, and others who took time out of busy schedules to answer questions and provide feedback. In addition, I thank readers and staff at Manchester University Press for insightful and helpful comments.

Archivists, of course, are central to the success of any historical project. I benefited from assistance from Jennifer Thorp, curator of the Highclere Castle archives, the curators of the John Johnson Collection at the Bodleian Library, the staff at the British Library, National Archives, Guildhall Library, London Metropolitan Archives, Huntington Library, Lewis Walpole Library, and Folger Shakespeare Library. This project emerged during an archival digital revolution and since its beginning, revisiting essential documents from London archives has become easier due largely to the efforts of Tim Hitchcock and Robert Shoemaker. I want to extend my appreciation to these two scholars for their successful implementation of vitally important digital archive collections.

No project is possible without financial assistance, and I wish to thank the American Historical Association for the Bernadotte E. Schmitt research grant, UC Irvine School of Humanities and Department of History, Eastern Kentucky University, and California State Polytechnic University, Pomona for funding various stages of this project. Thanks also to Starlyn Vrigo and David Baeza, my graduate assistants.

I am most grateful for my family's much needed support. I am indebted especially to Maia and Cian for their understanding and patience and to David Sheridan, for his emotional support, steadfast encouragement, humour, and willingness to read and comment on successive drafts of chapters during each stage of writing. In thanks for his tireless dedication and love, I dedicate this book to him.

Introduction: Making a mannered metropolis and taming the 'perpetual fair'

England hath Fairs and Markets in abundance, and, in general, all Sorts of Means and Conveniencies for Trade. Bartholomew Fair is the greatest in London; indeed there is no great Business done at it, but the City of London it self is a perpetual Fair.[1]
(Henri Misson, London, 1719)

In 1738, a caravan containing a collection of wild beasts travelled along Cheapside as it made its way – most likely from Bartholomew Fair in West Smithfield – to Southwark Fair. The showman escorted his cargo through this neighbourhood of merchants, shops, and 'occasional gentlemen', when a wagon wheel broke and animals spilled out of their cages. Businessmen and women were so alarmed that they considered closing their shops, despite it being the noon hour. This threatened disruption to Cheapside, the central commercial street in London, at the peak of the workday was narrowly avoided when the showman collected his animals and proved to the local businessmen and women 'that his Beasts were securely chain'd down'. Once local fears were 'dispers'd [and] a new Wheel [was] fix'd ... the Caravan [was] convey'd safely to Southwark'.[2] Contradictory forms of commerce existed in early eighteenth-century London.[3] This September noonday, London's transient business of peddling curiosities collided with business conducted in brick shops. From the perspective of shopkeepers and city officials, streets free of wild beasts or other dangers were the ideal setting for polite and orderly commerce.[4]

Eighteenth-century London saw the emergence of a thriving commercial network of shops and services, many of which were housed in permanent and, in some cases, grand new buildings in both the City and the newer West End.[5] Even as London's shops and industries boomed, outdoor commerce thrived along London streets and at the city's many spring- and summer-time fairs. Increased availability of consumer goods and a growing pool of labourers who entered London each day fuelled both transient and fixed industries.[6] As people continued to recognize opportunities to profit in the mobile commerce of fairs, urban authorities found it difficult to enforce their own preference for one type of commerce above another. This book analyses urban debates regarding the place of festivity in the metropolis. London's fairs were discussed in city records, sermons, and pamphlet literature. These sources reveal diverse opinions about the roles of commerce and festivity in the city and reflect shifting understandings of what constituted appropriate public behaviour in urban spaces. Arguments about the worth of fairs are often gendered – they reflect understandings and expectations of urban authorities and spectators of what was appropriate male or female urban behaviour, and also demonstrate fears about the containment of festive (and often unruly) masculinity and femininity. An analysis of London-area fairs reveals how the potential of urban spaces and practices to disrupt idealized gender hierarchies and relations attracted city authorities' notice. At the same time, these locations provided participants a venue in which to contest or claim and gather status from idealized understandings of gender.[7]

Festivity was one of the primary attractions of early modern London, which was rich in civic and royal pageantry. The city offered plenty in the way of theatrical and musical entertainment, was full of coffee houses and taverns, and was the site for many spring- and summer-time fairs. Even public punishments, such as whippings or executions, drew crowds.[8] Festive occasions provided Londoners from all social backgrounds opportunities to express urban identities. Whether structured by civic agendas, as were Lord Mayor pageants, unstructured and impromptu, such as the unchartered Tottenham Court Fair, or coordinated by entrepreneurs providing entertainment for a fee in places such as Sadler's Wells or Ranelagh House, festivity provided Londoners spaces to comment upon, profit from, and interact with each other and their changing urban environment.[9] Meanwhile, festive London spaces came to represent the overall vibrancy, diversity, and potential of the growing metropolis. Fairs, in particular, represented London in microcosm to many social commentators. Urban festivity drew the types of large crowds only found within Britain in London – men, women, labouring and elite, soldiers and civilians, criminals and religious – all among monsters, rope dancers, hawkers, gingerbread sellers, gamesters, musicians, and actors. Such gatherings demonstrated London's potential and resources that urban officials likely hoped could be harnessed and directed in an orderly fashion, yet fairs were also contrary – they were difficult to contain and embodied disruptive social and cultural potential.

Over the course of the seventeenth century, London's population grew from about 200,000 people to half a million.[10] Most of the growth occurred in suburban areas outside of the City's jurisdiction, but population growth and the expansion of the metropolis meant more than physical changes to London's urban landscape. This expansion was attended by social and cultural changes, as well. New housing arrangements, patterns of consumption, traffic, and pollution shaped urban experience at all levels.[11] The changing spaces of metropolitan London influenced how individuals located 'themselves – mentally and geographically – within the city' during this remarkable period of transformation.[12] Through an analysis of metropolitan fairs, this book explores the ways in which people's use of streets for seasonal festivity changed and gained new significance during a period marked by urban transformation.

Fairs were sites that existed between two worlds. As institutions with medieval and religious origins, they had transformed to largely secular events dedicated primarily to commercial entertainment by the early eighteenth century. Most fairs also crossed social boundaries. Fairs do not fit neatly during a time in which historians argue we see social distancing and a demarcation between 'popular' and elite entertainments. Fairs complicate this narrative because Londoners of all social backgrounds sought diversion at fairs. While eighteenth-century Londoners continued to enjoy the business opportunities and leisure offered at fairs, social commentators were increasingly worried by the possibility that they were unstable events representing a style of commerce and popular practice that was not easily contained. Drawing large crowds and encouraging drinking and a host of other immoral behaviour, fairs seemed particularly dangerous in a city growing faster than could be captured in maps and street directories.[13] Commentary about fairs and legal attempts to regulate them reveal the larger negotiations undertaken by those who lived within the 'strange mélange of new and old' that London had become by the early eighteenth century.[14]

Festive use of city spaces examined within the context of commentary about that use reveals the ways in which particular urban spaces acquired meaning.[15] Men and women of various social backgrounds and ages attended and worked at fairs. There, they utilized fairs in ways that suited their own needs or interests, but did so within a society that ascribed particular gendered meanings to their behaviours at fairs. Social commentary conveyed prescriptions about what men or women 'ought' to do (or not do) at fairs. Men and women carried on in their use of that space, upon occasion revealing that they did understand the gendered significance of their behaviour at fairs.[16] People's use of fair space at times flouted conventional ideas about appropriate use of those spaces, but often it did not. A historical examination of the everyday use of fairs within the context of gendered prescriptions attempting to circumscribe that behaviour provides insight into the way in which spaces became gendered and how 'gender roles as actually lived were complex interactions of ideas and material circumstances'.[17]

Local urban authorities did what they could to curtail fairs, but beyond issuing orders their efforts were largely ineffective. London was governed within the City and Southwark by the Court of Aldermen – a group of men, each elected for life, to lead individual wards established by royal charter. Each year, one Alderman served as Lord Mayor. From among the Aldermen, City magistrates were chosen to hold the sessions of the peace eight times a year. The areas outside of the City were governed by the magistrates from those counties. From the Thames north, the Middlesex magistrates oversaw the metropolis.[18] These two jurisdictions, the City and Middlesex county, both of which saw an increase in fair entertainment, are the focus of this book. Enforcing urban orders and ensuring public safety depended upon constables and night watchmen, who often found this an overwhelming task, especially during times of urban festivity.[19] These men were joined in their efforts by groups of reform-minded Londoners, often members of reforming groups promoting the reformation of manners, who policed city streets informing on any illicit activities they witnessed. Despite official and voluntary urban reform efforts, London festivity continued and became increasingly popular. The struggle among urban authorities, business men and women, and fair-goers, all who continued to partake in this seasonal festivity, was intense. This contestation over festive uses of urban space was instrumental in determining the place, appropriateness, and function of amusement in the 'modern' metropolis.

Dissolute, disorderly, and immoral: Urban festivity and social order

Urban authorities who hoped to preside over a mannered and 'polite' city consistently encountered the everyday reality of the metropolis.[20] Eighteenth-century writers such as John Gay wrote about dirty streets peopled with 'clashing wheels, lashing whips, dashing hoofs, hawkers' cries' and the trampling feet of 'crouds heap'd on crouds', and this was during an average London day.[21] During fairs, streets became even more crowded, dirty, and noisy. City fathers and social critics with idealistic hopes that city streets could be mannered according to their own polite understandings found such notions meant little when juxtaposed against the everyday life of the city. Discourses regarding polite urban behaviour taught that as city leaders controlled their actions and words, and adopted pleasing, clean and fashionable personae, so might other Londoners who followed their lead. Polite men and women did walk along city streets and even entered fair grounds on occasion. Here, though, they might meet a similar fate to that of the cook, Joseph Underwood, who, while dressed in his finest and helping a female member of his party cross the street, was assaulted by a crowd of unruly men and stripped of his wig, walking stick, and watch.[22] Both local and national authorities viewed late seventeenth- and early eighteenth-century London as a centre of 'dissolute immoral and disorderly practices', which they believed fairs encouraged.[23] Such practices not only endangered the safety of local inhabitants, they were perceived also to be a national problem. To be sure, polite men and women faced personal dangers when they walked in urban fairs. Here, they became noticeable targets for pickpockets or other criminals, but to authorities the broader and more potent threat was uncontained, impolite masculinity, which threatened London's and the nation's order in ways which were dangerous beyond a few cuts and bruises, the loss of personal property, and damaged pride. This sort of threatening masculinity was not controlled by dictates of politeness, challenged social hierarchy, and was not fully productive because it often involved men who were not regularly employed.

After the English Civil War, London's Great Fire in 1666, which destroyed nearly 80 per cent of the City of London, and the 'Glorious Revolution', government officials in England, both local and national, became concerned with cleaning up, regulating, and ordering city spaces.[24] Unruly masculinity encouraged by the temptations of fairs seemed particularly dangerous in the context of England's late-Stuart transitions of power. As 'foreign' rulers, William and Mary faced resistance to their authority as they assumed the English monarchy. When the Roman Catholic Stuart monarch James II was ousted, his Protestant daughter and her Dutch husband succeeded him. Though James II was in France, groups of his supporters, or Jacobites, loyal to him and his heirs, remained in England. Monarchs from William and Mary to the Hanoverians faced the threat of Jacobite plots intended to replace them with James II's heirs, and many times crime and Jacobitism coalesced.[25] Highway robbery, smuggling, and poaching were all associated with Jacobitism in the form of 'social banditry', or crime undertaken by 'plebeians motivated by social grievances', instead of necessity.[26] In London, this was a special concern, and fairs seemed ideal locations for such rioting. During the summer months, fairs were frequent sites of rowdy criminal activities including theft, rioting, assaults and, in surrounding areas, highway robberies. National authorities were concerned that disorderly public gatherings could easily become locations for Jacobite plotting and social disturbance.

Urban authorities responded to royal decrees to regulate public amusement, but their attention to unruly activities was motivated by an immediate concern with maintaining order. Frustrated authorities realized their limited means of enforcing orders against fairs and festivities continued despite them. Fairs had only been successfully curtailed during plague years, in 1665 and 1666 for example, in the interest of public safety, and they even appear to have continued in a limited version during the Commonwealth.[27] With the restoration of Charles II, for whom festivity was not a primary concern, fairs predictably increased in duration and number. Both Bartholomew and Southwark fairs lengthened well beyond chartered days and many new fairs appeared. By the time William and Mary and later, Anne, began to put the brakes on Restoration frivolity, celebrations such as Bartholomew Fair extended two weeks instead of the chartered three days. Reform-minded monarchs issued decrees against disorderly amusements in the hopes that their proclamations would encourage public morality and foster the social and political stability they associated with uncontested Protestant leadership. Legislation issued by the City of London echoed higher royal concerns. From the late seventeenth century, City and county officials issued order after order in an effort to curtail unchecked fairs. Though the orders were sometimes successful, fairs continued and by 1763 it seemed that though the largest 'beasts' of Bartholomew and Southwark Fairs could be tamed (Southwark Fair was abolished), it would be difficult to rid London of this type of amusement. Not only were 'pretend' fairs (or fairs held without charters) springing up in areas of the metropolis, but fair-type amusement was becoming commercialized in the form of tea gardens and pleasure gardens oriented towards all classes of Londoners.

Historiographies of a 'modern' metropolis

London and wider England's politically and socially tumultuous seventeenth century has intrigued historians who look at the city as an example of an emerging modern metropolis, though they debate the extent to which it became modern.[28] Some scholars view this period in London's history as one in which events such as political and economic changes, disease, and natural catastrophes worked together to initiate a break with previous social arrangements, architectural styles, and manners. According to this familiar narrative, during the eighteenth century London emerged as a well-populated and commercially influential world centre. As London changed, so too did elite notions about the appropriate use of urban space for amusement. To some observers, spaces of public amusement represented a threat to more than just industry – customary fair entertainment threatened a delicate social and gender system, something many felt was crucial to the maintenance of order in the burgeoning metropolis.[29] As authorities struggled to control the growing London population, they drew from new discourses such as 'politeness', as well as religious discourse. A focus on an eighteenth-century 'break' with pre-modern society obscures our understanding of the ways in which elite notions of appropriate and productive urban behaviour were informed by long-standing religious beliefs just as often as they were informed by new notions of politeness.

A growing literature examines London's transition from a medieval to a 'modern' metropolis.[30] Art historian Elizabeth McKellar's work *The Birth of Modern London* examines London's architecture in the period 1666–1720. She traces the development of new building in London especially after the Fire of 1666, although she argues new building projects were already underway before the fire. Her focus on architecture allows her to demonstrate how London's 'tightly packed warren of medieval buildings' metamorphosed into a 'modern landscape of regularized streets of brick-built properties'.[31] In the process of following changing architectural styles, McKellar introduces a contemporary human perspective all too easy to ignore when the focus is on buildings. She argues against believing London's new building style ushered the city easily into the modern world. By populating this new London, McKellar suggests that much uncertainty accompanied the post-Fire building frenzy. London's inhabitants were particularly worried about the disappearance of open spaces surrounding the city and the types of activities – recreation, food production, military training – these spaces allowed.

Although McKellar's project (as an art historian) remains urban development and design and is never entirely focused on the culture and society of this changing London, she challenges the idea that London developed into a modern and polite city with little opposition and was accepted by contemporaries as the inevitable conclusion to the Great Fire or as an inevitable product of 'modernity'. She emphasizes, instead, the tensions accompanying urban development and the mental impact London's seemingly unfettered urban growth had on the inhabitants of both the city and the larger nation.

Miles Ogborn's work, *Spaces of Modernity, London's Geographies 1680–1780*, also focuses on London's transition to a 'modern' metropolis. Ogborn engages with modernity theorists who see a totalizing movement from communal, agricultural, corporately-ordered societies to capitalist, industrial societies composed of people (men) who see themselves as individuals agreeing to participate in civil society. He examines London as a test case in order to suggest that modernity does not, in actuality, emerge in a totalized and inevitable fashion. Here, he supports Kathleen Wilson, who argues that modernity is not '*one* particular moment, whose "origins" and characteristics can be identified with certainty and mapped onto a specific temporality between the sixteenth and twentieth centuries'. Instead, Wilson sees modernity as a 'set of relations that are constantly being made and remade, contested and reconfigured'.[32] Ogborn supports Wilson's configuration with his analysis of several London spaces – the Magdalen Hospital, the street, the pleasure garden, 'excise geographies', and the Universal Register Office. In these spaces, Ogborn traces the ways in which processes of modernity, such as 'individualization, commodification and bureaucratization' developed and were reacted to in various contexts on an everyday level.[33] He argues that modernity emerges slowly and differently depending upon the historical context. There is no overarching 'modern' which emerges everywhere the same.

Karen Newman continues to dismantle the notion that urban modernity happened with an abrupt rupture. In her study of the cultural spaces of early modern Paris and London, Newman finds these cities featured temporal changes in demographics, economics, and technology that shaped urban space and gave rise to 'forms of cultural capital and articulated certain discursive figures, modes of subjectivity, and enunciation usually claimed solely for modernity'.[34] In the spaces of early modern London – and in particular at its fairs, I argue – one finds the type of nineteenth-century 'Metropolitan subjectivity' theorized by Georg Simmel. This sort of subjectivity was 'a problem of the individual attempting to assert autonomy in the face of metropolitan simulation and distraction: noise, traffic, a market economy, the crowd'.[35] Newman does not advocate moving back the 'Big Ditch' that marks the beginning of modernity; rather, she wants to demonstrate continuities between medieval and 'modern' urban environments. Through an analysis of literary and visual representations of early modern London and Paris, Newman reveals how 'productive relations among city, subject, and text often claimed for the nineteenth century, and more recently the eighteenth century, are already at work in the verbal and visual cultures of early modern London and Paris'.[36]

Early modern London was clearly a city transforming demographically, politically, and culturally, and much recent work examines shifting perceptions of London during this period. Increasingly, many scholars are beginning to interrogate not just the changing shape of the metropolis, but the ways in which individuals lived within and experienced the context of early modern London's shifting urban environment.[37] Scholars not only interrogate London's emerging 'modern' topography, but they locate bodies within that space. London, to early modern contemporaries, 'was not an easily described, neatly enclosed metropolis but a bewildering and disorienting collection of places and spaces, people and commercial items, frustrated desires and unmet expectations'.[38] How people lived within, visited, or imagined this confusing metropolis is not often the focus of studies that examine the emergence of London's architectural or administered modernity. Contemporary critics and legal authorities had much to say about what should have been ideally occurring in London's early modern streets, but these records tell us little about how ordinary Londoners experienced a city imaginatively and literally in flux. While urban development did alter spaces in London, physical changes did not necessarily equate behavioural change. Fairs and the practice of fair-going demonstrate that some urban traditions continued and merely adapted to new contexts. When examined in the context of late Stuart and early Georgian London, commentary regarding fairs as well as the actual practice of fair-going reveal the ways in which Londoners of all classes imagined their relationship to the metropolis, their expectations about what they might gain from or encounter within their city, and their understandings about themselves and their social obligations in the context of the urban environment – or, more concisely, the 'nature of metropolitan experience'.[39] A focus on people's experiences at fairs provides a glimpse of how both male and female Londoners of all social backgrounds negotiated between their expectations of some of London's most cacophonous spaces and the people, behaviours, and spectacles they actually encountered there.

This book continues to challenge understandings of the emergence of modernity in early modern European cities, but from the perspective of popular amusements. An analysis of urban authorities' attempts to control urban amusements reveals the social side of London's changing environment. Just as there were disruptions to the uniformity of London's new topographies in the shape of older buildings, markets, and institutions, there were also disruptions to new conceptions of proper urban behaviour. There was no unified approach behind elite regulation of London festivity, nor was there a uniform response to regulatory efforts. Struggles to define appropriate urban entertainment were met by alternative understandings of festivity held by diverse Londoners. If we abandon the quest to seek the origins of the 'modern' city in late seventeenth- and early eighteenth-century London, and instead seek to understand the ways in which people lived within a constantly shifting and rebuilding environment, the process of creating what we recognize as 'modern' becomes more inclusive, involving diverse Londoners, male and female, working and elite, who defined and utilized urban spaces through the everyday practice of living, working, and surviving.

Before a coherently understood 'modern' London emerged, it played out in urban spaces such as fairs – the city was 'enacted before it was visualized, it walked before it was drawn'.[40] If our objective is to comprehend the way in which London 'became' modern, then we must understand the way in which new spaces were 'consumed'.[41] New styles of architecture, new fashions, new theatres, or new public amusements such as pleasure gardens all communicated elite understandings of what was appropriate and polite behaviour for the eighteenth-century urban environment.[42] Yet, at the same time, long-standing entertainment venues such as fairs remained popular. New entertainments and styles did not replace the old, but rather merged with them and, at times, did successfully break from them. People who attended, consumed, and profited from London's amusements helped define the boundaries of what became 'modern' London festivity.

Investigating the attempted regulation of public amusements tells us a great deal about the ways in which gender was crucial to the regulation and ordering of the urban setting. Historians such as Lena Orlin, Laura Gowing, Susan Amussen, and Lyndal Roper discuss the extent to which gender was essential to the maintenance of social order in post-Reformation Protestant Europe. These scholars demonstrate that as Church authority declined and the influence of Church courts diminished, the family increasingly became the central site of social discipline. Fathers became 'bishops' of their own families – ensuring order both within their households and, by extension, in the villages and cities beyond the walls of their own 'castles'.[43] Existing historiography of early modern gender order and social discipline does not dissolve gradually into similar work written about gender order in the nineteenth century, a time during which social order and women's behaviour was more institutionally overseen by secular courts, police forces, and bureaucracy, as well as by husbands and fathers. An abrupt transition in gender historiography moves from a corporately ordered society to an industrial organized one.

Much work remains before we can understand the process by which gender and ideas about the family's role in society gradually gave way to (or coexisted with) institutionalized means of social control during the transitional period of the late seventeenth to mid-eighteenth centuries. In a quickly expanding urban centre such as London, city authorities attempted the regulation of social behaviour in public places. For a time, customary means of social discipline existed alongside increased city-sponsored regulation. Recognizing the means by which gender expectations worked alongside and sometimes against social regulation allows us to measure the extent to which ideas of order were gendered. Spaces were assigned gendered significance – being present as a 'man' or 'woman' took on particular meanings in various spaces. These meanings varied according to the class and occupation of the individual, as well as to the hierarchical position of observers.[44]

The chronological limits of my study are from the late seventeenth century (a period which marked increased attention to the regulation of public amusement) to the mid-eighteenth century. This period is often overlooked by scholars of London's amusements in favour of the later eighteenth century – a period in which it is easier to focus on only polite entertainment and its meaning for the middling sort.[45] Prior to analysing fairs, Chapter 1 describes them for the twenty-first-century audience. This chapter examines what made fairs fascinating to the men and women who attended them. Spectacles and services at London fairs targeted different audiences – though some were enjoyed equally by both men and women, others were targeted to a specific sex or particular class. It is important to understand what happened at fairs before we can comprehend the gendered significance of consuming particular fair exhibits. Examining the fairground reveals, also, the gender hierarchies and class relationships that existed there. Therefore, this chapter reconstructs the rich and varied experience of fair-going from printed accounts and images of fair spectacles describing everything from the pressing crowds to food and drink to rope-dancing women. This analysis demonstrates just how urban festivities disrupted the usual workings of the city and begins to explain why fair entertainment appealed to a wide social spectrum of Londoners. Understanding the amusements of fairs and the logistics of attending them helps us understand what motivated urban officials to regulate them and why they successfully resisted regulation throughout the early eighteenth century.

Chapter 2 turns from fairs and their entertainments to debates about their dangers. In late Stuart England, some notable and polite London men fashioned themselves into urban patriarchs. Reform movements provided middling London reformers incentive to observe the city around them from a moral high ground. From this perspective, London's fairs seemed dangerous – they threatened social order particularly because they encouraged behaviours contrary to reformers' own notions of polite masculinity. Middling men had available to them two discourses that motivated their urban reform attempts: religious sermons and tracts and satirical periodical literature. Men who heard sermons or read pamphlets regarding the dangers of vice and public immorality looked around them at London's post-fire urban landscape in disarray. Sermons calling for religious renewal or cleaning up social ills and avoiding 'lewd' behaviour took on a specific meaning as they were preached, printed, and disseminated in a city undergoing the constant fluctuation of post-Fire reconstruction. Men who participated in urban reform movements considered London's fairs disorderly events that threatened their gendered ideals. Becoming 'Heroick' Christian informers and policing urban amusements, middling men made themselves essential to the urban environment.

Chapter 3 examines more closely regulation attempts by London's Court of Aldermen and efforts by Middlesex magistrates to curtail fairs. London's Aldermen and Middlesex county authorities believed fairs threatened social and commercial order in London. It is clear that London City and Middlesex county officials shared concerns of social reformers that fairs undermined masculine productivity and encouraged unruly male behaviour. In the era before a uniform, professional police force in London, disorderly fairs contributed to a tenuous social situation in the quickly expanding metropolis. London authorities repeatedly attempted to regulate what they saw as a growing nuisance in the capital city, but men from various social backgrounds contested their attempts. Officials viewed such men as unruly and potentially threatening to local and national order. Ordinary men literally threatened public safety or commerce with their participation in fair amusements while the urban elite who sanctioned fairs flouted local governance in different ways. Court documents reveal a long struggle between urban officials and those who profited from or enjoyed fairs. These records illuminate social reasons beyond discourse that influenced official attempts to regulate fairs. Though much of London was rebuilt after 1666, the city's reconstruction was never implemented according to an overarching plan and an older order remained. Some rebuilt areas may have been constructed along classical lines or featured new improvements, but ordinary men and women's use of these spaces was much slower to change. Londoners continued to use urban spaces according to their customs, occupations, class, and gender.

Literary and artistic representations of the danger of London fairs prominently featured unruly or immoral women. Chapter 4 examines how women's bodies were used to represent the overall danger London's fairs presented the city and even the nation. This chapter provides an overview of the unflattering literary and artistic depictions of women providing services or enjoying the spectacle of fairs, and analyses their significance in terms of early modern notions that gender order was the foundation for a stable society. Fears about the unpredictability of urban amusement were embodied in representations of women who tempted men or flouted gender hierarchy at fairs. Court records, periodicals, pamphlets, sermons, and newspapers relating to London's fairs reveal that social critics shared assumptions that upsetting gender order threatened metropolitan social order. Representations of women at fairs reveal, also, how early modern views of women were adapted to and continued to be invoked in an increasingly modern environment.

Chapter 5 considers whether or not gendered understandings of women's behaviour at fairs developed by elite male writers and artists had any real impact on the lived experience of women who worked at fairs. Though representations of women at London's fairs contributed to negative stereotypes of working women, opportunities for women to profit at fairs remained into the middle of the eighteenth century. Their ability to partake in fair commerce is revealed in court documents (and in one case, in a little-used Pie Powder court record for Bartholomew Fair), lease documents, and even Parliamentary records. As this chapter reveals, though social critics believed women were a dangerous presence at fairs, this discourse had little effect on women's abilities to find work at them. Eighteenth-century representations of the 'fair sex' at work tell us more about gender expectations and social order than they do about women's actual experience at fair grounds.

Though urban officials and middling social reformers believed fairs threatened local and national order, they were in fact instrumental to celebrating local and national events. Chapter 6 examines what a popular audience of London's inhabitants – elite and non-elite – gained from their consumption of fair amusements. Print evidence of fair culture reveals the messages ordinary men and women consumed at fairs. These messages reflected and helped shape gendered understandings of men and women's appropriate place in Britain. Theatrical entertainments and fair exhibits such as clocks or mechanical pictures reveal themes of local and national significance. In the context of international conflicts, fair exhibits communicated notions of one's role in the increasingly global community of Britain. The fair ground was also a site at which a popular audience encountered ideas about 'science' and nation at exhibits and spectacles. While there was certainly not an 'official' popular scientific culture at fairs, during the late seventeenth century, fair-goers who could afford it saw some of the same curiosities also exhibited at court. These curiosities contributed to fair-goers' understandings of the larger world and their place, as Londoners and Britons, within it. Fair exhibits disseminated to popular audiences notions of local and national identity through plays, waxworks, clocks, and other exhibits illustrating national victories, royal lineages and masterpieces of British architecture, and the natural landscape. The visual and popular culture of fairs demonstrates that Britons of various economic and ethnic backgrounds actively contributed to national imagining. National identities were not consolidated only in the world of print or in strictly political contexts.

Opportunities for public urban entertainment remained a central and visible aspect of London life from the late seventeenth through mid-eighteenth century. While occasions for festivity grew, so did new understandings of the usefulness of urban entertainment. Perceptions of public amusement tell us much about how various groups imagined how London's urban spaces should be used and by whom. Debates about public amusement in court records, printed literature, and sermons reveal conflicting understandings of the appropriate organization and uses of urban space. From eighteenth-century Vauxhall, to the nineteenth-century Crystal Palace, and today's South Bank featuring the 'London Eye', popularly accessible amusement has been an important aspect of London life. This book explores the process by which public amusement was institutionalized as one aspect of London's and by extension, England's (and later, Britain's), national identity.

London's eighteenth-century amusements are often understood as something consumed by members of the increasingly polite middling sort, who used new entertainment venues to showcase their personal wealth, learn about style, or attract a spouse.[46] This study avoids focusing solely on middling consumption of public amusements and looks at fairs, instead, because diverse Londoners frequented them. It is this wide appeal that makes fairs ideal locations to examine usages of urban space for amusement. Public amusements were more than a forum for middle-class or elite identity formation – they were also locations of identity formation for working or unemployed people. Fairs were centres of vital business networks providing not only entertainment but also food, lodging, and shops connected with or supporting fairs. At spaces such as fairs, Londoners formulated common understandings both in relation to the objects and pleasures they consumed as well as to each other. Beyond identity formation, a focus on both the consumption and production of fair entertainment provides a lens through which we can explore the development and function of sociable space in a transforming metropolis.

Notes

1 Henri Misson, M. *Misson's Memoirs and Observations in his Travels over England. With Some Account of Scotland and Ireland. Dispos'd in alphabetical order. Written originally in French.* (London, 1719), 77.

2 *Daily Post,* 9 September 1738; *The Weekly Miscellany,* 15 September 1738.

3 Peter Earle describes the demographics and topography of Cheapside in *A City Full of People: Men and Women of London, 1650-1750* (London: Methuen, 1994), 13-14.

4 Wild beasts spilling out onto Cheapside had particular meaning because, as Paul Griffiths has argued, the central thoroughfare was a symbolically important space. It was both a commercial centre and, 'political space where verbal and visual statements of meanings of order were emphasized, and a key point on the map of civic and royal ritual, as well as on the route followed when offenders were led around the city for public punishment in busy locations': see 'Politics Made Visible: Order, Residence and Uniformity in Cheapside, 1600-45', in Griffiths and Jenner (eds), *Londinopolis: Essays in the Cultural and Social History of Early Modern London* (Manchester: Manchester University Press, 2000), 176.

5 Roy Porter, *London: A Social History* (Cambridge, MA: Harvard University Press, 1994), 142-4.

6 A.L. Beier and Roger Finlay, 'Introduction, The Significance of the Metropolis', in Beier and Finlay, *The Making of the Metropolis, London, 1500-1700* (London and New York: Longman, 1985).

7 In Amanda Bailey and Roze Hentschell (eds). *Masculinity and the Metropolis of Vice, 1550-1650* (New York: Palgrave Macmillan, 2010), the editors demonstrate that the 'early modern city' offered men, in particular, 'myriad opportunities ... to gain from, reject, or even revise patriarchal dictates', 3.

8 Robert Shoemaker, 'Streets of Shame? The Crowd and Public Punishments in London, 1700-1820', in Simon Devereaux and Paul Griffiths (eds), *Penal Practice and Culture, 1500-1900: Punishing the English* (New York: Palgrave Macmillan, 2004), 232-53. Interestingly, the continuation of public punishment was debated due to similar concerns regarding the appropriate use of London's streets and obstructions to commercial interests.

9 Jean E. Howard argues that theatre also importantly shaped how early modern Londoners made sense of their changing city, in *Theatre of a City: The Places of London Comedy, 1598-1642* (Philadelphia: University of Pennsylvania Press, 2007), 2.

10 R. Finlay, *Population and Metropolis: The Demography of London, 1580-1639* (Cambridge: Cambridge University Press, 1981); R. Finlay and B. Shearer, 'Population Growth and Suburban Expansion', in Beier and Finlay (eds), *London 1500-1700: The Making of the Metropolis*; J.F. Merritt (ed.), *Imagining Early Modern London: Perceptions and Portrayals of the City from Stow to Strype 1598-1720* (Cambridge: Cambridge University Press, 2001), 1-2.

11 Merritt, *Imagining Early Modern London*, 1-2. See also Griffiths and Jenner, *Londinopolis*, 1-3.

12 Merritt, *Imagining Early Modern London,* 2. Scholars are increasingly considering not just the demographics or political significance of the sprawling metropolis, but

'how early modern contemporaries themselves viewed the city and its sprawling suburbs'. Chris R. Kyle, 'Remapping London,' *Huntington Library Quarterly* 71, no. 1 (March 2008): 244.

13 Merritt, *Imagining Early Modern London*, 8–9.

14 Ibid., 5.

15 Amanda Flather discusses the theories of anthropologist Doreen Massey and their application to thinking about space in early modern England in *Gender and Space in Early Modern England* (London: Royal Historical Society/Boydell Press, 2007), 2.

16 See for example Elizabeth Pulwash (Pate), whose rape outside of Tottenham Court Fair in 1736 is discussed in Chapter 6.

17 Flather, *Gender and Space*, 8–9. In her study of London-based comedy, Jean R. Howard demonstrates how the city frequently featured as 'a place where both status and gender relations were constantly being renegotiated', *Theatre of a City*, 27.

18 Both the government and policing functions of London are described in J.M. Beattie, *Policing and Punishment in London, 1660–1750: Urban Crime and the Limits of Terror* (Oxford: Oxford University Press, 2001).

19 See David Cressy, *Bonfires and Bells: National Memory and the Protestant Calendar in Elizabethan and Stuart England* (Berkeley: University of California Press, 1989); and Beattie, *Policing and Punishment*, Chapter 3.

20 Literature on the development of 'politeness' in London and wider Britain is numerous and includes Lawrence Klein, *Shaftesbury and the Culture of Politeness: Moral Discourse and Cultural Politics in Early Eighteenth-Century England* (Cambridge and New York: Cambridge University Press, 1994); Paul Langford, *A Polite and Commercial People. England 1727–1783* (Oxford: Clarendon Press, 1989); J.G.A. Pocock, *Virtue, Commerce and History* (Cambridge and New York: Cambridge University Press, 1985); Tim Hitchcock and Michèle Cohen (eds), *English Masculinities, 1660–1800* (London and New York: Longman, 1999); Philip Carter, *Men and the Emergence of Polite Society, Britain, 1660–1800* (Harlow, Essex: Pearson Education, 2001).

21 Earle, *A City Full of People*, 5–6.

22 *Old Bailey Proceedings Online* (www.oldbaileyonline.org, accessed 10 April 2004. Hereafter OBP), 5 December 1744, trial of William Brister, et al. (t17441205–34).

23 London Metropolitan Archives (LMA), Middlesex Sessions of the Peace, MJ/SB/B/69, January 1711–12.

24 Concern over the establishment or maintenance of order in London was nothing new. As Peter Lake demonstrates, early modern commentators and playwrights may have praised London at times, but they were at the same time 'frightened and alarmed' by the city's potential to corrupt social and cultural order. See 'From Troynouvant to Heliogabulus's Rome and Back: 'Order' and its Others in the London of John Stow', in Merritt, *Imagining Early Modern London*.

25 Paul Kléber Monod, *Jacobitism and the English People, 1688–1788* (Cambridge and New York: Cambridge University Press, 1989), 111–19.

26 Ibid.; See also E.P. Thompson, 'Eighteenth-Century Crime, Popular Movements and Social Control', *Bulletin for the Study of Labour History*, 25 (1972).

27 Henry Morley, *Memoirs of Bartholomew Fair* (1880; reprint Detroit, MI: Singing Tree Press, 1968), 142–3.

28 Beier and Finlay, *The Making of the Metropolis*; P.J. Corfield, 'Walking the Streets:

The Urban Odyssey in Eighteenth-Century England,' *Journal of Urban History* 16, 132–74; Neil McKendrick, John Brewer and J.H. Plumb (eds), *The Birth of a Consumer Society: The Commercialization of Eighteenth-Century England* (London: Europa Publications, 1982); Miles Ogborn, *Spaces of Modernity, London's Geographies, 1660–1780* (New York: Guilford Press, 1998); Elizabeth McKellar, *The Birth of Modern London, The Development and Design of the City, 1660–1720* (Manchester and New York: Manchester University Press, 1999); Peter Borsay, *The English Urban Renaissance: Culture and Society in the Provincial Town, 1660–1770* (Oxford: Oxford University Press, 1989); Peter Borsay, 'The Rise of the Promenade: The Social and Cultural Use of Space in the English Provincial Town c. 1660–1800' *Journal for Eighteenth Century Studies* (Fall 1986), 125–39.

29 For an analysis of how urban authorities managed the London population and its associated crime problem, see Beattie, *Policing and Punishment.*

30 See note 8 above. See also Cynthia Wall, *The Literary and Cultural Spaces of Restoration London* (Cambridge: Cambridge University Press, 1998); Dana Arnold, ed., *The Metropolis and Its Image: Constructing Identities for London, c. 1750–1950* (Philadelphia: University of Pennsylvania Press, 2001), and Griffiths and Jenner, *Londinopolis.*

31 McKellar, *The Birth of Modern London*, 23.

32 Kathleen Wilson, 'Citizenship, Empire and Modernity in the English Provinces, c. 1720–1790,' *Eighteenth-Century Studies* 29, no. 1 (1995): 69–96.

33 Ogborn, *Spaces of Modernity*, 28.

34 Karen Newman, *Cultural Capitals: Early Modern London and Paris* (Princeton, NJ: Princeton University Press, 2007), 4.

35 *Ibid.*

36 *Ibid.*

37 Merritt, *Imagining Early Modern London*; Ian Munro, *The Figure of the Crowd in Early Modern London: The City and its Double* (New York: Palgrave Macmillan, 2005); Emily Cockayne, *Hubbub: Filth, Noise and Stench in England, 1600–1770* (New Haven, CT: Yale University Press, 2007); Karen Newman, *Cultural Capitals*, especially Chapter Four, 'Filth, Stench, Noise.'; Vanessa Harding, 'Recent Perspectives on Early Modern London', *Historical Journal* 47, no. 2 (2004): 435–50.

38 Deborah Harkness and Jean E. Howard, 'Introduction: The Great World of Early Modern London'. *Huntington Library Quarterly* 71, no. 1 (March 2008): 2.

39 Merritt, *Imagining Early Modern London*, 3.

40 Andrew Gordon, 'Performing London: The Map and the City in Ceremony', in Andrew Gordon and Bernhard Klein (eds), *Literature, Mapping, and the Politics of Space in Early Modern Britain* (Cambridge: Cambridge University Press, 2001), 70.

41 Michel de Certeau, *The Practice of Everyday Life*, translated by Steven Rendall (Berkeley and Los Angeles: University of California Press, 1984), xii–xiv.

42 Many of these polite venues and fashions are explored in Langford, *A Polite and Commercial People.*

43 Lena Orlin, *Private Matters and Public Culture in Post-Reformation England* (Ithaca, NY: Cornell University Press, 1994); Susan Dwyer Amussen, *An Ordered Society* (New York: Columbia University Press, 1988); Lyndal Roper, *The Holy Household: Women and Morals in Reformation Augsburg* (Oxford: Oxford University

Press, 1989). Gendered imagery in political discourse is explored in Rachel Weil, *Political Passions: Gender, The Family and Political Argument in England, 1680–1714* (Manchester, 1999).

44 See Laura Gowing, '"The Freedom of the Streets": Women and Social Space, 1560–1640', in Griffiths and Jenner, *Londinopolis*; Robert Shoemaker, 'Gendered Spaces: Patterns of Mobility and Perceptions of London's Geography, 1660–1750,' in Merritt, *Imagining Early Modern London.*

45 Examples of this emphasis on urban amusement as 'polite' in the eighteenth-century: McKendrick, Brewer and Plumb; John Brewer and Roy Porter (eds), *Consumption and the World of Goods* (London and New York: Routledge, 1993); Langford, *A Polite and Commercial People.*

46 See for example Langford, *A Polite and Commercial People.*

1

'London's Mart': The crowds and culture of eighteenth-century London fairs

N early forty years before William Hogarth painted *Southwark Fair* in 1733, London's Aldermen and Common Council began their campaign to curtail the popular fair from two weeks to its legally chartered three-day duration. During the late seventeenth through early eighteenth centuries, fair entertainment was routinely attacked by London City and Middlesex county officials, as well as social critics, all of whom considered this amusement socially destructive. In Hogarth's

1.1 *Southwark Fair*, 1733 (engraving), William Hogarth (1697–1764). Guildhall Library, City of London/The Bridgeman Art Library.

painting (engraved the same year), he depicts beneath a Union Jack the people, activities, and occupations found at a London fair. His representation is a rich social document, both for its record of actual fair activities and also for its warning of the explosive and disorderly potential of fairs. As Hogarth portrayed the fair, it was a social 'safety valve', but one near the point of boiling over, a concern shared by City and Middlesex county authorities.[1] Fairs and other popular amusements were long tolerated as safety valves. Some authorities believed that when working people had opportunities to participate in contained occasions for disorderly behaviour (during festival days and fairs), they would be less inclined to act out while living and working during their ordinary daily lives.

The trouble in Hogarth's London, however, was that an institution once tolerated as a break from ordinary life was becoming routine. In *Southwark Fair*, Hogarth visually represents a common concern that fairs threatened to spill out of their confines, both physical and temporal, just as the Greek army spilling out of the Trojan Horse depicted on the centrally-located advertisement for Lee and Harper's 'Siege of Troy'. Art historians often refer to the theme of a 'fall' or 'descent from good fortune to calamity', in this painting.[2] Not only is Troy about to fall, but to the right of this advertisement is another for a puppet show depicting a separate fall – that precipitated by Eve, who is shown tempting Adam above an image of Punch pushing Judy toward the jaws of Hell.[3] This is echoed on a lantern advertisement for *The Fall of Bajazet*, located metaphorically just below the collapsing platform of players. Reversing fortunes are repeatedly represented across the picture from a 'procurer ... enticing a pair of country girls to their ruin', to a farmer losing money in a game of dice.[4] Hogarth's portrait of Southwark Fair underscored a general fear of city officials and social commentators that fairs threatened to swallow up 'rational' commerce, overtake the urban environment and lead to the destruction of London (and, by extension, the nation) if not properly contained.[5] This painting also aptly depicts the social and gender disorder urban officials feared would result from unconfined urban festivity.

Unlicensed fairs and popular amusements associated with fairs were profitable at all times of the year, especially from spring to early fall. Even licensed fairs such as Southwark (or 'Lady Fair') and St Bartholomew's Fair tested the limits of their charters, extending well past the original three-day Church festival days around which they were founded. Both fairs commonly lasted at least fourteen days, if not longer. With some charters dating back to the Middle Ages, London fairs were established as annual markets devoted to specific types of trade, though entertainment always accompanied business. Such fairs were usually associated with Church feast days. By the late seventeenth century, commercial development in London had made the trade of yearly fairs less necessary, and reform of the Church had long made obsolete the celebration of feast days associated with the pre-Reformation church.[6] The primary draw by this time was the entertainment, and London authorities were disturbed by the disruptive potential of large gatherings devoted primarily to diversion. London crowds provided City and Middlesex county officials much to critique – their enjoyment of these summertime amusements continued in spite of the concerns and decrees of both local and national authorities.

This chapter looks behind official efforts to regulate fairs and asks why orders against fairs and their amusements faced concerted popular resistance. An examination of the physical and emotional appeal of fair entertainment to fair-goers from diverse walks of life helps shed light on the resiliency of this form of urban amusement. Government regulation of urban festivity in a rapidly growing metropolis made sense – not only was there no regular London metropolitan police force to oversee social order at large gatherings, but local and national officials viewed crowds as potential shelters for dissident political conspirators, who might turn such crowds into rioting mobs supporting the 'Pretenders'.[7] However, legal restrictions did nothing to repel fair patrons. Fairs were institutions embedded in the seasonal lives of Londoners who resorted to and worked at them throughout the summer months. Fair workers, showmen and women, and fair-goers consistently evaded orders to partake in this urban amusement. An analysis of what people did and saw at fairs provides insight into popular understandings of the importance and desire for urban festivity. This analysis demonstrates that fairs remained in early eighteenth-century London important gathering points at which people exchanged not only goods and services, but also social and cultural information and ideas.

The everyday practice of attending, working at, encountering, or even avoiding fairs shaped the summertime lives of ordinary Londoners walking the city streets during times devoted to these festivals. The preparations for fairs overtook the areas in which they were held. Newspapers at times reported on the progress of fair preparation. In 1701, a newspaper advertisement describes the entertainment that will happen in a 'large Booth' already constructed a week before the beginning of Bartholomew Fair.[8] A 1726 news item reports that at least two weeks before Bartholomew Fair a carpenter – Mr Evans, aged 60 – fell to his death while building a fair booth.[9] Some fair booths were constructed weeks before fairs began, and were distractions in the areas in which they were built. Londoner and diarist Stephen Monteage recorded the start and end of many London fairs and described encountering fairs during his regular walks around the city. In 1746, he watched as 'about 5 or 6 Booths' were built in Smithfield the evening before the fair began.[10] Monteage considered fairs and other curious London exhibits appropriate entertainment for his domestic servant Margaret, and in 1743 he records giving her '1/8 for to see the fairs'(by which he meant Bartholomew and Welch Fairs) and he sent her in 1741 to 'Mr. Garratts in Cheapside to see the Show'.[11] Samuel Pepys, the noted chronicler of London life, also described fairs in his diary, which he attended alone and with family members and friends.[12]

A close examination of descriptions of fairs and their customers reveals the complexity of this type of urban sociability. Largely understood as a form of 'popular' culture, this amusement was frequented in fact by Londoners of many different backgrounds – poor, working, middling, and elite. By no means, however, were fairs a purely democratic space. Though different people may have been present at these events, fair entertainment provided each group opportunities to define themselves and their group identity against others present in the same space. At the same time, an analysis of the everyday offerings of fairs contextualized against the backdrop of increased local and national interest in curtailing them reveals the place such festivity held in the lives of Londoners during this period of 'early modernization'.[13] This analysis considers the practice of urban amusement an important aspect of our understanding of the ways in which European cities and their inhabitants experienced transitional 'moments of modernity'.[14] Such a focus reveals, also, that the process of ordering the city, controlling its people, and rebuilding its spaces was not a rapid process. Instead, it took place in fits and starts and was contested by people's customary use of the urban environment.

Fair spaces

Fairs were held during late-spring and summer months in all regions of London, central and outlying, and were a type of amusement and commercial activity enjoyed in both urban and rural areas. St Bartholomew's Fair occurred in the City ward of Farringdon Without, which lay just outside the old city walls but within its jurisdiction. The charter for this festival was granted by Henry I to his former jester, Rahere (or Rayer), who was then a monk who had also founded the Priory of St Bartholomew.[15]

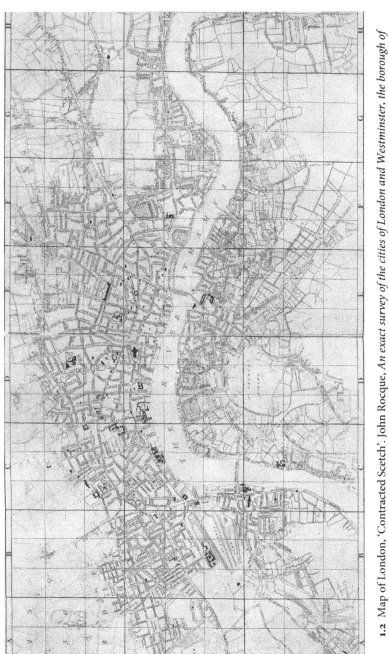

1.2 Map of London, 'Contracted Scetch'. John Rocque, *An exact survey of the cities of London and Westminster, the borough of Southwark, with the country near ten miles round*, by permission of the Folger Shakespeare Library.

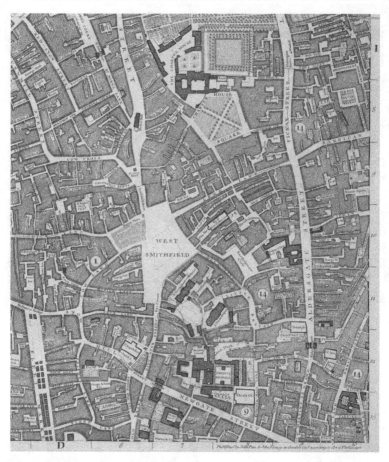

1.3 West Smithfield. John Rocque, *An exact survey of the cities of London and Westminster, the borough of Southwark, with the country near ten miles round,* by permission of the Folger Shakespeare Library.

The fair was held beginning on St Bartholomew's Eve in late August since 1133. Taking place in West Smithfield, the fair grounds were located in and around the old priory, including the area near the hospital once attached to the priory before it was founded as a separate institution for the poor and infirm.[16] Sir Richard Rich, 1st Baron Rich, who purchased the priory and its grounds, maintained rights to the fees of the fair's Pie Powder Court as well as fees from letting the ground within the old priory and from the cloth fair. The City of London retained rights to grounds or structures let within the confines of the hospital and its

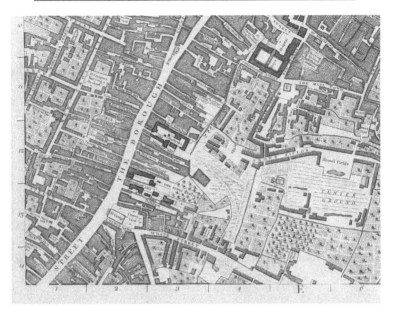

1.4 Southwark. John Rocque, *An exact survey of the cities of London and Westminster, the borough of Southwark, with the country near ten miles round*, by permission of the Folger Shakespeare Library.

cloisters. Once at the edge of the city, by the late seventeenth century, West Smithfield was surrounded by suburban development. By then, it became more common for people to move from their places of business in the city and to the residential areas being built outside of the City centre.[17] The area around Bartholomew Fair was devoted to commerce or city governance. Within close walking distance were the Guildhall, Bank of England, and Newgate prison – still closer were the London Bridewell, the Old Bailey, and St Bartholomew's Hospital, against the gate of which fair booths were frequently constructed. At the edge of the City's commercial, financial, and governing nucleus, Bartholomew Fair was the most urban of the city's fairs.

Just across the river from the City in Bridge Ward Without, Southwark Fair occurred at the edge of the City's jurisdiction. Chartered by the City of London under Edward IV, this fair was traditionally held beginning on 7 September.[18] The fair extended along Borough High Street and stretched from St Margaret's Hill to St George's Church and beyond. This area of town was most known for numerous inns and taverns and the Marshalsea and King's Bench prisons. Beyond the margins

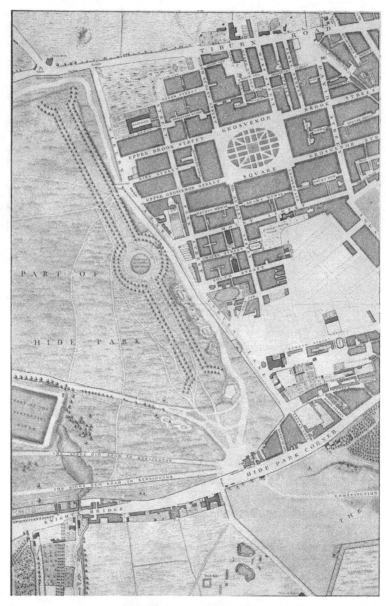

1.5 Hyde Park and surrounding area. John Rocque, *An exact survey of the cities of London and Westminster, the borough of Southwark, with the country near ten miles round*, by permission of the Folger Shakespeare Library.

of the fair were open fields used both for various types of leisure and industry, including bowling greens, gardens, felt making or cloth manufacture, tanning, and farming.[19] Southwark was a traditional space in the city for pleasure and diversion. The area featured many brothels, bear gardens, and bowling greens, therefore a fair did not seem out of place here – nevertheless, it was targeted by City officials in the early eighteenth century and until its final suppression in 1763 as a distraction from industry.

The third of London's largest and most well-known chartered fairs was May Fair, founded later (1688) than the previously mentioned fairs when Sir John Coell received a charter. This charter was not unexpected because a previous fair, St James's Fair, had been held at the site since the reign of Charles I.[20] May Fair was notorious for its bawdy amusements and rowdy, young crowds. Edward Ward, who visited the fair, described it in his early eighteenth-century work, *The London Spy*. May Fair took place near the south-east corner of Hyde Park in the West End of London, an area eventually known as 'Mayfair'. Facilitated by Charles II's fondness for the palace of St James, elite interest in this side of town increased and builders constructed housing suitable for wealthy clientele – St James's Square, streets around Piccadilly, Hanover Square, and Mayfair were all popular among London's elite.[21] By 1708, Edward Shepherd, an architect, had acquired the rights to May Fair and it continued, though it was closely watched by Westminster and Middlesex county officials. This fair eventually fell victim to London's suburban growth and the festivities, which had been curtailed by the Court of Common Council in 1762, were finally confronted in 1764 by a resident powerful enough to quell them: the Earl of Coventry. He purchased a home in the neighbourhood and then complained about the 'unceasing uproar during the month of the fair'.[22] Shortly after, the amusements of this fair ceased.

Beginning with May Fair on the first of that month to St Bartholomew Fair held in late August through Southwark Fair held during the first weeks of September, these were the three largest festivals of the spring and summer season. Though officially chartered for specific amounts of time, fairs bled from one to the next and were punctuated by various unofficial 'pretend' (or unchartered) fairs. One such fair, Tottenham Court Fair, held on the northern outskirts of London usually happened for fourteen days beginning on 4 August. Welsh (or 'Welch') Fair in Clerkenwell, also frequently held in August, and Mile End and Bow Fairs were held at the end of summer, especially during the 1730s.[23]

It is not possible to accurately approximate how many people crowded into the streets in and surrounding the areas chartered for regular fairs, but the numbers were great enough to prompt much literary and visual commentary. In 1746, we get a glimpse into fair numbers when the Middlesex Sessions recorded, in an order against unlawful suburban fairs in the northern suburbs, that 'several thousands', or a 'great Concourse' of people, 'tumultuously assembled' at fairs such as Tottenham Court Fair.[24] While official numbers are not recorded, urban authorities expressed anxiety about the great numbers present at all London fairs. Literature describing fairs nearly always comments upon their closely packed crowds, which obviously fascinated both writers and readers. Hogarth's 'Southwark Fair' most famously captures the over-crowded festival. Not only does the packed foreground give a sense of the bodies crammed into the space, but in the distance, we see a separate group gathered in another area of the fair. Although it is not possible to estimate attendance numbers of fairs, it is clear that if crowds had not been large, London officials would not have been as concerned with this London tradition. A lease book kept by the Earl of Warwick, who inherited from the Rich family an entitlement to one part of Bartholomew Fair as well as real estate and buildings in West Smithfield, notes that people who leased rooms in shops for fair booths did so for seven days 'upon the feast day of St. Barthollomew the Appostle and three dayes next before and three dayes next after the said feast'.[25] In leases relating to ten out of twenty of his buildings located along Long Lane and Cloth Fair behind St Bartholomew the Great on the north border of Bartholomew Fair, Warwick stipulates that lower rooms must be made available by the leasers to fair exhibitors (who also leased from Warwick) during the fair.[26] Warwick's leases relate to only two streets used during Bartholomew Fair. For this particular fair, then, we can expect that those who came into town to sell goods or entertainment in ten of the buildings owned by Warwick remained in London for at least seven days. For a week (or, most likely, more), those leasing booths added to the already burgeoning population of London. Added to those leasing from Warwick were others who attended fairs, acted, danced, and sang in performances, or leased ground in and around permanent structures.

Balconies, windows, and doors of shops located within the boundaries of fairs were turned into or lined with booths, pedlars, and performers, all seeking to attract customers' attention from the numerous other entertainments and goods. A 1671 lease book held in the Guildhall Library lists shops and doors let to fair exhibitors year round, or only during the fair. This suggests that, at least in 1671, the City of London had similar lease agreements exempting the days of Bartholomew Fair from their regular leases.[27] Anywhere there was ground upon which to build, elaborate booths were constructed, sometimes two stories high with their own balconies on which fair performers advertised themselves and their shows. In order to attract the crowd's gaze, players and exhibitors above ground or at street level often employed sound to draw attention. In Ward's *The London Spy*, for example, his middling protagonists describe the dissonant noise of May Fair. Here, they encountered 'the harsh sound of Untunable Trumpets, the Catterwauling Scrapes of Thrashing Fidlers, the Grumbling of beaten Calves skin, and the discording Toots of broken Organs'.[28] At Bartholomew Fair, the cloisters of the hospital were even filled with entertainment, though in this hidden location, such diversions consisted of gaming and prostitution.[29] With any available space devoted to the commerce of fairs, spectators who attended these yearly festivals were overwhelmed with sights, sounds, and smells inducing them to part with their money. Fairs presented many opportunities to spend money. Entertainments cost anywhere from a few pence to a few shillings, depending upon what one chose to see or do. Food and drink, of course, were also available as were trinkets, pamphlets, and fair souvenirs, and gambling offered one a means of disposing of any amount of money.

The visual culture of fairs

Hogarth meant his presentation of Southwark Fair as a moralistic statement about the potential danger of fairs, and he used painstaking detail to make his point. His representation of individual fair activities and entertainments, however, subverts this message. Though a scaffold of players will momentarily hit the crowd below, interrupting the pleasures of the fair, the print's viewer can avert their focus from this impending disaster and find evidence revealing why London fairs such as Southwark Fair were popular. Just as Hogarth's crowds seem unaware of the real threat from above – perhaps they are more focused on the thrill of imagined danger facing tightrope walkers and 'flying' men – people who attended fairs were not concerned with how city officials or social commentators interpreted their merriment. They attended fairs looking for amusement, sociability, spectacle and, for some, profit. When we consider the place fairs held in the social lives of Londoners, Hogarth's print best represents the physical as well as emotional appeal of these venues.

Printed commentary about fairs illuminates anxieties and fears about the rapidly shifting demographics, economics, and social order of London. At the close of the seventeenth century, urban populations grew at a phenomenal rate. Between 1670 and 1750, migration to cities increased and England's urban population grew from thirteen to nearly

21 per cent of the country's total population.[30] By 1700, London was a major metropolis of 490,000 inhabitants and in 1750 it surpassed Constantinople as Europe's largest city with its population of 600,000 – nearly 10 per cent of England's total population.[31] Fair amusements were a popular target for some writers who evoked representations of fair disorder to punctuate their more general view that such entertainment was inappropriate and dangerous for a metropolis the size of London. Satirists juxtaposed commerce and amusement, country and city, mannered and ill-mannered to convey to increasingly mannered audiences the humour they found in fair entertainment. Writers, artists, and readers who produced or consumed these representations defined their own identities as opposed to those who participated in the spectacle of fairs.

Hogarth's print as well as less formal depictions of fairs, including a fan sold as a souvenir at Bartholomew Fair, provides a sense of the visual world experienced by fair-goers. Combined with literary descriptions of fair amusements as well as information gained from court books, leases, and other documents, these sources give us a sense of the overwhelming spectacle of London's largest fairs. At the same time, visual and literary depictions of fairs reveal that Londoners viewed them – at once pre-modern and modern institutions – as one of the unique features of London life. Representing fairs, their entertainments, the crowds that attended them, and the bodies on display was one means by which social commentators constructed a sense of shared London identity and projected what it meant to be a Londoner to those living outside of the city.[32]

By the early eighteenth century, few European cities could have hosted fairs with the numbers of people who attended and worked at London's fairs. A familiar tradition with roots in England's medieval past, fairs in London represented simultaneously customary amusement and new urban spectacle. Though much focus has been given to eighteenth-century London as a 'modernizing' city, we often do not acknowledge vestiges of pre-modern institutions existing in the centre of this slowly changing metropolis. Existing in both urban and rural areas of wider London, urban fairs complicate our understanding of the emergence of the 'modern' as well as our notions of the separateness of 'country' and 'city'. As an institution of sociability, if not commerce, fairs bridged the pre-modern and modern worlds and spanned the city and the country; fairs occupied an 'intermediate space', in the capital's culture.[33] Britons' continued patronage of fairs reveals how some customary practices continued within new London city spaces. The eighteenth century marks a transitional moment between fairs as places that combined essential marketing days with religious festivals and celebration to the early nineteenth century, which saw the emergence of commercialized centres of sociability shaped along lines of class or gender.[34] Fairs contained many aspects of these later amusements institutionalized in the long nineteenth century.

Early eighteenth-century printed accounts of fairs are similar to Hogarth's visual representation of their multifarious entertainments. Acting as urban spectators, writers did their best to record the extraordinary spectacle of London fairs for their audiences. Londoners who would not otherwise attend these festivals or people who lived too far from the city to ever attend could be virtually present through such literary descriptions. Journalists directed vivid descriptions toward middling or elite audiences in London as well as those outside of the city who would have been unable to attend fairs on a regular basis. Popular literary forms for descriptions of fair amusements were songs, short pamphlets, and mock heroic poems in the tradition of Alexander Pope.[35]

In such sources, it is possible to recover the experience of attending fairs in one of Europe's largest metropolitan centres. These sources are particularly useful in the absence of any reliable attendance figures at London fairs. Records reveal who purchased licences (though it is not always clear for what purpose they were purchased), what entertainments were advertised, and what city officials thought of fair entertainments, but no existing record reveals the number of people who attended fairs. Literary and print evidence demonstrates, however, that crowds at fairs were large enough to provoke commentary from numerous writers.[36] Print and literary sources provide, also, evidence of the types of entertainment one found at fairs, especially when read alongside existing newspaper advertisements and playbills regarding fair entertainment.[37] Posters advertising fair entertainments were commonly posted throughout London. In May Fair, for example, posters were so large that 'he that runs may read them'.[38] Many playbills or advertisements have been preserved by collectors who copied advertisements into scrapbooks.[39]

Advertisements as well as literary descriptions help us better understand the nature of fair entertainment. These sources shed light on what sort of activities city officials called lewd or dangerous in court documents, and they work together to provide a complex picture of the visual world of fairs, particularly when descriptive accounts of fairs highlight instances in which entertainment or exhibitions failed to live up to advertised promises – and even situations when they did. From Edward Ward's 'London Spies' to Samuel Pepys's first-hand accounts of the rope dancer Jacob Hall, narrative descriptions of fair entertainment enrich our knowledge of fair entertainment.

Many accounts reflect, as in the case of Hogarth's *Southwark Fair*, the perspective of middling men who describe fairs for the sake of satire, moralizing, or both. This elite perspective shades depictions of fairs, exaggerating the differences between protagonists (usually middling) and the 'average' (more common) fair-goer. Though enough elite men and women attended fairs that their presence is mentioned in newspaper accounts, and even sometimes described their visits in diaries or correspondence, there are often very few people from middling to above social status depicted in these narratives. Accounts of fairs are nevertheless significant sources for reconstructing fair culture, as long as information is teased out from beneath the elite perspective.

Crowds 'as close as a Barrel of Figs'

John Bancks' 1738 poem, 'To Mr. Hogarth: on his Southwark Fair', captures Hogarth's visual depiction in verse and begins with a colourful description of the sights and sounds of the fair:

> Each rival Stentor roars aloud, To drown the Rest, and dupe the Croud: The tinsel'd Heroes catch the Sight, and Andrew's mimic Tricks invite; Contending Drums and Trumpets sound, At once to charm, and to confound.[40]

Elaborating a common theme among illustrators of London's fairs, Bancks presents fairs as locations of sights, sounds, entertainments, and people that are both captivating and raucous. This literature conveyed the experience of fairs to readers who encountered them vicariously through the author's narrative. Common motifs of this literature are descriptions of moving within crushing and disorganized crowds, experiencing unusual, thrilling, and sometimes ludicrous sights, encountering unsavoury smells, even more unsavoury people, and loud, unpleasant sounds. Other than at fairs, Londoners had few occasions to witness people from all walks of life – from 'garter'd Knights to the ungarter'd Shoe-Boy'[41] – in one small area; the crowds who attended fairs were a spectacle in and of themselves. In piece after piece, late seventeenth- and early eighteenth-century depictions of fairs highlight the experience of not only witnessing but also joining the multitudes at fairs.

Visual and written descriptions of London fairs treat crowds as curiosities in themselves – almost as if these multitudes were the main attraction of fairs. Those who wrote about fair crowds often adopted detached perspectives, similar to a later ethnographical style. Through their descriptions and analysis, elite journalists and artists examined fair crowds and activities for the 'truths' they revealed about the life in a metropolitan centre. The juxtaposition of food, objects, people, and entertainments from England, the British Isles, Europe, and the world within the confines of fairs became for literary observers who recorded 'London's Mart', a location at which the city's unique character was on display.[42]

Utmost among the topics writers discussed in order to best convey the experience of attending a fair was the sensory experience. With displays presented overhead as well as on the ground, food cooking, beverages being served, and people crowded close together, a fair-goer's senses were overwhelmed. One writer commented that at fairs 'various Objects strike [a person's] ravish'd Senses/The Eyes, the Ears, the Nose, the Tast [sic], the Touch ...'[43] These sensory experiences only hinted at in court records are accessible in literary descriptions, which provide insight into what drew people to the uncommon and festive experience of fairs. At the same time, writers' and artists' accounts demonstrate the ways in which middling to elite Londoners distanced themselves from certain tastes, smells, and habits of the common people who attended fairs.

The differences satirists found between themselves and other fairgoers often broke down along lines of a more 'cosmopolitan' view of urban life versus a rural and more naive perspective. Differentiation between social classes within London was accompanied and often overshadowed by understandings of a common urban identity consolidated against conceptions of outsiders having their first, or rare, taste of London life at a fair. The understanding that living in London imbued people with a perspective not shared by outsiders is reinforced in periodical literature such as *The London Spy*, in which a man from London shows his rural friend the sights of the city, and in popular songs such as 'Roger in Amaze – A Country man's ramble Through Bartholomew Fair'. In this song, a man from the country reflects upon his visit to Bartholomew Fair, where as a member of the crowd he experiences 'Zuch thrusting and squeezing, [that] Was never known.'[44]

Though denoting differences between rural and urban dwellers is a common theme in visual and literary depictions of fairs, it was the crowd at fairs that most fascinated writers and artists. Banck's description of Southwark Fair characterizes the crowd as a 'motely Throng', made up of 'Knaves, Jilts, Buffoons, Dupes old and young', all of whom are taken in by the fair spectacle and dangerously divorced from rational action.[45] In one essay, a writer begins his description of the fair with commentary about the crowd, which he calls, 'a numerous, tho confused Multitude, huddled together as thick as an assembly of religious

Bretheren, and holy Sisters at a *Covent-garden* Conventicle, or Quakers Meeting house'.[46] This writer obviously operated from an Anglican perspective as he compares the irrationality of fair crowds to people with Roman Catholic and dissenting religious practices – and he especially highlights the disorder and danger of the crowd by evoking female religious imagery in which he employs a traditional Protestant trope equating nuns with prostitutes. This perspective reveals how social critiques of fairs buttressed critics' own understandings of themselves and like-minded Anglican middling men as mannered and orderly. This particular type of mannered Anglicanism is similar to criticisms found in sermons and pamphlets issued by London societies for the reformation of manners.[47]

Writers' descriptions of fair crowds frequently equate people's physical characteristics with their social station. In *The London Spy*, Ward repeatedly refers to the bodily experience of attending a fair – both Bartholomew Fair and the more unruly May Fair. At the later fair, his protagonists could find few men of rank among 'many Thousands', and were dismayed by the 'Beggarly, Sluttish Strumpets', who were also 'Enemies to Cleanliness'. Among these women, the spies could not find 'one Whore that could have the Impudence to ask above Six-pence Wet and Six-pence Dry, for an Hour of her Cursed Company'.[48] Ward employs classed and gendered imagery equating the general disorder of the fair with the collective identity of its crowd, which he depicts as consisting of lower servants, working men and women, and unsanitary prostitutes, though we know that crowds were much more diverse, particularly because London elites such as Ward, Pepys, and Hogarth themselves joined these crowds. Dirty or unruly fair patrons upset Ward's and other middling men's notions of properly ordered bodies, yet at the same time social critics were fascinated by such disorderly crowds. According to the London spies, Bartholomew Fair was less despicable than May Fair, but their perception of the people who constituted the crowds remained informed by their own middling notions of cleanliness and taste, which transcended the 'rural' or 'urban' differences between themselves. In the case of the *London Spy*'s protagonists, both spectators agreed upon their own masculine and polite expectations of proper public behaviour and this common identity sometimes trumped differences stemming from their roots. These men's common identity was reinforced as they sat above the crowd in a Smithfield tavern. Here, they watch the 'Innumerable Throng', who in pursuit of festivity did not mind being 'Ancle deep [in] filth and nastiness', and were 'Crowded as close as a Barrel of Figs, or Candles in a Tallow Chandlers Basket, Sweating and

Melting with the heat of their own Bodies'. Worse were the 'unwholesome Fumes of [these] uncleanly Hides, mix'd with the Odoriferous Effluvia's that arose from the Singeing of Pigs, and burnt Crackling of over-Roasted Pork'. Had it not been for the two men's 'use of the fragrant Weed, Tobacco', they would have 'been in danger of being suffocated', once they joined the crowd.[49]

Fair crowds were not only made up of individual bodies 'shuffled together with as confused a mixture as little Boxes in a Sharpers Luck in a Bag', but writers who described fairs were also intrigued that the throng seemed to take on a life of its own.[50] One writer 'found it difficult to stear [sic] [his] course above three Yards in half an Hour's time', and it also took Ward's London spies a good amount of time to learn how to navigate their course in the crowd at Bartholomew Fair.[51] Once they 'launched' themselves into the 'Tempestuous Multitude', they were 'hurry'd along, from the Ground, by a Stream of Rabble, into the middle of the *Fair*, in as little time as a forward Beau may make a Fumbler a Cuckold'.[52] Besides highlighting the unpredictable nature of the crowd with a comparison to sexual behaviour and male honour, Ward evokes images of water and currents while his two main characters resign themselves to having to '[swim] down with the Tide', in order to get from one entertainment to the next. Later, they again refer to the 'throng' as a 'Stream of Rabble', that '[poured] into the Fair from all adjacent Streets', while the people among the crowd '[contended] to repel the Force of its Opposite Current, who were striving, like Tide and Stream, to overcome each other'.[53] As difficult to control and direct as floods of water, indiscriminate crowds swept their way through the streets and empty spaces of fair grounds, upsetting anything and everyone in their wake. Objects and people in the way became flotsam.

Ward's comparison of fair crowds to rushing currents reiterated what many thought was a danger of fairs. One might attend them as a reasoned person, but it took great effort to avoid being moved from one entertainment to the next against one's will. Satirists described navigating fair crowds as a chaotic experience, which must have resonated with those who had spent a day among the multitude at the fair. At the very least, such accounts, which made merely walking into the crowd at a fair seem like a thrilling act, increased the appeal of urban fair-going. As a spectator in crowded fair spaces, one risked their ability to make rational decisions. In particular, this literature appealed to men increasingly faced with expectations for polite urban behaviour – in crowds, a mannered individual was (against his will) separated from circumspect behaviour and able to enjoy the disorder, dirt, and potential pleasure of fairs. Legitimate danger did exist, however, as a 1733 newspaper attested. The *Daily Journal* reported: 'On Monday Night Last a Woman who delivered out Bills at Mrs. Lee and Harper's Booth in Borough Fair [Southwark] was so terribly squeezed by the people crowding in upon her that she soon after expir'd'.[54] That a woman fell victim to the crowd likely reinforced any growing notions of the unsuitability of fair entertainment (or especially fair work) for women. Not only was it a woman 'terribly squeezed' by the crowd, but this was a woman employed by a female fair booth proprietor.

Fair crowds interested writers beyond the way they seemed to take on a life of their own. Inhabiting a crowd was titillating and, sometimes, dangerous. It threw people from all stations and both sexes together. Within the crowd, one might encounter a pickpocket, but one also might enjoy the pleasure of close proximity to desirable strangers. Hogarth depicted a pickpocket at work among the crowd, which was a common fear of fair-goers. Before throwing themselves among the 'rabble', the two London spies buttoned up their pockets 'as securely as a Citizen does his Shop Windows when his Family goes to Church'.[55] With pockets secured, the middling protagonists of fair literature entered crowds in pursuit of their attending visual and sexual pleasures. For the author of *A Walk to Smithfield*, this included the thrill of squeezing himself between the 'soft Bellied Femals, just like a fatt Man thro a narrow stile, so that with artifical Hipp work and Thigh work, [he] labour'd as hard as ever any furious Lover did to niggle himself between the Knees of a coy Mistress'.[56] This protagonist makes his way to Pye Corner in Bartholomew Fair, only after by 'Storm and much Fatigue', he escaped the 'confused mixture of Hips and Buttocks'.[57] This sexualized description of the crowd at fairs conveyed to voyeuristic readers the physical excitement of not being able to control one's direction while mingling among closely-pressed bodies.

A description of the sensory experience of fair-going is not complete without mention of the food and drink people consumed at these events. Fair dining was such an unusual experience that Ben Jonson created a well-known character: Ursula, the Pig Woman, who sells cooked pork at Bartholomew Fair.[58] Perhaps due in part to this exaggerated seventeenth-century depiction, late seventeenth- and early eighteenth-century commentators on fairs perceived dining there (and especially enjoying pork at Bartholomew Fair) as essential to the fair-going experience. Dining at fairs provided the opportunity to indulge in large amounts of greasy food not ordinarily consumed in daily life. However, eating food prepared by transient pedlars of sometimes unknown origins made eating at fairs a dangerous activity that potentially threatened one's well-being, or, at the very least, one's intestines.

Fair dining was such an anticipated event that the author of *Bartholomew Fair: An Heroi-Comical Poem* devoted a page to this experience. The first person the author encounters upon entering the fair is a 'greasy Cook, of monst'rous Size'. Once near him and his culinary product, the author notices how people are overcome by their 'craving Stomachs', which take on a life of their own and cause them to '[cast] a greedy Eye ... [towards] the turning Spit, Where Veal and Pork, and Beef, promiscuous meet'. The cooking food is sensuously described as the various meats 'Each other baste; and dainty Kitchin Grease/Froths up, and browns the delicate fav'rite Piece:/With greasy Knife is cut the bounded Meal/Of Beef or Mutton, or the coarser Veal'. This bounty of meat is served to waiting human 'stomachs' on plates full of gravy and fat by 'dirty *Molly*, or the greasier *Kate*', from whose dirty hands one gladly risked receiving food in pursuit of the unique taste of fairs.[59]

Ward's London spies are less forgiving in their depiction of fair cuisine. Informed by their own 'refined' middling tastes, these two men have an unsavoury experience at Bartholomew Fair. Expecting 'tolerable Meat, and cleanly Usage', they enter a shop with expectations high. Though hoping to 'accommodate [their] Stomachs with good Entertainment', they were soon disappointed. Instead, they found a 'suffocating Kitchen', run by a 'swinging fat Fellow, who was appointed Over-seer of the Roast'. In amazement, the London spies witness this man 'standing by the Spit in his Shirt, Rubbing of his Ears, Breast, Neck, and Arm-pits with the same Wet-Cloth which he apply'd to his *Pigs*'. This brought a 'Qualm over [the] Stomach', of one of the spies, and he had 'much ado to keep the stuffing of [his] Guts from tumbling into the Dripping Pan'. Vowing to look for more sanitary dining conditions, these two men hastily left the shop.[60]

Whether or not these accounts of dining at fairs reflect reality is not discernible from existing sources. What they do reveal is how certain foods and eating experiences were associated with fairs and a particular social class. At fairs one found a variety of meats and other treats not always readily available, especially not in the quantities found at fairs. Just watching food cooking or the process of preparation during London's summer months was a spectacle for fair patrons. With a cornucopia of food and drink available to festive consumers, much of their time spent at fairs involved food – from smelling the aromas of different cooking foods while passing kitchens and open-air grills, to consuming as much as their stomachs, income, and discretion would allow.

Dexterous bodies and monstrous displays

The unique experience of dining at fairs, experiencing mingling scents and unusual sights, travelling through crowds, and perhaps enjoying the pleasure of close physical contact were not the only corporeal thrills of fairs. Plenty of unusual and attractive bodies were displayed for people's visual consumption. Audiences delighted in watching the disciplined displays of acrobats and rope dancers, who put themselves into precarious and seemingly dangerous positions in order to attract audiences. Rope dancing was particularly associated with fairs and this attraction was popular with Londoners from all backgrounds. Rope dancing is specifically noted in the seventeenth-century diaries of both Pepys and fellow diarist John Evelyn.

Rope dancing was a popular attraction of fairs from the mid-seventeenth century, when Jacob Hall became the first 'celebrity' rope dancer. Pepys mentions seeing Hall perform in Bartholomew Fair in 1668, and he called his display 'a thing worth seeing, and mightily followed'.[61] He went again to watch Hall at Southwark Fair that same year. In a span of a month, either Hall had added new feats to his routine or Pepys's anticipation of the spectacle was exceeded by the performance – he describes Hall's Southwark Fair performance as an 'action as I never saw before, and mightily worth seeing'.[62] Pepys was particularly enthused when meeting and speaking with Hall in a tavern near Southwark Fair. Here, Pepys interrogated the rope dancer about the danger associated with his trade. Asking him whether or not he had 'ever any mischief by falls in his time', Hall answered, 'Yes, many, but never to the breaking of a limb'. Perhaps a bit awed by the rope dancer and his acrobatic abilities, Pepys sums up his interaction with Hall saying, 'he seems a mighty strong man'.[63] Hall intrigued notable Londoners other than Pepys. Famous not only for his daring and agility on the ropes, but also for his 'handsome face' and 'symmetrical form', the rope dancer was rumoured to have had relationships with the well-known actress Nell Gwynne and the Countess of Castlemaine, both of whom were also mistresses of Charles II.

By the late seventeenth century and after Hall's death, rope dancing was common enough that one man's feats above ground were not enough to attract an audience. Advertisements grew more detailed and promised everything from complicated tasks and acrobatics performed on the rope to acts featuring troupes of graceful or courageous female dancers from England and the wider British Isles, the continent, and beyond. From 1698 to 1705, at least three companies of rope dancers performed regularly at both Southwark and Bartholomew Fairs, and in

1698, the fair-booth managers Barnes and Appleby featured a company of,

> the most famous Rope Dancers of Europe, ... the English, High German, Dutch and Morocco Companies, who perform strange and wonderful things of the Rope, the German Maiden out-doing all Men and Women, that ever Danc'd before her, both for high leaping and fine Dancing.

The German woman was particularly noted as being able to perform 'side, upright, cross or back Capers' at a 'prodigious height'.[64] Another advertisement promised that 'At the Famous Dutch Woman's Booth, over against the Hospital Gate' in Bartholomew Fair 'you will see a Wonderful Girle of 10 years of Age, who walks backwards up the sloaping Rope, driving a wheelbarrow behind her'.[65]

Rope dancing retained its popularity during the late seventeenth and early eighteenth-centuries. During this period, newspapers featured numerous advertisements promising entertainments on the rope supposedly more entertaining and thrilling than any other seen. In 1704, Pinkethman's Company of rope dancers featured 'two famous French Maidens and the Indian Woman', as well as performances of 'Mr. Evans' who 'walks the slack Rope and throws himself a somerset through a hogshead hanging eight foot high'.[66] At Southwark Fair in 1705 a booth featured two *other* 'famous French Maidens', the 'Lady Isabella and her sister the finch of Ropedancing'. These women had a questionable reputation as skilful performers, revealed in the statement that they were 'much improved of late'.[67] Rope dancing accompanies many other fair entertainments, including presentations of drolls or puppet shows. Lee and Harper accompanied their presentation of *The History of Darius King of Persia* with a company of rope dancers and tumblers 'just arrived from Holland, what outdoes anything that ever was seen in that nature'.[68] The 'conjerour', Fawkes, presented a yearly 'medly' of entertainment, which always featured rope dancing. In 1726, Fawkes's Southwark Fair display entertained 'his excellency Sid Mahomed Ben Aly Abogly, Ambassadour from the Emperour of Morroco and several persons of Quality'. This display featured 'Mrs. Vilante and others who has had the honour to perform before most of the foreign princes ... such exercises on the Ropes which have not been seen in this kingdom before'. Hoping to attract customers with the promise of novel and risqué rope-dancing displays, Fawkes describes this performer's routine in detail. Vilante performs:

> with two flags, one in each hand, which she displays as fine as any ensign can upon the ground and for her last exercise, there is a rope

made fast from the stage to the upper gallery which she walks up to the top and then comes down backwards. Next is a child of five year old which will dance a minuet upon the rope as perfectly as on the floor.[69]

Sexuality and the exotic helped fair-booth proprietors sell rope dancing exhibits. Rope dancing managers spun narratives in advertisements, detailing attributes of performers or performances that might attract curious customers. These advertisements reveal a common equation of foreignness and femaleness, adding a mysterious appeal to female rope-dancing displays. Such advertisements contributed to two concurrent trends in eighteenth-century London. First, they played upon traditions in which women's true nature and motives were thought to be constantly changing and, therefore, unknowable. Scientific understanding dictated that women were ruled less by reason than by feeling, and people imagined their bodies to be potentially explosive or easily inflamed, especially because they were ruled by their uteruses, which were in turn ruled by the moon.[70] Early modern conceptions of women as figures who embodied disorder and threatened male productivity and control made female rope-dancing displays seem particularly dangerous.[71] From this perspective women were as equally 'foreign' as people from outside England. At the same time, proprietors who advertised rope dancing played upon public understandings that dancing maidens clad in breeches and tights were not at all innocent performers, rather they seductively entranced audiences by their incomprehensible skill and uncertain origins.

The threat of the unknown in women increased when a ropedancer was also labelled foreign. 'French Maidens', 'Indian women', 'Moroccan Companies', even precocious children [and we might think of childhood as a 'foreign land' to eighteenth-century people], all promised spectators the thrilling and out-of-the-ordinary experience of watching potentially disruptive people executing risky manoeuvres. Proprietors appealed to customers' desire to witness seemingly hazardous spectacles at fairs. Not only would performers exhibit acrobatics on ropes above the ground, but some performers would be female *and* exotic. For some social critics, including Hogarth and Swift, foreignness and the exotic were associated with moral decay.[72]

Rope-dancing advertisements also situated public performances by women before a 'male gaze', thus contributing to emerging gendered notions of spectators as 'male' and spectacle as 'female'.[73] In order to perform acrobatics on ropes, women dressed in clothing that differed from everyday female dress. More than one writer discusses the voyeuristic thrill of watching women in breeches perform above ground while imagining these women's secret sexual motives behind their costume. The author of *Bartholomew Fair, a Heroi-Comical Poem*, immortalizes rope-dancing women as 'airy Females [who] in short Breeches dress; Their secret Limbs procure them a Caress. A well-shap'd Leg, and round handsome thigh, In white Silk Stocking, ravishes the Eye'. Thus, revealingly dressed, this rope dancer is potentially destructive because she 'soon bewitch th'amourous Standers by'.[74] The author entered the rope-dancing booth 'thoughtless of Disgrace', at least partly for the promise of sexual titillation. His description of the rope-dancing display reveals delight in watching the display both for its sexual pleasure and potential danger.

'Active Virgins' astride 'slacken'd Ropes', who vaulted 'with nimble Heels', and 'famous skill' excited viewers below. Successful rope-dancing proprietors sold this potent combination of sex and danger. Spectators were delighted and thrilled as the rope dancers 'dang'rous hang' and 'fright the Mob below'.[75] Audiences were thrilled by 'divers sights', from the 'famous Black' who 'well performs her Part', by dancing a jig on the rope 'grasp[ing] the Pole', assuming 'various Postures' and 'despising' all dangers jumping through the air to the 'Infant' (a child) who 'could hardly speak, yet there she nimbly danc'd'. As the audience watched the child 'Each Breast [pained] for th'adventuring Brat', who 'dauntless trod the stiffen'd Rope, when she deserv'd the Rod'.[76] This passage reveals what audiences who watched rope dancing might have witnessed, and also demonstrates that audiences preferred extraordinary feats. Booth proprietors sought to please crowds with diverse displays. In the quest for profit, proprietors struck a balance between expected entertainment and novel execution of that entertainment.

A woman's success as a rope dancer was measured according to the extent to which she projected femininity even while dressed in breeches. Exposed thighs were only worth a look if they were attached to someone who otherwise fulfilled male notions of beauty. The legendary rope dancer 'Lady Mary' was certainly a woman whose appearance and agility attracted fairground admirers. Beyond her skill, however, Lady Mary was made more attractive to fair audiences by her biography. Mary's story was a cautionary tale for reputable young ladies who assumed fair entertainment to be an innocent amusement, yet it is her supposed fall from an elite and chaste upbringing that increased this rope dancer's fame. In one account Lady Mary is described as a 'daughter of noble parents, inhabitants of Florence, where they immured her in a nunnery'. Carelessly, these parents allowed her to see a 'Merry Andrew' at a fair, 'a clandestine intercourse took place, and elopement followed'.

Her husband taught Mary his 'infamous tricks', which he forced her to exhibit for profit.[77] 'Lady Mary' was, in fact, the wife of the rope dancer and fair-booth manager Finley, who offered popular displays of rope dancers during the early eighteenth century.[78] No doubt, the two recognized the profitability of a good origin story. Lady Mary had become so popular in 1700 that during an epilogue at Drury Lane the actor William Pinkethman complained 'whilst the Rope-dancing sway'd' he 'made grimace' at the playhouse to 'empty Benches':

> 'Gad; I began to think my Charm decay'd;
> And that the Beaus resolv'd a new Vagary
> To go and live and die with Lady Mary.

When the dancer fell and hurt her foot, he thought 'Such dire concern was then, such desolation, As if 't had been the downfall of the Nation'.[79]

Female rope dancers not only were popular for their beauty and physical feats, but also found themselves objects of public concern beyond their performance life. A famous rope dancer, 'Isabella', was rumoured to be subjected to a very cruel husband.[80] Rumour told that her life ended because her husband 'impatient of delays or impediments to profit', forced her to perform while eight months pregnant. This alone, if true, would have added to the attraction and thrill of her dancing. Not only did she have to balance extra weight and different proportions, but pregnancy itself was proof that women's bodies could not always be controlled. A woman performing on a rope while visibly pregnant literally presented female unpredictability and vulnerability.[81] According to the legend, Isabella's excess weight caused her to fall from the rope 'never more to rise; her infant was born on the stage, and died a victim with its mother'.[82]

In a posthumous biography of Lady Isabella printed in 1810, the author provides the rope dancer's heartbreaking story, likely romanticized. This nineteenth-century author asks his readers to sympathize with the eighteenth-century woman because her life had been negatively shaped by a succession of caretakers who had not lived up to their obligations: inattentive parents, guardians at the nunnery, and a profit-driven husband who not only ruined her life, but his own child's. The story of Isabella dying while pregnant after being forced to work by a ruthless husband underscores her helplessness. She is vulnerable both to her involuntarily changing body and to her cruel husband. This retelling is interesting because it can be read as a morality tale buttressing nineteenth-century notions of separate work spheres for men and women and women's biological unsuitability for work. Beyond reinforcing notions of separate spheres, however, this story is rooted within an early modern tradition of cautionary tales that represented wronged women's 'patient submission'. Isabella, a victim of her ineffectual parents, an abusive husband and circumstance, suffers in similar ways to female characters in popular ballads and pamphlets from early modern England and Germany. These earlier women are victimized by husbands whose actions harm not only the female characters, but also their unborn children.[83] If this story were told during the early eighteenth century, audiences most likely understood them as echoing themes of this earlier street fiction as well as evidence of the ways in which women's biology made them unsuited for public work. The story of Lady Isabella's demise interestingly bridges between seventeenth- and nineteenth-century views of public women. Lady Isabella's story reminds us that the possibility rope-dancing women might be pregnant added another level of fear, drama, or even amazement to their performance for audiences.

Theatre at fairs

Perhaps the most popular and well-documented fair entertainment was fair theatre. Play booths were the central attraction of fairs from at least the late seventeenth century. Puppet shows, rope dancers, singers, and performances by groups of strolling players were common to London fairs until the late seventeenth century. By 1698, however, the nature of play-booth entertainment changed when actors and theatre mangers from the patent theatre began regular performances at London fairs. Patent theatre actors and managers saw in the fairs an opportunity to supplement their income while the theatres were closed for the summer.[84] William Pinkethman from Drury Lane was the first actor to realize the economic potential of performing at Bartholomew Fair.[85] He opened a booth in 1698 and began a long trend of professionalization of the theatre of London fairs, culminating in 1736, the last year before theatrical entertainment outside of the patent theatres was curtailed by the licensing act and limited only to licensed, permanent theatres. Though play-booth proprietors eventually devised means around the restrictions of this act, involvement of theatre professionals at London fairs declined after 1737.[86]

Professional theatre proprietors were only one type of theatrical-booth manger at London fairs. After the late seventeenth century, strolling company managers or those which existed only to provide entertainment for the London fairs remained, but their method of presenting entertainment at the fair was challenged and directly impacted by the appearance of professional theatre actors and managers at fairs. Once play-booth managers with the backing and resources (including props, costumes, actors, and money) of London theatres at their disposal began hiring fairground for performances, they raised expectations for all performance at the fair. Play-booth managers who did not meet the challenge lost customers. Theatre at fairs included dancing, music performances and, above all, drolls – or shortened versions of popular plays. The average play-booth presentation was about thirty minutes long and took place either in temporary booths constructed days in advance or inside lower rooms of taverns.[87] At some venues, managers sought elite clientele who could afford to avoid crowds by arriving in coaches using separate passageways. In 1722, for example 'Walker, from the Theatre-royal' advertised that at his Southwark Fair booth there would be a new 'commodious passage for the reception of Ladies, etc. paved and beautified with large open rooms on each side adorn'd with lamps. Also, a proper number of servants to guide the company to their coaches and prevent disturbances'.[88] Not all play booths featured such accommodations, however, and they thrived nevertheless.

London's fairs were traditions embedded in the city's seasonal life. Though their once established association with Church feast days was all but lost on post-Reformation revellers, they remained important festivals at which people both worked and played. The entertainments, tastes, and multifarious pleasures of fairs appealed to a wide spectrum of people. Artists and journalists concerned with urban disorder or who merely wanted to represent London's unique attributes focused on fairs to underscore their themes, all the while consolidating their own understandings of themselves as mannered and separate from the people they saw at fairs. Men and women from various backgrounds found many opportunities to work and socialize at fairs, and they continued to partake in this amusement despite official efforts to control them. At the same time, the increasing popularity and duration of fair entertainment alerted city officials who were concerned with the social disorder and distraction from commerce encouraged by fairs. In an era concerned increasingly with order and categorization, crowds and unpredictable gatherings were obvious targets for reform efforts. Fairs disrupted neat categorization of urban locales because they spanned across rural and undeveloped London locations, the City centre, and areas of new post-fire suburban development. Unchecked, popular enjoyment and patronage of this ubiquitous summertime amusement threatened to become embedded in the modern cultural life of the metropolis. As fairs continued despite criticism and concern, they fostered sociability and encouraged their own commerce of amusement. They remained, also, centres at which Londoners learned about themselves, their country-men, and the world.

Notes

1 Chris Humphrey argues this concept tends to 'hinder rather than help our inter-pretation of [festive misrule]', and that we ought to see 'performances of misrule as meaningful in their own right', rather than assuming to know they functioned as 'safety valves'. Here, I recognize that there was some understanding among late seventeenth- and early eighteenth-century authorities that fairs functioned as a type of social safety valve, though they were held too frequently for that to be their only purpose. At the same time, I examine fair entertainment in its 'own right'. *The Politics of Carnival: Festive Misrule in Medieval England* (Manchester and New York: Manchester University Press, 2001), Chapter 1.

2 E.D.H. Johnson, *Paintings of the British Social Scene from Hogarth to Sickert* (London: Weidenfeld & Nicolson, 1986), 26.

3 *Ibid.*

4 *Ibid.*, 26–7.

5 Christina Kiaer's analysis of Hogarth's *Southwark Fair* was particularly useful here and informed my own. See her 'Professional Femininity in Hogarth's *Strolling Actresses Dressing in a Barn*', in Bernadette Fort and Angela Rosenthal (eds), *The Other Hogarth, Aesthetics of Difference* (Princeton, NJ and Oxford: Princeton University Press, 2001).

6 Keith Thomas, *Religion and the Decline of Magic* (Oxford and New York: Oxford University Press, 1971; reprint Weidenfeld & Nicolson, 1997), 618.

7 J.H. Plumb, *The Growth of Political Stability in England, 1875–1725* (Baltimore, MD: Penguin, 1969), 60–1.

8 *Flying Post or The Post Master*, 19–21 August 1701.

9 *Daily Journal*, 13 August 1726.

10 London Guildhall Library, Diary of Stephen Monteage, London Guildhall Library, MS 205, v. 7, 1746.

11 *Ibid.*, MS 205, v. 5, 1741; MS 205, 1743.

12 See Robert Latham and William Matthews (eds), *The Diary of Samuel Pepys. A New and Complete Transcription* (Berkeley, University of California Press, 1970).

13 London's 'modernity' is debated in: Miles Ogborn, *Spaces of Modernity, London's Geographies, 1660–1780* (New York: Guilford Press, 1998); Elizabeth McKellar, *The Birth of Modern London, The Development and Design of the City, 1660–1720* (Manchester: Manchester University Press, 1999). For economic developments in early modern London see, Joseph P. Ward, *Metropolitan Communities: Trade Guilds, Identity, and Change in Early Modern London* (Stanford, CA: Stanford University Press, 1997).

14 This issue is debated in Kathleen Wilson, 'Citizenship, Empire and Modernity in the English Provinces, *c.*1720–1790,' *Eighteenth-Century Studies* 29, (1995): 69–96, and Ogborn, *Spaces of Modernity*.

15 Henry Morley, *Memoirs of Bartholomew Fair* (London: Chatto and Windus, 1880), 1.

16 John Stow, *A Survey of London* (1598), reprint edn Henry Morley, LLD (ed.) (Routledge, 1912; reprint Stroud: Sutton, 1999), 344–45; Morley, *Memoirs*, 88–9.

17 Roy Porter, *London, A Social History* (Cambridge, MA: Harvard University Press, 1994), 98–9.

18 Sybil Rosenfeld, *The Theatre of the London Fairs in the Eighteenth Century* (Cambridge: Cambridge University Press, 1960), 71.

19 This is based on John Roque's representation of Southwark and surrounding areas reprinted in Harry Margary, Lympne Castle, Kent, in association with Guildhall Library, London, *The A to Z of Georgian London* (Ashford, Kent and London: Headley Brothers, Invicta Press, 1981).

20 Rosenfeld, *Theatre of London Fairs*, 108.

21 Porter, *London*, 106–7.

22 Rosenfeld, *Theatre of the London Fairs*, 107 and Chapter 6.

23 *Ibid.*, 121–33.

24 LMA, Middlesex Sessions of the Peace, MJ/O/C/005, 10 April 1746.

25 TNA, E 164/54.

26 *Ibid.*

27 Receipts and Expenditures at Bartholomew Fair, MS 3465, London Guildhall Library.

28 Edward Ward, *The London Spy*, Part VII (London: J. How, 1709), in Randolph Trumbach (ed.), *Marriage, Sex and the Family in England 1660–1800* (New York and London: Garland Publishing, 1985), 171.

29 See *The Cloyster at Bartholomew Fair: or, the Town Mistress Disguis'd. A Poem* (London, 1707), for example, a treatise on types of prostitutes available to London customers. Though it says very little about Bartholomew Fair, it is interesting to note that the occupation is associated with this particular place and festival.

30 E.A. Wrigley, 'Urban Growth and Agricultural Change: England and the Continent in the Early Modern Period,' in R.I. Rothberg and T.K. Rabb (eds), *Population and Economy* (Cambridge: Cambridge University Press, 1986).

31 A.L. Beier and Roger Finlay, *The Making of the Metropolis, London 1500–1700* (London: Longman, 1986), 4.

32 Here, I borrow Vanessa Schwartz's understanding of the 'visual representation of reality as spectacle', in *Spectacular Realities: Early Mass Culture in Fin-De-Siecle Paris* (Berkeley, Los Angeles and London: University of California Press, 1998), 6.

33 Elizabeth McKellar, *The Birth of Modern London, The Development and Design of the City, 1660–1720.* (Manchester: Manchester University Press, 1999), 188–9.

34 In the late eighteenth and early nineteenth century, commercialized centres of leisure targeted to specific class audiences were plentiful. Such institutions included pleasure gardens, music halls, circuses, and museums. See Richard Altick, *The Shows of London* (Cambridge, MA and London: Belknap Press, 1978); Warwick Wroth, *The London Pleasure Gardens of the Eighteenth Century* (London and New York: Macmillan, 1896). Fairs were also seen as class-specific amusements catering to the working class. See Catriona M. Parratt, *'More Than Mere Amusement': Working-Class Women's Leisure in England, 1750–1914* (Boston: Northeastern University Press, 2001).

35 For more about the mock-heroic poem, a popular eighteenth-century literary form,

see Ulrich Broich, Trans. David Henry Wilson, *The Eighteenth-Century Mock-Heroic Poem* (Cambridge: Cambridge University Press, 1990).

36 Besides Edward Ward, there were numerous eighteenth- and nineteenth-century accounts of fairs, especially Bartholomew Fair. These works included *A Peep at Bartholomew Fair; Containing an interesting account of the amusements and diversion of that famous metropolitan carnival* (London: R. MacDonald, 1837) and *An Historical Account of Bartholomew Fair: containing a view of its origin, and the purposes it was first instituted for. Together with a concise detail of the changes it hath undergone in its traffic, amusements, &c. &c.* (London: John Arliss, 1810); and others cited later in this chapter.

37 Studies such as Henry Morley's on Bartholomew Fair and Rosenfeld's on London's fair theatre construct the history of fair entertainment from newspaper advertisements.

38 *Reasons for Suppressing the Yearly Fair in Brookfield, Westminster; Commonly Called May-Fair* (London, 1709), 9.

39 There are scrapbooks on Bartholomew and Southwark Fairs held at London's Guildhall Library, in the British Library, and the Borough of Southwark Archives.

40 John Bancks, *Miscellaneous works, in verse and prose, of John Bancks* (London, 1738. Reprinted in Eighteenth Century Collections Online, Gale Group), 97–8.

41 *Bartholomew Fair: or, A Ramble to Smithfield. A Poem in Imitation of Milton.* London, 1729, 4.

42 *Bartholomew Fair: An Heroi-Comical Poem.* London, 1717, 2.

43 *Ibid.*

44 *Roger in Amaze; or The Country-mans Ramble through Bartholomew Fair.* London: 1705.

45 Bancks, *Miscellaneous works*, 103.

46 *A Walk to Smith-field; or, A True Discription [sic] of the Humours of Bartholomew-Fair, with the many comical Intrigues and Frolicks that are acted in every particular Booth in the Fair, by Persons of all Ages and Sexes, from the Court Gallant to the Countrey Clown.* London: 1701, 1.

47 This is elaborated in Chapter 2.

48 Ward, *London Spy*, 173.

49 *Ibid.*, 237.

50 *A Walk to Smith-field*, 1.

51 Ward, *London Spy*, 237.

52 *Ibid.*, 239.

53 *Ibid.*, 246.

54 *Daily Journal*, 12 September 1733.

55 Ward, *London Spy*, 239.

56 *A Walk to Smith-field*, 1.

57 *Ibid.*, 2.

58 Ben Jonson, *Bartholomew Fair*. ed. Suzanne Gossett (Manchester: Manchester University Press, 2001).

59 *Bartholomew-Fair: An Heroi-Comical Poem*, 3–4.

60 Ward, *London Spy*, 246–7.

61 Pepys, 29 August 1668, quoted in: Thomas Frost, *The Old Showmen and the Old London Fairs*. (1881; reprint Ann Arbor, MI: Gryphon Books, 1971), 44.

62 Pepys, 21 September 1668 quoted in Frost, 45.

63 *Ibid.*

64 *The Post Man*, 13 September, 1698.

65 *Ibid.*, 19–21 August, 1701.

66 *Daily Courant*, 18 September 1704.

67 *The Post Man*, 13 September 1705.

68 *Daily Post*, 20 September 1722.

69 *Ibid.*, 16 September 1726. (This was also advertised the following year, revealing that claims of these entertainment's novelty were often exaggerated. The 'five year old' child was still 'five' in 1729.)

70 Phyllis Mack, *Visionary Women: Ecstatic Prophecy in Seventeenth-Century England* (Berkeley: University of California Press, 1989), 23; Merry Wiesner, *Women and Gender in Early Modern Europe* (Cambridge: Cambridge University Press, 1993, reprint 2000), 33. For additional information about early modern perceptions of women's bodies and minds, see Robert Shoemaker, *Gender in English Society, 1650–1850* (London and New York: Longman, 1998).

71 Joy Wiltenburg, *Disorderly Women and Female Power in the Street Literature of Early Modern England and Germany* (Charlottesville and London: University Press of Virginia, 1992), 18–19.

72 Beth Fowkes Tobin, *Picturing Imperial Power, Colonial Subjects in Eighteenth-Century British Painting* (Durham, NC and London: Duke University Press, 1999), 37.

73 Kristina Straub, *Sexual Suspects, Eighteenth-Century Players and Sexual Ideology* (Princeton, NJ: Princeton University Press, 1992), 19–20.

74 *Bartholomew Fair: An Heroi-comical Poem*, 14–15.

75 *Ibid.*

76 *Ibid.*

77 *An Historical Account of Bartholomew Fair*, 11–12. BL 11644 c 55. 13.

78 Rosenfeld, *Theatre of the London Fairs*, 109.

79 *Ibid.*

80 This legend is recounted in *The Atheneum; or, Spirit of the English Magazines*. Vol. XIII, April to October (Boston: Munroe and Francis, 1825), 246–7.

81 Wiltenburg, *Disorderly Women*, 177.

82 *Ibid.*; Also see Rosenfeld, *Theatre of the London Fairs*, 110.

83 Wiltenburg, *Disorderly Women*, 92–3.

84 William J. Burling, *Summer Theatre in London, 1661–1820 and the Rise of the Haymarket Theatre* (London: Associated University Press, 2000).

85 Rosenfeld, *Theatre of the London Fairs*, Chapter 2.

86 *Ibid.*

87 Morley discusses the length, as does Rosenfeld.

88 *Daily Post*, 13 September 1722.

2

'Heroick Informers' and London spies: Religion, politeness, and reforming impulses in late seventeenth- and early eighteenth-century London

I n 1698, the *Flying Post or the Post Master* reported the Lord Mayor's concern regarding disorderly behaviour at that year's Bartholomew Fair. His fears were echoed by members of voluntary reform groups, who believed fairs encouraged immoral and irreligious behaviour. The Lord Mayor was particularly alarmed by 'great Swearers and Cursers' frequenting the fair and 'issued out Warrants to several Constables to apprehend them'.[1] Joining the constables were 'sober Persons ... willing to promote a Reformation of Manners'. This joint force 'positioned themselves in divers places of the Fair, and took up a great Number of Persons, for profane Cursing and Swearing'. Many were put in the Bartholomew Close stocks, 'where some Thousands came to see them'. A 'great many lewd Women', however, were not shamed so publicly and were instead taken to Bridewell.[2]

This concerted effort to apprehend dissolute people at Bartholomew Fair was motivated by a late-Stuart concern with public morality.[3] During the late seventeenth and early eighteenth centuries, London magistrates did what they could to support royal proclamations motivated by the 'Zeal and desires of Reformation', to prevent, 'the deplorable increase of Prophaness Vice and Debauchery in this Kingdom'.[4] In particular, the Court of Aldermen believed their attempts to reform or abolish Bartholomew Fair supported 'the honour of almighty God of the King and of this City and the good Government thereof'.[5] This chapter examines reforming impulses directed at London and London-area fairs and asks why reformers of various backgrounds found fairs to be morally dangerous and socially damaging as institutions that might potentially increase crime or disorder, especially among the poor.[6] London and Middlesex officials believed orders against urban fairs supported royal reform campaigns, but in practice they found their legal efforts to alter urban festivity largely ineffectual. Voluntary social and religious reformers were confounded, also, as ordinary London revellers at fairs refuted their notions of a properly ordered metropolis. Seasonal festivity continued despite efforts to redefine urban practice according to religiously and socially motivated understandings of polite and moral use of urban space.

On 25 June 1700, London's Court of Aldermen made their latest in a succession of late seventeenth- through mid-eighteenth-century orders against 'Profaness Vice and Debauchery to [sic] frequently used and practiced in Bartholomew Fair'.[7] City officials' legal and social struggles to abolish, or at least curtail, seasonal festivity reveal complex and differing understandings of appropriate urban behaviour. London's authority figures acted as elite urban patriarchs overseeing physical and moral order in the metropolis. Joining them were middling men who, buying into emerging ideas of moral masculinity, supported urban reform as an aspect of their class identity. Both efforts were opposed in practice by contrary popular understandings of the use of urban space and suitable masculinity. Efforts to reform and reorder urban festivity in London never coincided easily with royal proclamations against unruly morality. Rather, campaigns to 'reform' seasonal festivity in the metropolis reveal the limits of not only royal but also local authority when faced with practices established over years as central to London's festive culture.

Attempts to control London's fairs were not only motivated by a wish to rid the city of immoral behaviour. In fact, such campaigns were more immediately informed at a material level by the common damages and theft associated with these unruly occasions. Reformers who took up the cause against vice in the city were concerned, in particular, about criminal activity undertaken by London's poor.[8] Such fears increased during years of peace or high prices. After the Treaty of Ryswick in 1697, for example, the Navy discharged an estimated 15,000 sailors within a few months.[9] Many of these men were discharged near London, where they would have gone to look for work – during the same period, however, many men were out of work in London-area dockyards.[10] The economic and social realities of demobilization after peace treaties fed into fears of what young and unemployed men might do, especially at fairs, which encouraged disorderly public behaviour. Anxieties regarding destructive public behaviour at fairs were shared by reformers, both official and voluntary, concerned with policing the growing urban population.

There is evidence in London court records and literary commentary about fairs demonstrating that theft and property damage went hand in hand with these institutions; concerns about property informed increased efforts to police early modern London.[11] Fairs were targeted on a practical level because criminal activity increased for their duration in and around the areas in which they occurred. Reformers derided fairs because they were obvious centres of criminal activity that presented seasonal interruptions to London's usual business. Beyond being disruptive to commerce, fairs encouraged immoral and disorderly behaviours such as public drunkenness and sexual freedom. Reformers likely viewed these activities as linked, because drinking was thought to increase criminal activity among labouring people.[12] Fairs were an obvious target for London's social reformers and their attention to their regulation is not surprising. The types of arguments reformers made against fairs reveal how middling reformers petitioned for their particular interests and goals for the city in the hope they would be taken seriously and implemented by civic officials.[13]

Though largely unsuccessful, efforts of London authorities and reform-minded individuals to regulate and control London's many fairs reveal their own understandings of ideal masculinity. Reformers' attacks against disorderly urban behaviour were shaped not only by emerging notions of polite masculinity, but also by religious belief and theories of urban and social order. City and county efforts to create an orderly and productive city reveal shared assumptions that urban space best served Londoners when used to undertake appropriate commerce. Appropriate for urban reformers meant commerce that reflected the sort of polite and controlled masculinity expounded by reform societies and religious discourse. Commercial exchanges were orderly when they occurred in urban spaces dedicated to trade and free of festivities that might divert Londoners from their usual business.[14] Crime encouraged by 'temptations' of the city, such as fairs, corrupted servants and apprentices, and authorities thought that fairs promoted social disruption attending drinking and festivity. Fairs were also spectacles that distracted men from their occupations, obligations, and proper social place.[15] In the justices' view, festivals lessened the overall commercial and moral strength of London.

The campaign to regulate festivity was a gendered project. City fathers and social reformers who operated according to emerging ideas of 'polite' masculinity wanted to shape London into a mannered metropolis, but their reform efforts met repeated resistance from fair-goers. Young men who used fairs for leisure or income (both legitimate and illicit) held contrary views regarding urban festivity. Their customary use of fair space as a location for drinking, carousing, profit, or sociability did not conform to new ideas about appropriate male urban behaviour. Despite regulation, many male and female business owners and pedlars

continued to see fairs as commercial venues where they worked in opposition to official regulation. Opposing views of the purpose and suitability of fairs worked against each other, and the campaign to regulate fairs
was turbulent.

Through legislation of fairs, London's Aldermen and Middlesex
county officials hoped to 'procure a thorough Reformation of Manners'.[16]
A reformation of manners, however, targeting traditional urban amusement was no easy task. Until the mid-eighteenth century, fairs, illegal
play booths, and curious spectacles exhibited by businessmen in the city
increased. City officials, social reformers, and critics informed by discourses of religious reform, politeness, and notions of urban order all
desired to regulate the duration and frequency of public amusements
while also controlling behaviour at these places. A desire to make the city
mannered and godly motivated many efforts to regulate amusement in
London, especially at the city's fairs.

London's officials as well as social reformers undertook their regulation of urban fairs in the context of royal proclamations against vice.
In the early 1690s, Queen Mary II wrote a letter to the Middlesex justices in which she appealed to parish officers and 'all other officers and
persons whatsoever, to do their part in their several stations, by timely
and impartial informations and prosecutions', to prevent disorderly
and ungodly public behaviour.[17] By 1692, when William III delivered a
'Proclamation Against Vicious, Debauched and Profane Persons' calling
for the regulation and suppression of 'blasphemy, profane swearing and
cursing, drunkenness, lewdness, breaking the Sabbath and other dissolute, immoral or disorderly practice', some of his subjects, particularly
members of London's societies for reformation of manners, were primed
to carry his message into the streets.[18] This royal concern that English
subjects were far too immoral continued under Anne, who wrote a letter
to the Westminster Quarter Sessions in January 1712. Here, the Queen
encouraged justices to enforce laws against 'irreligion', including those
prohibiting 'Blasphemy, Prophane swearing and cursing, Prophanation
of the Lord's Day, Excessive Drinking, Gaming, Lewdness and all other
dissolute immoral and disorderly practices'.[19]

The Middlesex and Westminster justices, London's Aldermen
and Lord Mayor, voluntary 'reform' groups, and periodical writers all
responded to these royal pleas to combat vice and immorality with their
own interpretations of which activities disrupted urban morality. Their
particular attention to regulating and suppressing fairs and amusements
associated with them was one outgrowth of this campaign. At fairs,
London officials found many irreligious and immoral practices frowned

upon by late-Stuart monarchs. In particular, fairs seemed to encourage illicit sexual behaviour, an ongoing central concern of late-seventeenth century efforts to curtail immorality.[20] Beyond royal decrees, two parallel impulses influenced urban reform efforts: politeness and renewed religious zeal. City reformers and social critics focused their vigilance on London's most obvious locations of vice, immorality, drunkenness, and gaming – fairs. There were many yearly fairs held in London, and among them were those operating without charters (which the Middlesex justices referred to as 'pretend fairs') as well as those that were licensed, but nevertheless disorderly. All of these were central targets of efforts to order the metropolis, and the efforts of London's Aldermen and Middlesex and Westminster officials to control fairs are examined in Chapter 3.

The late seventeenth- and early eighteenth-century interest in imposing a new moral physical and social order upon London is reflected in the writings of political philosophers and urban designers, who also voiced their anxieties about urban disorder. The Earl of Shaftesbury, Bernard Mandeville, and David Hume, for example, all shared concerns regarding the disorderly state of the metropolis, especially its streets. These men believed that the city streets were 'a matter of government, civility and self-control'.[21] Physically-ordering streets meant cleaning them of debris, paving, and lighting them. Concern with the physical attributes of streets extended equally to ridding them of unruly public gatherings, including fairs. Reforming London through attempts to make the city mannered by removing or reforming the city's disorderly and, therefore, impolite inhabitants as well as their traditions is a theme common to periodical literature describing the spectacle of London in the late seventeenth century. Concern with idleness and disorder on London's streets is found, also, in sermons preached at London societies for reformation of manners and to the City's Alderman and Lord Mayor. City officials' concerns regarding public amusements reflect a wider cultural debate about urban disorder and polite masculinity.

Men who conformed to emerging polite sensibilities and believed that London ought to be ideally ordered applied such notions equally to themselves. Such ideas are explored in scholarship focused on emerging polite society in the later Stuart years.[22] This literature views 'politeness' as a movement undertaken by middling to elite men and women to become 'well-polished', ordered, or accomplished in appropriate skills or personality traits according to one's sex.[23] Efforts to exhibit politeness were influenced by many factors including the growth of commerce and an infrastructure of shops devoted to fashion and sociability, as well as emerging feelings of nationalism, civic virtue, morality, and religion.

Polite ideas stemmed from and were reinforced by a growing body of conduct literature aimed both at men and women, although the most recent studies on the subject focus especially on the creation of a specifically masculine and polite identity in the eighteenth century.

How to control and make more polite a city the size of London was a matter of concern for national and local authorities, and it also occupied space in much of the discourse coming from and directed at middling men. Concern about imposing and maintaining order was particularly acute in London, a space in which thousands of people carried out their lives free of their 'natural' sources of discipline.[24] Regular opportunities for men and women to gather in the capital city for amusement worried urban officials and social reformers who believed such occasions encouraged behaviour they considered socially and religiously dangerous. These reformers also viewed such occasions as upsetting the city's usual commerce.[25] Popular recreations based around an agricultural calendar did not make sense in a world of wage labourers more oriented on industrial time.[26] Urban authorities struggled to discipline and regulate London's influx of working people, who had left the paternalist rule of their parishes and families behind in the country. By the late seventeenth century, London had outgrown the 'conventional machinery' of traditional, community-based moral policing.[27] In smaller communities, a familial-based gender order structured society and neighbours watched and put checks on public behaviour.[28] Such configurations were impossible in the shifting social context of late seventeenth-century London. In attempting to control the morality and public conduct of Londoners, urban authorities and reformers adapted traditional methods of keeping checks on urban morality to the social reality of their burgeoning metropolis.[29]

Economic trends between 1690 and 1750 contributed to urbanization and benefited Londoners involved in trade, industry, and commercial agriculture. Prosperous 'middling people', who now outnumbered England's traditional landed elite, empowered a rising consumer society.[30] People who prospered from trade, industry, or the professions made up this new group of neither gentlemen nor traditional labouring people. Such prospering folk were referred to by contemporaries as constituting 'the middling sort' or a 'middle station'.[31] Middling men and women were increasingly interested in material goods and leisure activities – they avidly consumed entertainment, services, and a new genre of print culture including novels, newspapers and periodical journals through which they developed shared understandings and sought ideas about self-improvement.[32] This increasingly economically prosperous group sought political influence within the metropolis.

One means by which middling men attempted to influence their city was through participation in groups such as societies for reformation of manners. Active participation was not required: any literate person, male or female, could participate virtually in the debate through print.[33] During the late seventeenth century, middling people sought literature focused on self-improvement, economics, and politics. Their demand for informative reading material motivated new types of literature, including newspapers and novels.[34] Sermons were an additional popular pamphlet subject and those preached to societies for reformation of manners were printed widely, as were tracts describing the agenda of these societies, such as Josiah Woodward's 1698, *An Account of the Rise and Progress of the Religious Societies in the City of London*.[35] Other printed critiques of urban life included satirical literature, engravings and paintings, and newspapers. Ideas about self-improvement gained from or con-solidated by this literature helped consolidate middling readers' concep-tions of mannered and acceptable urban behaviour. Informed by these notions in a growing metropolis that lacked the numbers of officials to fully enforce laws, reform-minded middling men stepped into the role of urban patriarchs in groups such as the societies for reformation of manners.

Enforcement efforts behind orders or warnings against urban festiv-ity were difficult to enforce in early eighteenth-century London. Orders against particular types of booths intended for performances, drink-ing, or gaming, for example, were openly ignored. Newspapers printed announcements that fairs were to be kept for chartered days only and that booths or land should be let only for 'Merchandizes, Trade and Commerce, according to the good Intents and Purposes designed in the Granting, Erecting and Establishing the said Fair'.[36] Trading in mate-rial goods was considered proper commerce, not entertainment, and this was reiterated in newspaper advertisements reminding Londoners of the commercial intent of fairs. A 1717 advertisement, for example, stipulated that commerce at the fair that year was limited to the sale of 'Cattle, Leather and other Goods', though the publisher added this was, 'to the great Afflicton [*sic*] and Mortification of poor Punch and all his Attendants'.[37] Nevertheless, Punch, along with the 'two German Maiden' rope-dancers, the Italian Scaramouch (and his dog), a feather-eating tiger, and various strolling players were not prevented from performing their shows and their performances continued to be advertised despite such orders on the part of city officials.[38] Though officials ordered a stop to shows at fairs, they continued to be tolerated.

It is clear that shows were tolerated within fairground booths and stalls.[39] In 1721, for example, a newspaper reported that London's Lord Mayor went in person to Bartholomew Fair and suppressed the 'gaming tables' while 'permitting' shows in 'the booth and in ... Houses' to continue a week longer. This was later retracted, but the statement reveals an understanding that prohibited shows were sometimes tolerated.[40] In fact, the Lord Mayor had given no such permission and the newspaper printed a correction in its following issue, but the false information continued to spread. The inaccurate report was repeated with further explanation in a rival newspaper, which proclaimed the advertisement *should* have read that booths and play houses, 'would have continued a Week longer, not that they were allow'd to continue a Week longer'.[41] The difference between continuing and being permitted to continue was commonly understood – and that London officials frowned on or did not allow entertainment at fairs did little to curtail that industry. Fair entertainment drew crowds despite proclamations made by urban authorities, proving festivity would continue and, from the perspective of reformers, provide an environment in which men and women could be easily tempted away from lives of economy and virtue.

Because fairs and their entertainment were difficult to curtail and people's behaviour in these spaces was policed unevenly throughout the metropolis, voluntary reformers attempted to fill in the gaps.[42] In some cases, morally and religiously minded reformers actively intervened when they witnessed behaviours they considered immoral, whether at fairs or not.[43] This method of keeping urban order is encouraged in Thomas Bray's 1708 sermon to the London societies for reformation of manners as the only means to curtail 'Sins of Uncleanness', such as cursing, swearing or sodomy, offences magistrates should 'Countenance and Encourage' any people to 'Inform against'.[44] However, as Faramerz Dabhoiwala has demonstrated, more often than actively policing public morality themselves, reformers provided financial support to existing officers or employed informers with money raised through subscription.[45]

Efforts to make London mannered coincided with the City's forced urban renewal initiated by the 1666 fire. In some fire-damaged areas, City planners rebuilt London and constructed new streets and buildings reflecting the latest architectural styles.[46] Consequently, according to Peter Borsay, 'cultural polarization' occurred along with this spatial 'urban renaissance'.[47] In a refurbished metropolis, some prosperous middling Londoners participated in a parallel effort to reform social practice, revealing how 'civilizing and social distancing ... went hand in hand'.[48] Making the city polite, however, took effort, for even in its post-fire refurbished spaces there was much about London in disarray, and the process was never complete. The population filling London was not necessarily mannered, nor was it gainfully employed. Social instability increased as unemployed or casually employed people found little relief. As Robert Shoemaker argues, the 1690s were the 'worst in the century' and were a time in which bread prices rose, wars disrupted trade, and the government manipulated coinage with disastrous effects.[49]

Religious and reform discourse

The emergence of societies for reformation of manners reflected a larger political and social concern with maintaining order in a climate of shifting traditions. Church officials took up the cause, as well as voluntary societies and justices of the peace who continued a campaign against vice through the middle of the eighteenth century.[50] These societies had special appeal for middling men, yet we cannot view them as being organized 'from below' because these men enjoyed the support of Churchmen, actively sought support from the upper classes, and enjoyed the support of many members of Parliament.[51] While not operating at a grass-roots level, the societies nevertheless provided a forum of action for some men who might not previously have had important roles to play in their city's governance, offering them a significant place in 'political intervention in the everyday life of the London streets'.[52] Members included a top level of reform-minded lawyers, MPs, and JPs, but also included a 'Second Society' of fifty men who were primarily tradesmen, a third group of constables, and a final group of 'informers', or tradesmen and artisans who remained on the lookout for incidents of vice and reported them to their local magistrates.[53] The tier of fifty select men compiled a yearly blacklist of those guilty of vice, and constables met regularly to devise the best possible ways to find and prosecute misbehaviour: all efforts were directed at ridding the urban environment of practices they recognized as immoral. Hunt has compiled information about offences prosecuted by societies for the reformation of manners from 1694–1738. Offences prosecuted included Sabbath breaking, profanity and swearing, drunkenness, keeping a common gaming house, sodomy (though rare) and, most commonly, 'lewd and disorderly practices', including prostitution.[54]

Societies for the reformation of manners provided middling men in London opportunities for active oversight of the urban environment, whether through financial support of moral causes or active policing, which they did with enthusiasm. Men who participated – the constables, justices of the peace, and residents of London, or 'informers' – quickly moved the societies' concerns beyond the founding members' desire to reform 'profane swearing and cursing and blasphemy'.[55] London had the most societies, with over twenty at one time during its nearly forty-year existence.[56] As members of these London societies, middling men gained influence as they reported 'vice' and also oversaw actions taken by parish officers and justices of the peace.[57]

The vigilant members of London's reform societies legitimized their existence within London as essential to national order. In a 1694 tract, *Proposals for a National Reformation of Manners*, the Society for Reformation trumpeted:

> What *Jerusalem* was of old unto *Judea*, and *Judea* unto other Nations, in like manner *London* is unto *England*, and *England* unto CHRISTENDOM. A *City* and *Nation* more favoured of God ... there is not to be found under the whole heavens.[58]

These men believed that England had been aided by divine intervention during the late seventeenth century, having survived an era that witnessed everything from political upheavals to natural disaster. Political shifts began with a mid-century civil war resulting in the overthrow of the monarch and establishment of the Commonwealth. In 1688, political turmoil was once again narrowly avoided with the 'Glorious Revolution' in which the Protestant William of Orange and his wife Mary Stuart filled the 'vacated' throne of Catholic (and French-supported) James II. As the century progressed, political parties emerged and fought for control of Parliament, middling people grew more prosperous, and in the midst of it all, the capital city was devastated by a fire in 1666. Because the city and nation had survived these major upheavals, the authors of the Society for Reformation's appeal asked Londoners to act responsibly. England was shown many mercies and '*God expect[ed] from England and London* a Publick or *National Reformation*, and nothing less than this, [would] be esteemed by him a *walking worthy* of these great mercys [*sic*] in all-becoming *thankfulness*'.[59]

Religious sentiment legitimized the work of reform societies. Sermons preached for societies for reformation of manners provided middling men justification for their self-proclaimed role as the city's moral force, a position mandated by their status not only as religious men, but also as 'good Citizen's and Country-men'.[60] The tracts combine Biblical lessons with proclamations about civic duty in an effort to provoke society members to 'aid and assist the Magistrates and Government in punishing Vice and Wickedness'.[61] The overwhelming message in such sermons was that London's order could not be ensured without the assistance of society members. Individual members were asked to inform on 'notorious Criminals, and to facilitate the seizing and arraigning of them for Lewdness, Blasphemy, Thefts and Murders'. In a time of unprecedented 'degeneracy and corruption', society preachers told their middling audience that the nation's health and safety depended on maintaining lawfulness in the metropolis.[62]

Society members looking for arenas of vice or degeneracy targeted obvious locations of both – the capital city's fairs. Similar to urban authorities, members of the London societies understood fairs as troubling institutions that were havens for the city's worst moral and religious offenders. In 1708, the same year London's Aldermen issued an order regulating the tenure and entertainments of Bartholomew Fair, Thomas Bray delivered a sermon addressing 'Outrages' against civic and religious law committed at Bartholomew and May Fairs.[63] Bray optimistically, if prematurely, proclaims that City officials had successfully '[overthrown ... and routed] that Seminary of Impiety and Debauchery Annually held in [Bartholomew Fair], *to the undoing* of the Youth, both of Town and Country', and praises the Westminster justices for their efforts to limit May Fair.[64] Bray may have hoped that city efforts to contain these fairs accomplished the final overthrow of impropriety at fairs. In fact, each fair had been only temporarily curtailed and both continued well past 1709 (when Bray's pamphlet appeared). Bray preached about this civic triumph (however temporary) as a reminder of the tangible social benefits of promoting good manners in the city. Reformers who heard and acted according to this speech not only helped purge London of social and moral disorder, but also ensured stable religious and political order. Bray emphasizes this by evoking the image of the old priory of St Bartholomew, the grounds of which hosted the fair he calls a yearly impious and debauched 'seminary'. This once Roman Catholic institution remained suspect to reform-minded Anglicans, for whom such festivals hindered the 'Cause of God against the Powers of Darkness'.[65] Though in his sermon Bray applauds city officials who regulated fairs for 'taking the *Outworks* of Satan's fortified Place among us', he warned that the '*Citadel* it self' was actually the play house, the place to which Satan's '*Militia* have now a Place to retreat'.[66]

Bolstering his message with militaristic imagery, Bray demonstrated for his congregation a successful assault on London's '*Spiritual Enemies*', fairs, and alerted them to the struggle yet to be won in London play houses.[67] With the help of the, '*Society for Reformation of Manners,* and their noble Band of *Heroick Informers*', Christ's 'Kingdom', would triumph and these warriors would meet the approval of not only their

Church and nation, but from 'so many Kingdoms and States Abroad'.[68] Combating the entertainments of fairs and playhouses seemed a tangible way for reform-minded Anglicans to maintain London's, their own, their nation's, and even the world's godly favour while ensuring social stability. This process provided them, also, vital roles in their city and nation's governance. As 'actively engaged' local 'informers', reform-minded men made themselves essential to the smooth and safe functioning of their local community.

Sermons delivered to societies for reformation of manners reinforced middling men's belief that they had a special policing function in their city, while also revealing specific areas and behaviours on which to focus their reform efforts. Reforming the city with godly intent is a trope repeated again and again. Though informed primarily by religious belief, these sermons reflect, also, audiences' emerging notions of politeness and proper urban behaviour. Ministers shaped Biblical lessons to appeal to their middling and increasingly polite audience. This late seventeenth- and early eighteenth-century concern with reforming lower orders led to little lasting legislation. However, reforming the manners of lower orders, especially in London, was one issue around which middling men coalesced and around which they forged new polite identities. Driven by a religious discourse, middling reformers sought to make their urban environment conform to their own emerging notions of an ordered metropolis. Making a mannered city was one way middling men influenced their urban landscape while in the process portraying themselves as actors in an important political debate.

Scholarship on politeness often de-emphasizes religious belief systems, which no doubt informed views of public amusements in London and their attending dangers. London's magistrates and justices inhabited a city and held offices in institutions closely allied with the Church of England. At civic events and during church festivals and holidays, these men attended sermons delivered by Church of England clergy who tailored their sermons to helping this audience fulfil civic duties in a godly manner. Their exhortations to magistrates demonstrated to these men not only their duty as officials imbued with the vast responsibility of insuring the godliness of the city and its inhabitants, but also gave them explicit instructions on how to secure God's favour for their city and, by extension, larger nation.

London Churchmen were part of an over twenty-year-long movement – an Anglican 'providentialist campaign for the reformation of national manners'.[69] Shaken by the events of the mid-seventeenth century, but from their re-established position controlling the Church and

State, Restoration Churchmen preached 'providentialism'.[70] Sermons delivered to London's Aldermen and Lord Mayor reflected their sincere belief that God had delivered their city and nation from the seventeenth century's troubles, from regicide to plague to fire. God restored order, but it was up to each individual to deserve and continue to earn God's 'divine providential care' for the entire nation.[71] With London's leaders in their congregation, these Churchmen made the focus of their sermons connections between the nation's and City's delivery from disaster and the religiosity of leaders. They preached to city leaders that they were responsible for ensuring continued civic blessings through their own divinely influenced governance. Without their guidance, the nation was imperilled.

Thomas Lynford delivered such a message in a sermon given at Guildhall Chapel on 24 February 1688/89. As summarized in a later printed version, Lyford demonstrated to the city's governors 'the necessity of God's Providence for the preservation of any City or Government, and consequently to persuade the Members thereof to use their utmost endeavours, for the securing to themselves, the divine favour'.[72] Lynford's discourse began with Psalm 127 v. 1, 'Except the Lord keep the City, the watchman waketh but in vain'. Throughout the sermon, Lynford reiterated the point that all efforts by individuals within the City did nothing for the larger good if leaders were not themselves Godly. To guarantee God's protection of the city, its governors had to avoid common errors of 'human weakness'. Such errors included not being wise enough to foresee potential dangers, avoiding 'factious temper[s] that ... take delight in embroiling the affairs of any nation', and causing general mischief for their own amusement. Above all, Lynford warned the city's governors that they should 'endeavor ... to provide for the Peace and Safety of any City of Government'. Bad governors, according to Lyford, ignore all laws, the rights and privileges of those ruled, and do everything according to their own whims. These type of men as rulers are the 'ruine of any State'.[73]

Other sermons delivered to the London Aldermen and Lord Mayor advise the leaders of their responsibility to be Godly. In 1696, Lilly Butler, who delivered sermons also to the societies for reformation of manners, preached on the occasion of the Lord Mayor's election from Proverbs 29, v. 2: 'When the Righteous are in Authority, the People rejoyce'. More directly than Lynford, Butler states, 'When those that have a lively and vigourous sense of God upon their Minds, and a sincere regard to his Divine Will, when Men of Conscience, Integrity, and Religion, when such Men are in *Authority*, they do highly promote the good estate of that Society they govern'.[74] Butler used the occasion to advise the Lord Mayor and Aldermen of the seven parts of a magistrate's office: the maintenance of people's property along with people's legal rights and privileges, liberties and immunities, to preserve public peace, to 'take care of their People's lives', defending them from assaults and abuse, to encourage industry, to maintain public charities and, above all else, to 'preserve and promote true Religion'.[75] Lynford and other ministers also mention many of these duties in sermons delivered to city officials. S.A. Freeman emphasized the maintenance of charity in an Easter sermon delivered to the Lord Mayor, Aldermen and 'Governors of the several Hospitals of the City' in 1698. W. Freeman preached on a variant of charity when he focused on the importance of the education of children.

When gathered to hear sermons at city functions or holy days, London's Lord Mayor and Aldermen heard repeated refrains of how and why they had the responsibility to execute their offices in a Godly manner. They were assured that their proper governance would bring order to the city and lessen some of London's struggles with poverty, crime, and general disorder. These messages often went beyond 'godly', however, preaching a type of Christian-influenced public civility. These Churchmen recognized the potential symbolic power Aldermen and the Lord Mayor had in portraying virtue and order to London's citizens. Through their demeanour they were told to exhibit qualities Gregory Hascard called 'the glew [sic] of Societies and Conversation, the best imitation of God and Christ, and the finest Livery and ornament of a Christian'. Hascard specifically referred to kindness, tender-heartedness, and readiness to forgive. All of these were characteristics exhibited by Christ and were, therefore, qualities the city's magistrates should emulate.

Hascard echoes refrains common also in conduct literature. Christian men had a duty to be in 'opposition to the contrary Vices of Anger and Wrath, Bitterness and Clamour, evil Speaking and Malice', all the expected religious duties. At the same time, however, they should exhibit self-control and 'pleasantness and easiness of Conversation', be courteous and have 'obliging temper[s]'. Above all, Christian men should not be 'sullen' or 'peevish' thinking this made them appear more religious. Hascard advised godly men to partake in amusement – they need not be melancholy because they understood how to avoid vice and could control themselves in any situation. These magistrates should even exhibit 'Gentleness when punish[ing]'. Punishment was an absolute necessity for the maintenance of law and order, but Hascard thought punishment should only go as far as needed in order to preserve Government and cause repentance – 'God and good men have never us'd utmost severity and destruction, which are due onely to the refractory and impenitent'.[76] By exhibiting all of these qualities and properly fulfilling his position, a godly magistrate avoided becoming a 'dark Lanthorn' only shining to himself. He was instead able to 'direct the Paths of the Simple'.[77]

Sermons emphasized the magistrates' responsibility to the wider community, but they also presented ideas of how a proper Christian community should function. God's favour could only be received if all members of the community played their part and fulfilled their obligations. City officials did their part by ensuring godly laws were passed and followed. They also served as examples of polite, Christian men for the populace who could secure God's favour for themselves, their city and nation by following the examples set by their leaders. Above all undesirable qualities among the inhabitants of London, these Churchmen agreed that idleness and lewd behaviour, especially in public, most welcomed God's disfavour. If a city was 'founded upon a rock' – or was governed by godly leaders – only half the battle was won. If God were to preserve any society, the 'Members thereof must not be idle, but must themselves use all necessary care for the preservation thereof'.[78] Not only should the leaders be conscious of how their actions affected their city, but urban inhabitants had also the responsibility to reform their own behaviour and avoid offending God. Lynford believed people could no better employ themselves than in joining 'publick Societies, and for the peace and quiet of others, as well as of themselves'. In so doing they would not hide their talents 'in a Napkin, and … depend wholly upon God's Providence, in the case of difficulty and danger'.[79] London citizens of all ranks had the ability to do something about their own city's godly status, and groups such as the societies for reformation of manners provided opportunities for them to be active in promoting their city's continued deliverance.

Hearing messages about how citizens should behave, London officials contrasted these messages with actual behaviour they witnessed in London's streets. As magistrates, they witnessed their share of disorderly and anti-Christian behaviour. Much of it was not synchronous with the idealized godly city presented to them in sermons advising them that God's favour and protection could only be secured if the city's inhabitants were 'kindly affected towards on another … [because] there is nothing more pleasing to God than Peace and Unity'.[80] Observing their city, London's Aldermen saw many inhabitants who were disorderly and indolent. In such a context, Butler advised them to 'incourage [sic] Industry' and to 'punish Vagrants and Beggars, and all Managers of such unlawful Games and Sports, as are wont to draw Men off from the useful Employment of their Callings, and to lead them into an idle and dissolute Way of living, whereby they become unprofitable and hurtful Members of a Society'. For evidence of idleness diverting people from their 'callings', officials had only to examine the City's many fairs – here Aldermen found peace and industry a rare commodity.

The security of London was not the only reason Aldermen were striving to become Godly leaders – they had as well a personal stake in making London safe. Sermons reminded them of the rewards to be reaped if they properly fulfilled their duties as Christian magistrates. Those who secured citizens' possessions, Industry and Zeal, who maintained people's rights and privileges, preserved the peace, defended the population, employed the poor, and suppressed wickedness would be 'honoured of God and Men; They will be as Signets on God's Right Hand, and Remembered when he maketh up his Jewels'. The sanctity and weight of their office was reaffirmed in these sermons as they were told, '[God] hath given you of his Power and Authority, and set you to judge for him upon Earth; and if you act for him faithfully and diligently ... he will make you partakers of his Nature and Glory, his Joy and Happiness in a degree far beyond what you can now conceive, and ye shall be like God in Heaven'.[81] Churchmen promised such rewards for dedicated and divinely inspired public service – divine deliverance for the City as well as themselves.

Preaching sermons to the Lord Mayor and Aldermen was an established tradition by the late seventeenth century, but what is unique about this period is most sermons were preached in newly constructed churches. By the mid-1680s, many of Christopher Wren's post-fire rebuilding projects were nearing an end. London's churches were being completed one by one. Many of the sermons were preached before the Lord Mayor and Aldermen at the Guildhall Chapel, one of the least damaged buildings and earliest reconstructed after the fire. Many others, however, were given in newly reconstructed churches. Delivered in these spaces, sermons were not the only message. The balanced classical interiors of these new churches reinforced messages heard in sermons delivered to the city's officials, especially those with themes devoted to the religious necessity of urban order.

Rebuilt churches reflected a wider revitalized Church in London. Before and immediately following the Restoration, fears of Catholic influence, the rise of Dissent, and Occasional Conformity motivated London's Churchmen to give their attention to a 'renewal of the Church in piety and edification, which they made the center of their own arduous and devoted pastoral care'.[82] Gordon Rupp calls this period of religious renewal in London a 'Small Awakening'. If engaging and socially concerned Churchmen revitalized religious life in London, this life must also have been influenced by the opening of newly rebuilt, and in some cases, congregationally-reconfigured churches. Throughout the 1670s and until the mid-1680s, churches were rebuilt and reopened. Eighty-seven churches had been destroyed by the Fire and while only fifty-one were rebuilt according to the Act of 1670 uniting several parishes, there were enough new churches in the city so that most communicating Christians would have at some point attended a rebuilt church. Because they were not publicly funded, but rebuilt by subscription or their own church funds, London's Churchmen had an immediate reason to make their preaching appealing in an effort to attract (paying) parishioners. Rebuilding churches provided one motive for religious renewal in the city. In this context, London's Aldermen heard sermons and made decisions about how to apply the religious lessons they learned.

New churches projected a semblance of Christian and Anglican order to anyone examining the city. By 1686 most of the churches had been rebuilt, although some steeples would not be replaced until the end of the century.[83] St Paul's Cathedral, which completed the skyline, was not finished until 1709.[84] Cynthia Wall describes London's skyline as the most visible evidence of London's post-fire order. While Wren's overall city plan was never achieved and London was not entirely transformed from its previous layout, the city's rebuilt skyline incorporated features that were both gothic and new. Sprawling along the river, the city was shaped by church spires rising over its surface, as they had for centuries. Wren's steeples evoked the previous Gothic spires, but along newer classical lines.[85] This skyline provided London a visual representation of the city's ongoing process of becoming new and projected the city's fluxuating identity. It retained Gothic elements from its past, but 'was also undeniable and unforgettably new, thus suggesting ... accommodation of the new urban space with traditional structures of social order'.[86] Continuing to exist above this reshaped city was the Church, and the Aldermen reflected this influence in their governance. There is perhaps no better visual representation of what London's Aldermen and Lord Mayor hoped to combat – disorderly urban spaces, some still old and others new, inhabited by people pursuing traditional amusements.

Twenty years after the Great Fire, London began to look again like a strong city, rebuilt in some parts according to the latest architectural styles. As difficult as it was to collect funds to rebuild London in a new, state-dictated style, impose a new order and functionality on its streets, and build classical churches, urban reformers found it even more difficult to impose that order on the people who populated these spaces. The reconstruction of buildings and streets coincided with the emergence of a fashionable polite middling man who used these streets and buildings to showcase his individual order and politeness. While middling and elite people may have experienced an 'urban renaissance' in London, working people continued to use these re-formulated spaces in traditional ways. London's most well-known traditional fair, St Bartholomew's Fair, took place in an area surrounding a city church untouched by London's fire. St Bartholomew's-the-Great is one of the few medieval structures that survived so close to the area consumed by fire. It is fitting that a tradition with medieval origins maligned by London's Aldermen took place in the shadow of one of the city's remaining medieval structures. This wooden former monastery and its grounds just outside of London's original walls was the site of a yearly fair. This fair was protected by the ancestral rights given by Henry VIII to the Rich family and their heirs. As such, the fair was literally and legally outside the all-encompassing reach of reform-minded city officials.[87] Despite the changing landscape of so many London streets, this fair held every August in West Smithfield near a surviving great church was a yearly reminder to city officials and urban reformers of the old city and the traditions they hoped to reform.

Discourses of reform in periodical literature

Cleaning up urban spaces and imposing a unique combination of new manners and old patriarchal order was a frequent topic of both reform societies and periodical literature written by urban spectators for a middling audience. While, as Alan Hunt points out, many writers including Edward Ward and Daniel Defoe criticized the moral efforts of the societies for reformation of manners, such work nevertheless illustrated aspects which London middling audiences thought required reform.[88] Through satire, periodical writers avoided the straightforward didacticism of ministers or reformers but still effectively communicated that London was unacceptably disorderly. They frequently wrote of London's urban environment and vividly portrayed the city's most tumultuous spectacles, especially the numerous outdoor markets and festivals, most notably Bartholomew Fair.

Londoners, however, did not need to join official reform-oriented societies to read about and become concerned with immorality. Metropolitan social problems concerned many urban spectators who documented or satirized such problems in periodical literature. During the late seventeenth century, periodical literature was increasingly popu-

lar, especially after the 1695 expiration of the Licensing Act, which subjected a writer's work to an official censor before it could be published.
At the expiration of the Licensing Act, weekly or often daily publications
appeared in bookstalls and coffee houses. Some of the era's most popular periodical works were the *Athenian Mercury*, the *Examiner*, *Tatler*,
Spectator and Ned Ward's *London Spy*.[89] Writers who hoped to make
a living at such work needed to effectively appeal to their readers' concerns. Writing for an audience of middling men and women often meant
echoing their concerns about London's disorder and vividly presenting
to them what, among the city's lower orders, required reform.

With such words as 'spy', 'tatler', or 'spectator' in the titles of their
periodicals, journalists reflected their readers' interest in surveillance.
Journalists often structured their periodicals in ways that made it seem
as if their readers received privileged information unknown to those
outside their audience.[90] They also echo traditions that maintained
England's social order and reformulated a primarily rural method for
social discipline to fit an urban setting. 'Spying' on one's neighbours
reinforced patriarchal social order and checked deviance in rural communities, but it was not as practical in a metropolis consisting of a fluid
and often masterless population. Without familial or parish ties to
constantly watch and censure disorderly behaviour, society (especially
represented by middling men) stepped in to ensure order. Periodical literature such as Ned Ward's work *The London Spy* (1698–1700) appealed
to the middling desire to critique and police London's population as
did tracts published by the Society for Reformation of Manners. These
works purported to reveal societal conditions requiring the intervention of politically conscious middling men. *The London Spy*, however,
also has an additional sensational side and demonstrates that middling
people consumed printed work for entertainment value, not only self-
improvement. Secrets revealed by 'spies' or 'tattlers' fascinated readers
while they also stereotyped certain urban people and spectacles as impolite. These overdrawn satires of inappropriate demeanour reinforced and
helped define readers' own sense of appropriate (polite) conduct.

Throughout Ned Ward's eighteen-volume periodical, the two men
visit almost every well-known site in London, including dress shops,
coffee houses, famous streets, St Paul's cathedral and Bartholomew Fair.
Ward devotes passages to describing individuals met by the two protagonists on their tour. The two men do not merely observe London's
sights; they enthusiastically participate in the town's activities and note
the character of all whom they meet. All the while, of course, the opinions of both the sophisticated urban dweller and his country cousin are

made known to the reader who might identify with either perspective – or both – depending on their origins. Middling men reading the series in London might think the text further justified a general reformation of the city's manners. Ward's 'London spies' surveyed the crowds and spaces into which they ventured, registering sights, sounds, and smells for the reader according to a 'polite' middling value system. Physical characteristics signified a great deal about 'true' character to readers. A religious idea familiar to most people in seventeenth-century England equated a person's visible bodily condition with the spiritual condition of one's soul. The realities of a person's or city's moral condition could be discerned in concrete physical characteristics.[91] This is evident in the ways in which the London spies vividly described and characterized the people and places they observed.

The outward appearance of individuals not only demonstrated each individual's morality, but was transferred, also, onto the meaning of their surrounding environs. When the two London spies visit Salisbury Court, for example, the reader quickly realizes this is one of London's immoral spaces based upon the residents found there. Ward describes these areas' inhabitants and the unclean, dimly lit space in which they are found with as many adjectives as there are to signify its similarity to Sodom. The people are 'figures' who look as if 'the *Devil* had Rob'd 'em of all their *Natural Beauty*' and nothing could be read in each person but '*Devilism* … *Theft, Whoredom, Homicide* and *Blasphemy* peep'd out at the very Windows of their *Soul; Lying, Purjury, Fraud, Impudence,* and *Misery* were the only *Grace* of their *Countenance*'.[92] Finding an unclean space inhabited by such godless people leads the protagonists to conclude the square is merely a 'corporation of *Whores, Coiners, Highway-Men, Pick-Pockets* and *House-Breakers*; who, like *Bats* and *Owls*, Sculk in Obscure Holes by Day-Light, but wander in the Night in search of Opportunities wherein to Exercise their Villany'.[93] The two make no effort to reform locations such as these when encountered, they merely move on, but the vivid illustration of such locales in the depths of Middlesex was certainly evidence that areas of London required reform.

Ward employs descriptions of people to signify the general character of public spaces in London. In spaces inhabited by labourers or men from the lower orders, the urban spectators describe disorderly 'mobs'. Such mobs represented a threat with real potential to any Londoner reading such a description. In the seventeenth century, London and other regions in England experienced occasional popular uprisings. These were dangerous events, particularly when remembered as aspects of the English Civil War, or as 'popish plots' threatening the security of England's recently established Protestant monarchs.[94] When the two London spies come across London's May Fair celebration, they describe a potentially dangerous 'Gazing Multitude'. Ward's spies watch this group in disbelief as they failed to follow the simplest directions when attempting to organize themselves as an audience for the 'Indian Rope-Dancers'. The show's coordinator tried to 'Collect the Stragling [sic] Rabble into their proper Order, yet, like an unmannerly Audience, they turn'd their Arses upon the Players, and Devoted themselves wholly to the Monkeys'. May Fair participants could not be successfully situated in order to enjoy a show, so how might this public group be organized in pursuit of something of benefit to the nation? Not easily, a reader might imagine. More perilously, though, characters stumbling upon May-Fair tantalized readers who remembered the 1702 death of a constable who was attacked there by a mob of soldiers while attempting to arrest prostitutes.[95]

Traditional and disorderly diversions such as May Fair did nothing to improve the event's participants. As the spies looked around themselves, they could not find 'one Man that appear'd above the degree of a Gentleman's *Valet*' and, in fact, had never seen 'such a number of Lazy, Lousie-look'd Rascals, and so hateful a Throng of Beggarly, Sluttish Strumpets, who were a Scandal to the *Creation* ... [and] Enemies to *Cleanliness*'.[96] Order was important to the health of the nation, and disorderly gatherings described in *The London Spy* seemed ominous to the polite middling reader.

Popular festivities were ideal locations for periodical writers to glean story ideas. Writers referred to them in ways that revealed immorality, economic waste, social, and gender disorder. Every August, Londoners were reminded of one vestige of their medieval heritage when Bartholomew Fair began in West Smithfield.[97] The lore surrounding the fair saw it as contributing to general disorder, providing a work space for pickpockets and prostitutes while also disrupting industry and encouraging working people's leisure in the middle of the City. Popularized widely by Ben Jonson's 1614 play *Bartholomew Fair*, the festival was known for its food, booths of curiosities, and puppet-plays, as well as for the impolite crowd it attracted. In the midst of late seventeenth-century reform movements, the fair was a primary target for anyone seeking proof of the general disorder and mayhem accompanying 'traditional' activities. For numerous reasons during the late seventeenth and early eighteenth centuries, the fair was increasingly the focus of public debate and official regulation.

The protagonists of Ward's *The London Spy* attend Bartholomew Fair. As they observe and participate in the festivities, the two men judge the multitudes they observe according to their own 'polite' (represented by the urban dweller) and 'traditional' (represented by the rural dweller) expectations. They reveal their individual codes of polite conduct as they journey through the fair and criticize the uncleanness, rudeness, vice, and gender and racial disorder they find rampant at the fair. The two men reveal their disgust upon arriving at the fair when they are overcome by the general mayhem. After having arrived by coach as a futile means of avoiding the 'Dirt and uneasiness of a Crowd', their senses are immediately insulted at the entrance, where they hear miscellaneous music mixed with cat-calls and penny trumpets 'made still more Terrible with the shrill Belches of *Lottery Pick-Pockets*'. The country man's senses were particularly shocked by Bartholomew Fair and he tells his urban-dwelling cousin that he 'should have been as much frightened at this unusual piece of Disorder, as Don Quevedo in his Vision, when he saw Hell in an uproar'.[98] While popular festivals were common in rural areas, the urban manifestation of this popular entertainment with its multitudes of people and exhibits was overwhelming. Ward's 'country' protagonist, with his rural sensibility, viewed London with amazement. His naive perspective reinforced for the reader the 'unnaturalness' of urban disorder. Despite the men's disdain for the conduct of crowds they understood to consist of urban men and women of lower ranks, the London spies eagerly immerse themselves in the crowd and its accompanying 'Filth and nastiness'.

Ward appealed to his readers' senses while transporting them to the fair. Bartholomew Fair was a popular summertime destination attended by many of his London readers as well as a popular literary subject discussed in English periodicals. A great many satirical prints and literature (poems, songs, and plays) also portrayed Bartholomew Fair.[99] The well-know seventeenth-century diarist Samuel Pepys visited the fair numerous times. He, his wife, and various friends enjoyed the pleasures of the fair, but his journal entries never describe the setting of Bartholomew Fair as vividly as do Ned Ward's two main characters. Pepys did not write his diaries for the general reading public, but it is relevant that he noted nothing unusual about the noises, odours, and dirt of the Fair.[100] Pepys accepted the environment of the fair – indeed, the promise of general disorder and escape from everyday life may have been what drew visitors from beyond the lower orders.

A middling fascination with fairs encountered either in person or through literary accounts reveals reluctance among some economically prosperous Londoners who were not quite ready to abandon customary amusements in a quest to become more mannered. Tensions inherent in middling people's acceptance of new roles and codes of conduct mirrored their economic standing. Consuming fair literature as well as attending fairs as voyeurs were methods through which middling people continued to enjoy this popular amusement. Though, in most cases, divorced from manual aspects of labour, these accounts reveal a middling desire to remain tactile in their play.[101] Fair literature catered to a wide spectrum of middling Londoners, from those new to the 'middle sort' just beginning to accumulate capital and live more comfortably than their working neighbours, to others who were more financially well off than many gentlemen. Along with their hierarchical positions within this newly constituting class, middling people would have had varying perceptions of fair amusements, from longing to participate to utter disdain.

Diverse portraits of Bartholomew Fair were intended for different audiences, but in much of this literature, and particularly in Ward's depiction, authors make almost nothing of the other middling people who must certainly have been among the multitudes enjoying the fair's sights and sounds. Ward's objective was to make the fair come alive for the reader, and reform-minded, polite middling men wanted to read about something unusual. Fascinating, disorderly, and dangerous festivals happening in the heart of London made better literary subjects than did descriptions of ordinary, expected events. *The London Spy* presented readers with ominous, unclean crowds needing reform, and for many readers these crowds represented traditional, impolite aspects of city life against which they defined their own gentility. In his periodical, Ward contributed to his society's cultural polarization and provided evidence to members of societies for reformation of manners that subduing London's vices was going to require the services of many middling men.

Tattling and informing, however, was only effective if accompanied by the concern of London officials who had power to legislate change in London. Though London's Aldermen heard sermons asking them to live up to a godly ideal of governance, in reality legislation was slow and public officials such as justices of the peace were overworked and often ineffective. Informed by ideals of urban order, peace, and London's moral health, Aldermen and middling reformers all worked to make their city mannered. Their efforts reflect religious and polite discourse and their own desires to make London's inhabitants conform to new ideals of urban order. These dangerous and unregulated centres of urban amusement frequently hosted violence, gender disorder and, of course, much vice and profanity. While London officials seemed motivated by the same desire to rid London of vice and immorality as members of societies for reformation of manners and periodical journalists, only London's Aldermen and other officials had political power to legislate according to these ideas. By examining their efforts to regulate fairs we see how their responses to urban disorder were influenced by cultural discourses stemming from religion and new understandings of politeness and urban order.

The discourse of middling urban informers reveals their attempt to impose a simultaneously 'modern' and 'pre-modern' order on metropolitan bodies. Informed by religious discourse as well as new understandings of polite urban behaviour, their urban reform efforts reflect the imposition of their new notions of self-regulation and cleanliness, as well as more traditional understandings of social and gender order. Through their participation in reform-oriented discourse, middling men made themselves vitally important as the new patriarchs of the metropolis. As London's new patriarchs, middling men attempted to join conventional authority figures – the aristocracy, Church officials, and fathers – as the city's caretakers. As 'heroick informers', middling men policed the city according to their own ideas of correct conduct while they ensured the virtue and godliness of both the city and nation with their vigilant urban oversight.

Notes

1 *Flying Post or The Post Master*, 6–8 September 1698.
2 *Ibid.* London's Bridewell prison and hospital was an institution founded in the sixteenth century to punish the urban poor. It also housed and trained poor children. For an overview, see the section on Bridewell in Tim Hitchcock, Robert Shoemaker, Sharon Howard and Jamie McLaughlin, et al., *London Lives, 1690–1800* (www.london lives.org/static/Bridewell.jsp, version 1.1, accessed 10 August 2012).
3 Robert Shoemaker has an extensive overview of the agenda of such reformers as well as reactions of their critics in Chapter 9 of *Prosecution and Punishment: Petty Crime and the Law in London and Rural Middlesex, c. 1660–1725* (Cambridge: Cambridge University Press, 1991). See also Faramerz Dabhoiwala, *The Origins of Sex* (Oxford: Oxford University Press, 2012), Chapter 1.
4 *Ibid.*
5 *Ibid.*
6 Shoemaker highlights material concerns motivating the reform efforts of the reformation of manners campaign in *Prosecution and Punishment*, 240. Though fairs certainly encouraged many activities reformers found immoral, we must consider the extent to which fears ultimately reveal a concern with rising crime in the metropolis.
7 LMA, COL/CA, Repertories of the Court of Aldermen (hereafter as Rep.), 104, 390.
8 Shoemaker, *Prosecution and Punishment*, 240.
9 J.M. Beattie, *Policing and Punishment: Urban Crime and the Limits of Terror* (Oxford: Oxford University Press, 2001), 46–7.

10 *Ibid.*, 47.

11 Elaine A. Reynolds, *Before the Bobbies: The Night Watch and Police Reform in Metropolitan London, 1720-1830* (Stanford: Stanford University Press, 1998), 5; see Chapter 3 of the present volume for court records that demonstrate the concerns of Aldermen and Justices of the Peace.

12 Dana Rabin, 'Drunkenness and Responsibility for Crime in the Eighteenth Century'. *Journal of British Studies* 44, no. 3 (July 2005): 457-77.

13 Shoemaker, *Prosecution and Punishment*, 240.

14 Developing notions of orderly, or 'polite' commerce are explored in David Alexander, *Retailing in England During the Industrial Revolution* (London: Athlone, 1970); Neil McKendrick, John Brewer, and J.H. Plumb (eds), *The Birth of Consumer Society: The Commercialization of Eighteenth-Century England* (London: Europa Publications, 1982); Paul Langford, *A Polite and Commercial People: England 1727-1783* (Oxford: Clarendon Press, 1989); for a description of the topography and demographics of commerce in London, see Peter Earle, *A City Full of People: Men and Women of London, 1650-1750* (London: Methuen, 1994).

15 Beattie, *Policing and Punishment*, 55-7.

16 Rep. 98, 303 (1693-1694).

17 Robert Shoemaker, 'Reforming the City: The Reformation of Manners Campaign in London, 1690-1738', in Lee Davison, Tim Hitchcock, et al., *Stilling the Grumbling Hive: the Response to Social and Economic Problems in England, 1689-1750* (New York: St. Martin's Press, 1992), 101.

18 *Ibid.*, 103.

19 LMA, Middlesex and Westminster Sessions of the Peace, No. 700, 21, January 1711-12, MJ/SB/B/069.

20 Dabhoiwala, *Origins of Sex*, 52.

21 Miles Ogborn, *Spaces of Modernity: London's Geographies, 1680-1780* (New York: Guilford Press, 1998), 78-9.

22 This literature includes: Lawrence Klein, *Shaftesbury and the Culture of Politeness: Moral Discourse and Cultural Politics in Early Eighteenth-Century England* (Cambridge: Cambridge University Press, 1994); Langford, *A Polite and Commercial People*; J.G.A. Pocock, *Virtue, Commerce and History* (Cambridge and New York: Cambridge University Press, 1985). Although she does not make 'politeness' her focus, Dorothy Davis discusses the growing retail trade in England in her *Fairs, Shops and Supermarkets: A History of English Shopping* (Toronto: University of Toronto Press, 1966); Michèle Cohen, 'Manliness, effeminacy and the French: Gender and the Construction of National Character in Eighteenth-century England', in Tim Hitchcock and Michèle Cohen (eds), *English Masculinities, 1660-1800* (London and New York: Longman, 1999); Stephen H. Gregg, '"A Truly Christian Hero": Religion, Effeminacy, and Nation in the Writings of the Societies for the Reformation of Manners'. *Eighteenth-Century Life* (25, Vol. 1), 2001.

23 This definition is taken from Philip Carter, *Men and the Emergence of Polite Society, Britain, 1660-1800* (Harlow: Pearson Education, 2001), 35.

24 Robert W. Malcolmson, *Popular Recreations in English Society, 1700-1850* (Cambridge: Cambridge University Press, 1973), 160-1.

25 These concerns are featured in two early eighteenth-century publications printed

in response to urban regulation of fairs: *Reasons for Suppressing the Yearly Fair in Brookfield, Westminster; Commonly Called May-Fair* (London, 1709) and *Reasons Formerly Published for the Punctual Limiting of Bartholomew Fair.* (London, 1711).

26 Malcolmson, *Popular Recreations*, 89.

27 Dabhoiwala, *Origins of Sex*, 40.

28 This is the argument presented in Susan Dwyer Amussen, *An Ordered Society* (New York: Columbia University Press, 1988).

29 Dabhoiwala discusses, in depth, how sexual policing adapted to this urban environment in Chapter 1 of *Origins of Sex*.

30 Davison, Hitchcock, et al., *Stilling the Grumbling Hive*, xxvi–xxvii.

31 Peter Earle, *The Making of the English Middle Class: Business, Society, and Family Life in London, 1660–1730* (Berkeley and Los Angeles: University of California Press, 1989).

32 *Ibid.*, 10.

33 *Ibid.*

34 *Ibid.*, 10–11.

35 Josiah Woodward, *An Account of the Rise and Progress of the Religious Societies in the City of London, & etc. And of the Endeavours for Reformation of Manners Which have been made therein* (London, 1698).

36 *The Observator*, 18–21 August 1703. Orders against London area fairs including May Fair, Bartholomew Fair and Southwark Fair appear throughout the late seventeenth and early eighteenth century. These include a number in 1708: *Post Man and the Historical Account*, 10–13 July 1708; *London Gazette*, 29 July–2 August 1708; *Post Man and the Historical Account*, 30 November–2 December 1708; Such notices continue and are especially prevalent in the early eighteenth century, though they continue to appear until the middle of the century. Examples include: *Weekly Journal or Saturday's Post*, 31 August 1717. *Weekly Packet*, 24–31 August 1717, *Aplebee's Original Weekly Journal*, 2 September 1721.

37 *Weekly Journal or Saturday's Post*, 31 August 1717.

38 *Post Man and the Historical Account*, 15–17 August 1699; *Post Man and the Historical Account*, 19–21 August 1701; *English Post with News Foreign and Domestick*, 5–8 September 1701.

39 Constables and other parish officials were frequently criticized for failing to fully carry out their duties. Shoemaker discusses constables' reasons for not adequately fulfilling duties, which include because they were only in office for a year, they 'were typically more interested in preserving good relations with their neighbors than with impressing the justices with their zealous behavior'. *Prosecution and Punishment*, 221–2.

40 *Daily Journal*, 29 August 1721.

41 *Aplebee's Original Weekly Journal*, 2 September 1721.

42 For a discussion of the gradual implementation of regular policing on London's eighteenth-century streets see Beattie, *Policing and Punishment*, Chapters 3 and 4. The Night Watch, for example, varied in its effectiveness according to 'local circumstances – particularly the wealth and social character of the ward', 177.

43 Julian Hoppit, *A Land of Liberty? England, 1689–1727* (Oxford: Clarendon Press, 2000), 237–9.

44 Thomas Bray, *For God, or for Satan: Being a Sermon Preach'd at St. Mary le Bow, Before the Societies for Reformation of Manners, December 27, 1708* (London, 1709), 10–11.

45 Dabhoiwala, *Origins of Sex*, 64.

46 Peter Borsay, *The English Urban Renaissance: Culture and Society in the Provincial Town 1660-1770* (Oxford: Clarendon Press, 1989), 37; Ogborn; Elizabeth McKellar, *The Birth of Modern London, The Development and Design of the City, 1660-1720* (Manchester and New York: Manchester University Press, 1999); Joyce M. Ellis, *The Georgian Town, 1680-1840* (New York: Palgrave, 2001).

47 Borsay, *English Urban Renaissance*, 285–86.

48 *Ibid.*

49 Shoemaker, 'Reforming the City', 100.

50 Shoemaker, *Prosecution and Punishment*, 238–9. Societies for reformation of manners developed within the wider context of late seventeenth-century Anglican moral reform movements. These coalesced with national attention to public morality. See John Spurr, 'The Church, the Societies and the Moral Revolution of 1688', in John Walsh, Colin Haydon, and Stephen Taylor (eds), *The Church of England c. 1689-c. 1833: From Toleration to Tractarianism* (Cambridge: Cambridge University Press, 1993).

51 Alan Hunt, *Governing Morals, A Social History of Moral Regulation* (Cambridge and New York: Cambridge University Press, 1999), 32–3.

52 *Ibid.*, 45.

53 *Ibid.*, 34.

54 *Ibid.*, 35–9.

55 Shoemaker, 'Reforming the City', 102.

56 *Ibid.*

57 *Ibid.*, 103.

58 Society for Reformation, *Proposals for a National Reformation of Manners* (London: John Dunton, 1694), 2.

59 *Proposals for a National Reformation*, 4.

60 *Ibid.*

61 Robert Fleming the Younger. *The Divine Government* (London, 1699), 70.

62 Fleming, *Divine Government*, 68–9.

63 Bray, *For God*, 11.

64 *Ibid.*, 11–12.

65 *Ibid.*

66 *Ibid.*, 12.

67 *Ibid.*

68 *Ibid.*, 13.

69 Spurr, 'Moral revolution of 1688', 41.

70 Although this Anglican discourse seems to resemble Puritan belief in providence and predestination, it differs in that it did not emphasize 'intense psychological experience in which every event was imbued with providential significance for personal salvation', but instead focused on God's providence as a means to encourage 'practical religion' and morality within the community and larger nation. *Ibid.*, 32.

71 *Ibid.*, 36.

72 Thomas Lynford, *A Sermon Preached before the Right Honourable The Lord Mayor and Court of Aldermen of the City of London, at Guild-Hall Chappel. February the 24th 1688/9* (London: Walter Kettilby, 1689).

73 *Ibid.*, 7–10.

74 Lilly Butler. *A Sermon Preached before The Right Honourable The Lord Mayor and Aldermen and Citizens of London at St. Lawrence Jewry On the Feast of St. Michael, 1696* (London, 1696), 10.

75 *Ibid.*, 12–14.

76 Gregory Hascard, *A Sermon Preached Before the Right Honourable the Lord Mayor Sir James Smith* (London: William Crook, 1685).

77 *Ibid.*, 5.

78 *Ibid.*, 17.

79 *Ibid.*, 17–18.

80 *Ibid.*, 27.

81 Butler, *Sermon*, 25.

82 Gordon Rupp, *Religion in England, 1688–1791* (Oxford: Clarendon Press, 1986), 48–9.

83 John Summerson, *Architecture in Britain 1530–1830* (Penguin, 1953; reprint New Haven, CT and London: Yale University Press, 1993), 192.

84 *Ibid.*, 188.

85 *Ibid.*, 198.

86 Cynthia Wall, *The Literary and Cultural Spaces of Restoration London* (Cambridge and New York: Cambridge University Press, 1998), 184.

87 The City did have a legal claim to part of the fair, but could not legally suppress it.

88 Hunt, *Governing Morals*, 52–3.

89 Howard William Troyer, *Ned Ward of Grub Street: A Study of Sub-Literary London in the Eighteenth Century* (London: Frank Cass, 1968), 7.

90 In her essay, 'The Pursuit of Pleasure: London Rambling,' Jane Rendell offers an intriguing analysis of 'spy tales' which were one part of the early nineteenth-century 'rambling genre'. She argues, 'spy texts were fascinated with the darker aspects of urban life'. In Neil Leach (ed.), *The Hieroglyphics of Space: Reading and Experiencing the Modern Metropolis* (London and New York: Routledge, 2002), 104–5.

91 Phyllis Mack, *Visionary Women: Ecstatic Prophecy in Seventeenth-Century England* (Berkeley: University of California Press, 1992), 22.

92 Edward Ward, *The London Spy* (London: J. How, 1709), fourth edition, in Randolph Trumbach (ed.), *Marriage, Sex and the Family in England 1660–1800* (New York and London: Garland Publishing, 1985), 155.

93 *Ibid.*, 156.

94 As late as 1678, members of Parliament and other London residents experienced 'hysteria' in the face of a 'Popish plot'. J.H. Plumb, *The Growth of Political Stability in England, 1875–1725.* (Baltimore, MD: Penguin, 1969), 60–1; John Coffey, *Persecution and Toleration in Protestant England, 1558–1689* (Harlow: Pearson Education, 2000), 182–4.

95 Hunt, *Governing Morals*, 53.

96 Ward, *London Spy*, 173.

97 William Addison, *English Fairs and Markets* (London: B.T. Batsfort, 1953), 50–1.

98 Ward, *London Spy*, 236–7.

99 Some examples are: *Bartholomew Faire, or Variety of Fancies* (London: Richard Harper, 1641); *Bartholomew Fair: An Heroi-Comical Poem* (London: S. Baker, 1717); *The Cloyster in Bartholomew Fair; or, The Town Mistress Disguis'd* (London, A Banks, 1707); *Roger in Amaze: Or The Country-Mans Ramble Through Bartholomew Fair* (London, n.d.).

100 Robert Latham and William Matthews (eds), *The Diary of Samuel Pepys*, Vol. IX, *1668–1669* (Berkeley: University of California Press, 1976).

101 See Peter Earle, *A City Full of People*, for a discussion of the types of work undertaken by the vast range of 'middling people' in London.

3

Regulation and resistance: Wayward apprentices and other 'evil disposed persons' at London's fairs[1]

Middlesex and Westminster justices and London Aldermen spent a good deal of the late seventeenth through mid-eighteenth centuries attempting to pass legislation they believed would conform London to their idea of an orderly and productive commercial centre. Seasonal fairs that disrupted commercial order in the metropolis concerned London officials working to establish productivity and commerce in the city. Urban legislation and reform discourse sought to reconfigure fairs. Both opponents as well as supporters of fairs looked for ways to shape these events into institutions reflecting their own idealized notions of early-modern urban order. Central to that reconfiguration was renegotiating gender order. Reform-minded Londoners worried that urban fairs had power to corrupt men, making them unproductive and, therefore, unfit as citizens and/or subjects. The anxiety of urban officials particularly focused on apprentices, who officials worried could be tempted away from productivity during London's festive summer months.

The concerns of urban officials likely reveal their response to underlying economic developments: London's population of apprentices had grown from 1,400 in the mid-sixteenth century to double that by the early seventeenth century and 30,000 by 1800.[2] Apprentices, though, were not the only male labourers in early modern London. During the same period, opportunities for wage labour unhindered by contracted agreements increased.[3] Perhaps in this context urban authorities were insecure about work arrangements protected by contracted obligations. Free men working for wages lacked restrictions imposed by apprenticeship, but at the same time, apprentices who did work according to contracted arrangements were not always kept industrious. Urban officials worried that masterless men as well as men with apathetic masters could be lured from lives of hard work by the festive offerings of London's fairs.

One case presented Middlesex officials with powerful evidence of the threat they believed fairs posed to commerce and industry in the capital. In the early eighteenth century, William Adams's parents apprenticed their son to Joseph Bidwell, a carpenter from St Giles-in-the-Fields. They assumed their son would learn his trade and eventually embark upon an industrious career.[4] By 1732, however, it was obvious to Adams and his parents that his training was not proceeding as planned; not only did he fail to receive the clothes promised him by his indenture, but he was also not given the opportunity to learn carpentry. Perhaps enticed by easy summertime profits, William's master 'employed him in driving a chair, with boys and girles [sic] in it for halfe pence a piece, drawn by two or three dogs [at] ... most of the little fairs about town'.[5] The Middlesex justices viewed Bidwell's misuse of his apprentice's labour with concern because they were engaged in a campaign to contain the frequently disorderly amusement of fairs, many of which extended well beyond their chartered days or were held with no charters.

For city fathers, an orderly city featured spaces in which productive men were visible. Festivity, in this ideal metropolis, was contained and isolated from commercial and productive spaces. Within a commercially well-ordered city, an apprentice was ideally subjected to the paternal authority of his master. Contained by this relationship, the apprentice was bound to obey his master, to avoid drinking, and follow other rules of conduct. Conversely, the master was bound to train an apprentice to become a skilled worker.[6] Adams' apprenticeship profoundly contradicted this notion of an orderly metropolis – the idea that a young man could be schooled in a trade while working at an eighteenth-century fair (long since an occasion for marketing) and in an occupation one could only describe as amusing children confounded urban officials. With little hesitation, the justices discharged William Adams from his nonproductive apprenticeship.[7]

The Middlesex justices could have filled sessions scrutinizing the duties of apprentices who did work other than what they were contracted to do. The Corporate apprenticeship system (within London's city companies) was waning during the eighteenth century.[8] Seventeenth-century events such as the Civil War, Plague and Fire had altered the configuration of the London apprentice system. Additionally, sixteenth-century population movement outside of the square mile of the City and the growth of suburban industry weakened London apprenticeships.[9] By the 1720s, apprentices were not controlled by an 'urban system of guild mutualism' and becoming an apprentice in London no longer ensured that a young man would be trained in a skill. In fact, an apprenticeship was more likely to 'be the means of organizing and [exploiting] young labour power'.[10] Eighteenth-century London's expanding economy demanded a large, free, and mobile work force.[11] In this context, more men found employment opportunities outside of apprentice arrangements. Wider London's urban authorities cited concern over young men's moral and financial welfare as their motive for urban reform efforts.

Urban officials worried particularly about the negative consequences fairs had on labouring young men. They saw a relationship between London's 'temptations' and crime and were especially concerned that the festivity associated with fairs had the potential to distract or, worse, ruin apprentices or servants.[12] Their concerns, however, were not shared by all Londoners who found themselves in supervisory roles over others. The breakdown of guilds and increasing numbers of servants in London helped shift the balance of power away from masters.[13] Frequently, commentators complained about the independence of their servants and other London workers.[14] Though there are many complaints in printed sources from the period regarding the non-deferential behaviour of servants, there is a lack of certain evidence regarding their numbers. However, historians agree that somewhere around one-thirteenth, or 7.7 per cent of the total population of the metropolis, was exclusively a domestic servant.[15] Peter Earle finds that over 25 per cent of London women were employed in domestic service.[16] Numbers of working men increased also during the eighteenth century. Growing workshops associated with manufacturing and the increasing amount of capital required to set up shop ensured a large supply of workers, not necessarily apprentices, who had little hope of becoming masters themselves. Ideally, city fathers hoped masters guided apprentices and servants in appropriate behaviour. In reality, patriarchal master-servant relationships were strained and demographically difficult in a growing city such as London. While Joseph Bidwell and others like him alarmed city fathers who saw that not all masters believed fairs threatened young men's moral development, most masters, journeymen, and apprentices likely found fairs nothing more than deserved breaks from usual working lives or profit-making opportunities.

London businessmen and women who profited from the fair industry encouraged its continuance. Their servants or apprentices surely supported them in catering to this industry, and when not at work in or around fairs, took time to play at them.[17] Those who made at least partial livelihoods from the commerce generated by fairs continued their work despite the city fathers' attempts at regulation, while their products of food, goods, and entertainment were heartily consumed by participants in London's festivity. Coexisting, yet contrary, views of the purpose and suitability of fairs worked against each other, and the campaign to regulate them was difficult. Through legislation and contestation, common, middling, and elite Londoners all helped define the place of amusement in their early modern metropolis.

City and county efforts to contain festive amusements in London are one of many examples that reveal the challenges of maintaining urban order in the face of London's growth. During the late seventeenth and early eighteenth centuries, policing throughout the City and surrounding counties varied by parish. During the Elizabethan era, traditional policing in London was undertaken by householders who took turns serving as constables or other officers.[18] Neighbourhood constables policed areas in which they lived, where they were aware of community dynamics and could practice a 'flexible' style of policing 'melded to neighbours' needs much of the time'.[19] Increasingly, this method of policing was strained by the complex realities accompanying a shifting and rapidly growing urban population. By 1700, as policing London became more taxing, hiring 'stand-in' constables and substitutes for the night watch became more common.[20] At the same time, new night-time entertainment venues placed increasing demands on those whose responsibility it was to police the night streets. Not every man who undertook traditional policing responsibilities was prepared to meet these increasing demands, though individual householders maintained a sense of personal obligation to oversee order in their neighbourhoods.[21] While this obligation motivated some men to continue to fulfil policing duties in person, others employed substitutes. Meanwhile, Londoners who enjoyed night-time entertainment expected protection and more effective policing.[22] Increasingly after 1735, night-time policing was done by a regular night watch, necessary as night-time leisure and entertainment opportunities increased not only at fairs but also at a variety of commercialized entertainment venues.[23] While policing efforts were not able to predictably regulate urban festivity in and around London, the increased need for officers and the payment of officers dedicated to law enforcement helped further the development of a professionalized police force.[24]

Policing evolved in response to the realities of living in a transforming metropolis, but nevertheless remained insufficient to carry out urban orders calling for the regulation, or abolition, of fairs. By 1809, the Lord Mayor ordered thirty paid men to attend Bartholomew Fair to prevent riots, but during the early eighteenth century this type of special policing happened infrequently.[25] Informal policing was undertaken or funded also, as discussed in Chapter 2, by members of voluntary organizations such as the societies for the reformation of manners.[26] As growing fears that crime and social instability was on the increase, urban officials desired to assert control over unruly areas of London.[27] Authorities' fears regarding unchecked masculinity at London's fairs were frustrated by strained methods of policing. At the same time, not everything that happened at fairs was illegal. Policing practices, therefore, could not solve the problem alone.

London, the nation, and the struggle to regulate fairs

In 1708, St Bartholomew's Fair's lease was up for renewal and this became the focus of much discussion by the city's officials. During the seventeenth century, the fair grew from its original length of three days to a full fourteen days and city officials hoped to return it to three. Efforts by London's officials to limit the duration of and control the types of booths present at Bartholomew Fair continued through the mid-eighteenth century.[28] Among those unhappy about this extended festival were several tradesmen who lived and worked in the area of the fair, West Smithfield, and found their business interrupted during its tenure, though other business owners in the area profited from the fair. Whether or not the lease of Bartholomew Fair should be renewed, and in what manner, was the subject of an anonymous tract directed at London's Lord Mayor and the Court of Aldermen and Common Council. This pamphlet did not call for a prohibition of the fair (legally, this was not possible and socially it may not have been desired). Instead, this pamphlet justified the limiting of Bartholomew Fair for some of the same reasons detailed by the societies for the reformation of manners. Urban fair space proved too disorderly for a polite city and at the turn of century, an urban festival Samuel Pepys once considered a pleasant diversion was viewed as an unruly event, threatening the precarious urban order. Echoing the societies' concerns, the *Reasons for the Limiting of Bartholomew-Fair* finds London's order instrumental to England's strength:

> The Happiness and Prosperity of the *Great* and *Wealthy* City of *London*, our August *Metropolis*, are so much the Interest and Honour of this whole *Island*, that every Inhabitant thereof is, by *Self-love* as well as *Duty*, bound to promote the Welfare of it, as he is capable.[29]

Promoting London's, and by extension England's, 'welfare' meant to London's city officials the promotion of 'good order and good manners', established only when 'honest citizens' assisted magistrates in restoring order to the 'visible occasions of Disorder and Misdemeanor' especially in such places as Bartholomew Fair, a 'meer *Carnival*, a season of the utmost *Disorder* and *Debauchery* by reason of the *Booths* for Drinking, Musick, Gaming, Raffling, and what not'.[30]

Notable men of various backgrounds supported London's efforts to regulate Bartholomew Fair. In a pamphlet discussing London's regulation of Bartholomew Fair, Charles Leslie, an Irish Anglican, celebrated the 'Reformation' begun in the city by the 'putting down' of Bartholomew Fair.[31] In his discussion of the fair, he responds to a dialogue that appeared earlier in John Tutchins's *Observator*. These men were from different sides of the political spectrum – Leslie, an Anglican nonjuror and Jacobite; Tutchin, a Dissenting Whig – but both men supported some form of regulation and reform for Bartholomew Fair. In print, they argued over the extent to which the irregularities of the fair should be blamed on the Anglican governors of St Bartholomew's Hospital, around which the fair was annually held. Not surprisingly, the hospital (and, thereby charity) benefited from profits derived from the fair. From a dissenter's perspective, the profit derived from 'debauchery' demonstrated Anglican corruption. To an Anglican, the fact that profits supported charity and were overseen by Churchmen made them appropriate. Leslie further points out that the hospital governors themselves had noticed the increasing corruption of the fair and had set up a committee to investigate establishing 'Useful, or at least inoffensive' activities at the fair. This, according to Leslie, supported Tutchin's own proposition that 'Manly exercises [should be] set up instead of the Shows, or such other Diversions might be Contriv'd as may be Inoffensive'.[32] Whether Tory or Whig, concerned men believed reform at Bartholomew Fair was overdue. Social commentators as well as London authorities focused particularly on reforming the style of masculinity encouraged by and practiced at fairs. The debate between Leslie and Tutchin reveals an implicit understanding that London's men needed festive space. Neither supports an outright ban on the fair; rather, they wish to replace immoral or disruptive entertainment with instructive, 'manly', or useful amusement. Festivity had an urban purpose: workers required respite – but without direction London patriarchs feared its consequences.

As the debate raged over the regulation of Bartholomew Fair, a pamphlet launched a similar attack against May Fair, which also notoriously withstood regulation attempts. The author of the 1709 tract, *Reasons for Suppressing the Yearly Fair in Brook-Field, Westminster; Commonly Called May-Fair*, depicts the fair as breeding disorder and calls it, 'a pregnant Nursery of *Treason* and *Rebellion*'. May Fair began on the first of that month – a date traditionally associated with festive misrule,

3.1 *Mayfair*, 1716. Courtesy of the Lewis Walpole Library, Yale University.

particularly involving apprentices.[33] In 1702, fair-goers violently attacked a special force of constables who had been sent to preserve order at the fair and its surrounding areas. This attack on officers of the law revealed just how powerless London's constables could be when they faced large crowds. The constables could do little against a riot of '30 Persons with drawn Swords', and the 'Mob' wielding 'Stones and Dirt'. One constable, John Cooper, was killed in the affray and eight other people were injured.[34] During a later attempt to quell the fair, a constable was, 'drag'd thro' a Horse-Pond', while policing the fair. Other constables had even been pursued, 'to the very Doors of the neighboring *Justices* of the Peace; and the *Justices* themselves have not been able to protect them, by reason of the *Numbers* and *Insolence* of the riotous Mob'.[35] Clearly, Middlesex policing efforts represented a drop in the bucket of what would have been required to effectively suppress this popular yearly festival. Rowdy fair-goers, it seemed, turned the tables of authority on constables, whom they chased out of the fair instead of the reverse. Such scenarios deeply troubled authorities. In the tract, the writer describes how 'sober' people, 'Lament, that in such a well-order'd Government as that of this Nation

... so pestilent and extensive an Evil as this should be deem'd *remedi-less*.[36] By failing to restore order at May Fair, the anonymous writer argued, government itself, both local and national, was made to seem like a '*May-Game*'.[37]

The 1702 May Fair exemplified the potential all fairs had to become dangerously unmanageable and, in particular, implicated unruly young men. Thomas Cook, executed on 11 August 1703, was signalled out among the crowd of thirty sword-wielding men as responsible for the constable, John Cooper's, death. He was a known prizefighter – the 'Gloucester Butcher' – and a self-confessed, 'grievous Sinner, a great Swearer and Drinker, an Adulterer, a Prophane and Lewd Wretch, and a sworn Enemy to those who were employ'd in the Reformation of Manners'.[38] This restless young man had been apprenticed to a London barber-surgeon for two years, ran away and returned to Gloucester, where he worked as a butcher and kept an inn. Uncertain of his future, he eventually retuned to London, but swore until his execution that he had, 'no Sword in his hand that day the Constable was kill'd, nor was in the least concern'd in the Company of them that kill'd him'.[39] Though professing innocence of the crime for which he was found guilty, Cook agreed that he had lived a disreputable life. His sins included drinking in May Fair and confronting a constable in the fair who was 'taking up men for swearing'. In fact, Cook was charged for the crime, in part, because he bragged to a Dublin victualler that people in London 'used' men affiliated with societies for reformation of manners 'like Doges'.[40] As proof, Cook described the encounter with the reforming Constable in May Fair and elaborated that he went up to the six men accompanying the Constable, drew his sword, and demanded the prisoner apprehended for swearing be released. After the resulting fight, Cook told the Dublin victualler that he 'wiped his sword and went away'. He was advised to leave for Ireland and stay until the trial in London was over.[41] Unfortunately for Cook, he found it difficult to maintain silence and 'made his braggs of what he had done' during May Fair. He was eventually apprehended, tried and executed for the crime.[42]

Thomas Cook's behaviour during May Fair revealed the trouble with such urban festivity. He was a restless young man, uncertain of his place in the world, who openly mocked attempts to control immoral public male behaviour. He embodied the type of man urban reformers found most threatened social order. According to the author of the tract calling for the suppression of May Fair, the festival was particularly troubling because it seemed to not only encourage, but also shelter such unruly masculinity. Literally protected within the 'nursery' of this fair, the author of the tract believes young men found sustenance for socially destructive behaviour. The author draws insightful conclusions about what complicated the regulation of May Fair and lists several explanations for why the fair had become so dangerously disruptive. The underlying difficulty was not only that fair-goers were young and male – but also that the fair was the first festival of the spring and summer fair season. Young men were encouraged to 'licentiousness' by the time of the year – early May. A mixture of seasonal feelings and festivity was so potent that the pamphlet's author describes how even innocent youth might spot the fair and decide to walk through it for 'Curiosity'. Once there, young Londoners who lacked fully-formed notions of godly and productive behaviour, 'fall-in' with the fair, where, once 'gotten within the *Circle* of Temptation, they consent to enter into a Booth, [where they] fall into ill Company, and are surrounded with Temptations'.[43] Temptations of the fair compounded upon each other until young innocents ran the risk of being, 'push'd into that *deep Ditch*, into which *such fall as are abhorred of the Lord*'.[44] The pamphlet continues to argue that the dangers of the fair not only tempted those who accidentally stumbled upon them, but people in the neighbourhoods bordering the fair, who were lured by '*large Papers* posted on the Gates, and chief Places of Concourse … printed in such large *Capitals*, that he that runs may read them'.[45] Even more destructive than playbills were actual fair amusements, the promise of which lured people into the fair, and then into booths. Worst of all were gaming booths which drew in and 'decoy'd' apprentices and other young people and then cheated them out of their money. As a means to recover and repair finances and, perhaps, reputations, these impoverished victims would have to go 'home to the Cash of their *Parents* and *Masters*'. This financial drain was met, if not superseded, by the evils of the, '*profane* and *licentious PLAY-HOUSE*', at the fair, where both the young and the 'meaner sort of People', might encounter corrupt ideas that would lead to their personal and moral destruction.[46]

Throughout the tract, the author avoids placing all blame with festive young men, and instead looks for a way to counter disorderly masculinity with polite male behaviour. Certainly, the author argues, there would always be, 'vain and wicked Persons [who] will not fail to partake of [fair entertainment], tho' they beggar themselves, starve their Families, and ruine their Souls thereby'.[47] Young men, whose moral choices were shaped by their age, required godly and mannered older men to steer them away from this temptation. Wiser men comprehended the ill effects of fairs on all sorts of young people, from novice apprentices to the 'meaner sort' of people, whom authorities did not expect to behave reasonably. This pamphleteer calls upon local residents of, 'true *Honour* and *Virtue*', asking them to assist in the fair's suppression.[48] With the help of local notables, the author of this pamphlet argued, the fair might be finally contained. This is similar to conclusions drawn in the tract discussing the limitation of Bartholomew Fair and by members of London's societies for the reformation of manners. Without a regular and large police force, there was little recourse but to rely on traditional notions of order – respected authorities with understandings of their own self-control and governed by religious principles would shepherd Londoners who they believed lacked both.[49] Central to this order was deploying men who embodied civility and controlled behaviour as moral models for London's youth.

Concern that May Fair was an especially dangerous festival was echoed in London newspapers from 1708 and 1709. Newspapers in these years printed reminders that all fairs were limited to three days. The *Post Man and The Historical Account* printed notices pertaining to May Fair, explaining why the fair was, 'worthy [of] the Care of those in Power and Authority'.[50] The newspaper particularly noted that the fair threatened young people, servants and apprentices – all of whom were susceptible to being misled by 'ill disposed', and 'Lewd' people undertaking 'disorderly' practices.[51] Beyond the typical moral hazards of fairs, this 1708 report reveals the unique danger of May Fair, which, being located in Brookfield, May Fair, was dangerously 'near Her Majesties Palaces', making the festival, 'very dangerous to Her Royal Person and Government, by Seditious and Unreasonable Men, taking there by an Occasion to execute their most Wicked and Traiterous Designs'.[52]

The dangerous potential of unrestrained masculinity (and inappropriate femininity, as well) prompted debates within London's Court of Aldermen and Common Council as well as the Middlesex county authorities for the two decades leading up to the 1708 and 1709 tracts on Bartholomew and May Fair. Almost each year, in either summer (before the fairs were held) or early autumn (after the fairs were held), officials addressed limiting fairs. Court records reveal urban authorities' concerns that fair booths presenting plays, exhibitions, music, and lotteries, or offering drink were places, 'to which the Worst and Lewdest of both Sexes resort'. They also believed that fairs were sites of 'frequent Bloodsheds, Tumults and Disorders [which] daily happen to the terror of the Inhabitants and others', and that at fairs, '… the Apprentices, Servants and Youth of and about this City are debauched'.[53] Such pamphlets and orders reveal a concern about the dangerous potential of uncontained, unfocused, and disorderly masculinity. Apprentices, servants, soldiers, and other young men were an ominous and unpredictable force if authorities failed to contain them. Such men threatened the security of all Londoners if their celebrations outgrew the spatial and temporal boundaries of fairs. Drunken revellers, seduced by the temptations of gaming and female spectacles such as ropedancers or attractive actresses threatened the peace and safety of their fellow, more controlled fair-goers as well as the neighbourhoods surrounding fairs. Worse, unruly groups of men might become susceptible to political movements, such as Jacobitism, which threatened the peace and security of the nation.

Some residents from areas surrounding fairs shared the concerns of urban authorities that fairs contributed to disorder and disrupted commerce. In July 1694, a group of residents who lived and worked in and around West Smithfield presented a petition to the Court of Aldermen, asking them to limit the duration of St Bartholomew's Fair.[54] Their daily business and ordinary routines were upset when the fair continued beyond the three chartered days. The Court responded by issuing an order limiting the fair to its original three days, as its 'ancient institution' stipulated. London's Aldermen argued such measures were necessary because the fair became too frequently an occasion for violence. For the Aldermen, this petition supported their notion that fairs exposed servants, youth, and apprentices to moral danger, but such a petition also allowed them to add that Bartholomew Fair, in particular, interrupted the everyday businesses and lives of West Smithfield residents. Bartholomew Fair 'exposed the Houses of the Inhabitants … to the continual danger of Fire', while interfering with locals' ability to continue their business. The Aldermen hoped their order would provide for the safety and security of the area's inhabitants and 'restore them [and the traders] to the full enjoyment of their Trades'.[55] In June 1707 London's Court of Common Council also considered the impact the fair had on those resorting to the fair for trade. They hoped restoring the fair to three days would prevent the 'traffick of the … traders and Fair keepers' from being 'interrupted and diminished' by the 'Tumults and disorders' that frequently occurred there.[56]

Several instances confirmed urban authorities' fears that London's fairs promoted violence and threatened orderly masculinity. When notable Londoners were assaulted at the fair, it revealed how uncontrolled the festivity had become. By the 1740s, there were several 'polite' venues in London frequented by fashionable middling or elite men and women. The Spring Gardens in Vauxhall, for example, catered to a discriminating crowd – or at least patrons wealthy enough to afford the admission fee. Nevertheless, seasonal fairs remained popular locations for all classes of Londoners. One genteel man, Joseph Underwood, the Duke of Montrose's cook, risked the entertainments of Bartholomew Fair the evening of 24 August 1744. He apparently believed the fair was a suitable venue for his sister and 'two other ladies', whom he escorted wearing the *accoutrements* of his politeness – a wig, silver watch, handkerchief, hat, and ivory-tipped walking stick.[57] While politely helping the women cross a channel in the road between the George Inn and the Swan, he was torn from his party, shoved into the crowd, and violently assaulted by 'nine or ten men'.[58] During the attack, Underwood was robbed of his walking stick, watch, and wig.[59] This man's polite manners meant nothing to rowdy and seemingly fearless criminals in Bartholomew Fair. If anything, the criminals took advantage of this man's manners – assaulting him just at the moment when his manners made him most vulnerable – while protecting female companions from harm or dirt and helping them across a street, he failed to protect himself.

Ann Wells, one of the women accompanied by Underwood, described the evening of the assault to the King's Commission of the Peace. From her description, and details provided by other witnesses, we get a sense of the visibility (between 9 and 10 at night), confusion, and crowds that contributed to this incident. The seven or eight men and one boy who attacked Underwood pushed the women into the crowd of the fair as they focused their assault on the man. When the attack commenced, Wells 'squawled out' and was then hit across the back, though she was unsure of whether the blow was intentional. The attackers seemed intent to not harm the women, instead focusing on acquiring valuable items from their male victim. These were pickpockets, not murderers. They typically gathered in crowds to pick pockets, but this evening their robbery became more violent. Wells's testimony is revealing when she discusses the crowd's response to the attack. While 'several gentlemen came to our [the three woman's] assistance', none of them, 'would go to Mr. Underwood's' because there were 'so many of the fellows'.[60] The danger, then, was that a large group of violent young men (between the ages of 14 and 26 – the ages mentioned in the narrative) proved too threatening to the crowds who watched. While the women were protected, they were also not targeted by the thieves. Clearly a gendered dynamic was at play in the crowd's response to the attack. Other fair-goers may have already experienced violence from Underwood's attackers and were afraid to interfere. Since 'dusk' the friends and troublemakers had, 'walked about the fair, hitting people over the head, and picking … pockets'.[61] After attacking Underwood and disappearing into the cloisters, this group of London young men bullied their way through the fair, ending the evening stealing gingerbread and making mischief in the Smithfield Rounds until 11 o'clock.[62] As for Underwood, he finally emerged from the crowd with a bloodied head, missing his hat, and carrying his wig (mentioned in the records of the Court of Alderman as having been stolen).[63]

This incident exemplifies that on the everyday level, masculine manners mattered little at fairs. Though men like Underwood may have hoped to use fair space to showcase their finery, many more men, such as William Brister, James Page, Theophilus Watson, and others (the men indicted for assaulting and robbing him) recognized fairs as a hunting ground for polite, easy prey. As for London men who attended the fair and whom authorities most likely hoped would help in community policing, this incident reveals just how ineffectual they were when groups of unruly young men took control.[64] As late as 1744, urban authorities had little control over fair crowds. Crime and a host of disorderly behaviours, such as rioting, prostitution, or gaming, continued despite authorities' prohibitions.

City officials did not successfully manage urban festivity until well into the eighteenth century, and in the case of Bartholomew Fair, the nineteenth. Until concerted and regular efforts to assign constables to policing fairs were successful, city and county officials typically resorted to pre-emptive efforts to manage fair entertainment. For example, in 1694, an order against Bartholomew Fair stating that it must be held for only three days was published five weeks prior to the fair. At times, forces of constables and volunteers could be mustered in efforts to police morality at the fairs. In 1698, the *Flying Post or The Post Master* printed a warning that constables and reformers would be out to apprehend disorderly people at Bartholomew Fair.[65] Nevertheless, London authorities found it difficult to control immoral and illegal behaviour at fairs. Their best effort involved reminding those who leased rooms or ground for booths that they must only let them for three days during the fair. Realizing that they competed against increased profits during the fair rather than deliberately lawless citizens, the court even discussed compensating leasers for any financial loss which accompanied this regulation, though whether or not they did is unclear. The president of St Bartholomew's Hospital was also encouraged to not lease shops in the hospital's cloisters for more than three days and was advised that hospital Beadles should 'clear the cloisters of Lude and disorderly persons'.[66]

Obviously, proactive attempts to curtail the business of fairs were not consistently successful; particularly because the City lacked the funds it would take to replace the increased income local businesses received during fairs. The profitability of fairs is evident in a 1732 case at the Old Bailey, in which Elizabeth Davil claims that during the time of Bartholomew Fair, her area victualling house took in an extra pint porringer of £12 a day.[67] The profit to be gained (and lost) at fairs is also revealed in the case of Joseph Forward, brought into court for stealing from his landlord. Ann Chapman and her husband attempted to profit by renting rooms during the fair. In 1734, the Chapmans had the misfortune to rent to a dishonest couple, the Forwards, who leased their room from the end of April through 'Bartholomew-tide'. This couple was in town to sell Gin and Black puddings during the fair season and agreed to pay 2s a week for their room. They remained for twenty-four weeks, paid only 12s., and 'used to come home drunk at all Hours'.[68] Financial gain was available, potentially, to those who let rooms during London's fair-season, but the nature of fair work and those who performed it was often ambiguous. There was certainly the potential for great profit for some, but easy profit attracted those who hoped to siphon some for themselves. This happened to Davil, who brought in her maid for stealing her extra cash, and in the case of the Chapmans, who incurred loss from their unpredictable pedlar tenants. In any case, the promise of the quick and bountiful profit to be gained from fairs was enough for some who worked at or near fairs to ignore court orders asking them to forgo that seasonal income.

London's Aldermen were as concerned with regulating Southwark Fair as they were with Bartholomew Fair, as their regulation attempts for this fair reveal. The fair was originally chartered for two full weeks, but in 1690, London's Aldermen curtailed the fair to only three days.[69] While London authorities frequently announced that fairs would be held for three days only, they very rarely effectively enforced this regulation. Classified newspapers' advertisements reveal entertainments being held from the beginning of Bartholomew Fair on 24 August until the beginning of September, just before the start of Southwark Fair on the south bank. Entertainments then moved across the river and at Southwark Fair they typically ran until almost the last week of September.[70] Londoners who attended or worked at Southwark Fair resisted regulations just as those who attended Bartholomew Fair, but some area residents grew tired of the disorder and commercial disruption occasioned by the yearly festival. On 14 September 1714, London's Aldermen heard citizens who voiced their annoyance with 'the irregularities and mishiefs [sic]' of Southwark Fair, which was continuing well beyond the regulated three days of 7, 8, and 9 September.[71]

At times, the regulation of fairs took on national significance. In

1714, much more than citizens' complaints motivated urban authorities to direct concerted regulatory efforts at this fair – four days after discussing Southwark Fair in court, the new monarch, George I, was due to make his triumphal entrance into London close to the time of Southwark Fair. In such a scenario, unchecked frivolity represented a threat to not only civic order, but to the accession of a new monarch whose rule was already contested by Britons supporting the Catholic Stuart line. London's Aldermen did not say as much in the official record, in which they complain that the 'Booths, Scaffolds and sheds ... now erected in the street under the pretence of the said fair will greatly obstruct the solemnity of His Majesties said Publick entrance into this City'.[72] However, these temporary structures on London's South Bank were an eyesore and symbolized much more than a blatant disregard for urban authorities. If we read between the lines of the Aldermen's record, it expresses their anxiety about the smooth transition of power. Temporary booths and scaffolds were 'dangerous to the spectators' of the monarch's procession in more ways than one. London officials surely worried that the continuation of festivities in Southwark sent the wrong message to their new Protestant monarch. Not only was this a fair with roots in the Roman Catholic Church (and located, fittingly enough, adjacent to St George the Martyr Church), but also city officials wanted to present the new monarch an image of a united capital city full of inhabitants who honoured, rather than contested, his arrival. To City officials, temporary booths and scaffolds symbolized its unruly patrons partaking in the fair beyond its 'customary usage'.[73]

The presence of temporary fair structures visibly detracted from the overall image of an architecturally orderly, permanent, and powerful city, which featured new classically inspired buildings and spaces rebuilt during the building boom following the city's 1666 fire. More importantly, however, the temporary structures of fairs were incongruent with the unified metropolitan image city fathers hoped to present: they were a tangible reminder that dangerously subversive elements loyal to the Catholic Stuarts remained in the political centre of the nation. Located on the opposite bank from the important centres of the nation's political authorities, the sheds, booths, and scaffolds of Southwark Fair must have seemed like an alternate city sheltering a disorderly society ready to contest the new monarch's legitimacy. These fears motivated the Aldermen to take swift action, and they ordered 'Mr. Hartley [the City's justice], and Mr. Marson, Bailiffe [sic] to cause the booths and scaffolds and sheds to be taken down ... or any others which shall be set up that may obstruct the said solemnity ...'[74]

It took an issue of national security, however, for urban authorities to successfully control urban fairs. During average years, orders limiting the fairs in Southwark and West Smithfield were made and printed by London's Aldermen, who faced the difficulties of limiting fairs and devising 'proper methods for prevention of the great Immorality and profanes generally [there] practiced'.[75] Coupled with logistical problems attending actual regulation of fairs were the new problems of unlicensed play booths and 'pretend' fairs operating illegally without founding charters issued by local or national authorities. Such festivals and illegal entertainments threatened to become permanent London institutions if not stopped.

In 1735, London's Aldermen fought against a new and increasingly popular un-chartered entertainment: illegal and temporary play booths, which were erected not only at fairs, but also in areas such as Hampstead at times of the year not associated with festivals. In an effort to quell illegal play booths and perhaps break the public's growing taste for this style of entertainment, the Aldermen paid special attention to their regulation at that year's fairs. Perhaps because there was also national interest in curtailing theatrical entertainment (evidenced by the proposed 1735 Playhouse Bill and later 1737 Licensing Act), London authorities focused some of their regulatory attempts on that specific amusement.[76] In their orders, they prohibited building fair booths to present 'illegal interludes, stageplays, Lotteries, Gaming, Tipling, Musick … or other profane pastimes'.[77] Additionally, playhouse bills were prohibited from being posted within the City or its liberties in July 1703.[78] This special attention to booths featuring performance reflected their larger concern with illegal playhouses. In particular, they feared the wide appeal of this entertainment, which was experiencing a surge of popularity in proportion to the increase in London's best-known actors and actresses appearing on the fair stage.[79] At the same time, London's theatre was more apt to make political critiques, which were hugely popular with London audiences. For example, the thinly veiled satire of the Whig government found in John Gay's popular piece *The Beggar's Opera* found its way in modified 'droll' form into the play booths of London's fairs. London's Aldermen certainly shared the concerns of national authorities when they called unlicensed play booths in fairs and other urban locales 'a growing evil' with 'mischievous consequences'.[80] This concern with unlicensed playhouses was echoed by the Middlesex justices, which will be explored below, and continued to be a concern until the 1737 Licensing Act legislated the regulation of these institutions.[81]

Though fairs did extend for only three days on some years,

entertainments such as plays, music, and other performances often continued well past the chartered days of a fair. This continued until 1735,
when the Aldermen began to investigate seriously their legal rights to
limit or abolish London's fairs. The Aldermen's intensified regulation
of London fairs coincided with the Playhouse Bill, which was before
the House of Commons that year. Beginning with Southwark Fair, the
Aldermen called for a search of court books to determine their rights to
physically restrain this fair to three days. After the City Lands Committee
investigated the rights to the fair and found they had complete jurisdiction over this fair, they issued a regulatory order for Southwark Fair
on 21 June 1735. This order stipulated the usual – that 'Lady Day Fair
in Southwark' should be kept for 'three days only'; but this order went
further, stating that, 'Booths which are nuisances [could] be pulled down
by the Bayliff'.[82]

After issuing their warning that 'nuisance booths' would be torn
down, one booth was actually destroyed. Hannah Lee and her family
had operated play booths at fairs for many years. In 1735, however, she
was singled out because she had 'erected a Booth in or near Southwark
wherein she continues to Act Plays and Interludes in defiance of the
law'.[83] In July, the *London Evening Post* warned 'the Magistrates of this
City have … thought fit to put the Fair, called Lady Fair, or vulgarly
Southwark Fair, under the … Restriction of three Days, according to the
original Grant thereof'.[84] On 23 September, nearly three weeks after the
official end of the fair, Lee was summoned by the court and ordered to
cease her entertainment.[85]

The bailiff who had been ordered to destroy such booths clearly
tolerated these entertainments in his jurisdiction, for newspaper advertisements, playbills, references to fairs in the Old Bailey Proceedings, or
literary accounts commonly reveal the continuation of fair amusements
long after the official end of the fair.[86] However, there is also evidence
that constables sometimes did police play-booth entertainment. In 1732,
the *Daily Post* printed news that Mr. Fielding's 'celebrated Droll of the
Fall of Essex', playing in Bartholomew Fair (in early September) to 'vast
Numbers of Nobility, Gentry and others', would not be presented at
Southwark Fair that year 'as reported' because at the previous Southwark
Fair he had 'receiv'd such continual Insults from the Constables of that
Place, that he is fully determined not to perform his said Droll any where
but in … Bartholomew Fair'.[87] This is the same year that Fielding had
been brought into Bartholomew Fair's Piepowder Court for failing to
obtain a license, and perhaps the incidents were linked.[88] Even after
being reprimanded for evading rules of licensing, however, his entertain-

ment continued at Bartholomew Fair, and well past the charted days for the fair. Play-booth entertainment was not easily regulated. It was obviously quite popular; had play-booth proprietors and actors not profited from their business, they would not have evaded city legislation so tenaciously. At the same time, London's Aldermen could not depend on the City's officials on the ground to care about and carry out their legislation. Southwark's bailiff, at least in 1735, was either not very good at his job, did not find play booths immediately threatening enough to regulate, or simply had no force or authority to easily 'pull down' illegal play booths. Someone, however, did inform the Aldermen about Hannah Lee's booth so that they could take legal steps to close it. This is a reminder that not all London inhabitants enjoyed or profited from unlicensed play booths – or that personal motives may have caused someone to inform on Mrs. Lee that year.

Combating 'Evil Disposed Persons' at 'Pretend Fairs'

While London's Aldermen and Lord Mayor debated their options for limiting Bartholomew and Southwark Fairs, the magistrates in Middlesex launched their own campaign against disorderly public amusements. They, too, believed they combated 'vice' in their repeated attempts at regulation, although they faced a much more difficult situation. Throughout the early eighteenth century, Middlesex officials confronted the problem of unlicensed play booths and playhouses in Middlesex, as well as many un-chartered and illegal 'pretend fairs' sprouting up in diverse locations throughout growing suburbs including Tottenham Court, Hampstead, and Clerkenwell.[89] These un-chartered fairs were sometimes regularly held, but often happened spontaneously, and their existence flouted local and national authorities with the sole authority to establish fairs.

Pretend fairs became customary festivals not because someone with authority established them for a given purpose – to sell a particular product, for example – but instead they emerged because common people took it upon themselves to establish them. These informal traditions threatened the root of order in London. At pretend fairs, city authorities believed people blatantly congregated for the sole purpose of entertainment (though many of those who attended sought profit, as well as, or in lieu of, entertainment). Middlesex authorities viewed such gathering places as sites of potential social disturbance. Gaming, theatrical shows, music, and festivity all encouraged drinking, which, in turn, promoted unruly or uninhibited actions.[90] Coupled with this was the fact that festive places might become gathering spaces for young and potentially disruptive men not engaged in any sort of commerce or trade. Justices concentrated regulatory attention to attempting to abolish these unlicensed festivals.

Efforts to control Tottenham Court Fair, a 'pretend fair' founded 'from below', exemplify the struggle between urban authorities and Middlesex fair-goers who enjoyed and profited from un-chartered festivity. At the crux of this struggle were competing notions of commerce and issues surrounding public safety. People who profited from running music, theatrical, gaming, or drinking booths at this pretend fair liked the festival: those who were assaulted or robbed here believed otherwise. Regardless of how people viewed Tottenham Court fair, it continued year after year – fair-goers evaded the Middlesex authorities' regulation attempts, but officials were not deterred from efforts to police this festival. An order made in July 1718 is typical of their feelings about this festival. The Magistrates prohibited 'common players of Interludes and Keepers of Gaming Houses and Gaming Tables at or near ... Tottenham Court in the Parish of St. Pancras ... which practice tended to the encouragement of vice and immorality and to the debauching and ruining of Servants and Apprentices'.[91] Even worse, magistrates argued that at this fair 'young or unwary Persons are defrauded of their Money's and that severall [sic] persons there permit ... Drunkeness and Cursing ... in their houses or Booths... and that [some] commit assaults affrays and other disorder'.[92] In 1724, the Middlesex magistrates undertook their most decisive action against this festival and ordered the high constable of Holborn accompanied by his petty constables to assemble at Tottenham Court. So assembled, this force was ordered to apprehend illegal exhibitors. If this raid was successful, it was only temporary. The 'evil disposed persons' returned the following year and continued the tradition of this unruly public assembly. Assembling a large force to police county orders was logistically difficult and very expensive, particularly because in order to suppress a fair of this size, large numbers of men (who would not, themselves, join in the festivity) would have to be paid to police the area around the clock for the duration of the festival.

From 1718, Middlesex justices made successive orders prohibiting suburban pretend fairs. Though their orders were printed in newspapers and posted throughout town, these spontaneous festivals continued and spread. One of the most disorderly fairs in Middlesex was Welch Fair, held in the Parish of St James, Clerkenwell. It reached the height of its unruliness in 1744, when William Griffiths 'unlawfully maliciously and contemptuously utter[ed] and [spoke] of and concerning John Elliott ... one of his Majesty's Justices of the Peace ... (being in the Execution of his office for Preservation of the King's Peace and to Suppress any unlawful assembly of loose, idle and disorderly Persons [at] Welch Fair)'. Griffiths was convicted of calling the justice of the peace a 'scoundrel' then challenging his masculinity with: 'I am a better man than you ... you may kiss my Arse'. He was also indicted, but not convicted, of assaulting and beating Francis Hole, another Justice of the Peace.[93] Griffiths' blatant contempt for local authority had significance beyond his insults and physical attacks. His disregard for urban authority and participation in the festivities of an un-chartered festival represented the wider threat these illegal festivals posed to the foundations of metropolitan order. The continued presence of such fairs illustrated local officials' limited control over policing festive urban space. Men who policed illegal festivals had tenuous authority from the perspective of male revellers who felt empowered to undercut social rank.

Not all participants in the amusements of pretend fairs were as overtly threatening as William Griffiths, though. Others who disregarded London authorities did so in their quest for profit. The casual commerce taking place in fair booths, shops, taverns, and wheelbarrows in and around London fairs was a small industry. Some Londoners desired even more opportunities to profit from this style of urban amusement. In 1743, George Shank came before London's Court of Aldermen to request a charter for a new fair he hoped to establish in East Smithfield. This 'Daily fair or Market' would offer opportunities to buy or sell 'Cloaths and Raggs', and Shank would have the privilege of collecting all tolls of this fair. Though city officials had tried for decades to limit fairs in London, they remained profitable ventures to men like Shank. Though his request was denied, a group of people had already been profiting from the buying and selling of 'Raggs' in Portsoken Ward, near Tower Hill at an illegal fair. A company of Merchant Tailors and inhabitants of this area complained to the Aldermen that 'Idle, Vagrant, Loose and Disorderly Persons', assembled at this location daily, except Sunday, from 'one or two in the afternoon until Night'. This assembly took place in a 'Tumultuous manner', and was held 'without any authority'. The only objects traded at this fair were, according to the petitioners, 'Raggs and old cloths which are [most likely] from Thieves or Robbers'.[94] The inhabitants complained that their own trades and occupations were hindered because 'customers [were] prevented by the Great Concourse of people who assemble there from coming to their shops'. Customers were not only prevented from gaining access to the area because of increased traffic, but they were also, 'in great Danger of being Robbed and pilfered by Rouges Thieves and Pickpockets who daily assemble there'.[95]

Portsoken inhabitants were concerned about this growing and disorderly festival. The fair prevented the continuance of everyday commerce, but inhabitants were powerless to do anything. Unable to suppress this illegal assembly themselves, the petitioners asked the court to use their 'authority and power to remove this great and Dangerous Nusance [sic]'.[96] On 2 June 1741, London's Aldermen finally issued an order regarding 'Ragg Fair'. They ordered two city marshals and constables of the area to 'take effectual care to prevent all such tumults and riotous Assemblies at this place or any other', asking them to bring any offenders before the Lord Mayor of his Justices of the Peace. Though this was ordered, the court found that the 'Nusances continued and increased', and so they 'Enjoyn[ed] the City Marshalls and all and every constables of this city to be careful and diligent in putting the said order in execution and preventing the several nusances ... and use best endeavours to apprehend all offenders'.[97] This order was printed and posted, but we do not know if it was followed by any of the area's official overseers. Struggles to regulate disorderly public gatherings and illegal fairs revealed to Londoners that urban authorities lacked real power to control large gatherings of people. The potential for social and political unrest, which might easily attend such popular disregard for urban law, worried both local and national authorities.

The problem of politics, urban play booths, and playhouses

The Middlesex Justices had attempted to regulate immoral and illegal public behaviour in the city since Queen Mary and Queen Anne's letters to the Middlesex Justices, but in April 1721, they had additional royal incentive to stamp out disorderly urban entertainments. In this year, George I worried about political dissent and issued a proclamation to the Middlesex and Westminster Justices of the Peace, asking them to be on the watch for any 'scandalous clubs or Societies of young Persons' in their jurisdictions. There was no specific mention of who were, exactly, the members of these scandalous clubs, but the King considered them dangerous because they 'meet together, and [in] the most impious and blasphemous Manner, insult the most Sacred Principles of our holy Religion, affront Almighty God himself, and corrupt the minds and Morals of one another'.[98]

Though the King's proclamation continued the earlier royal tradition of concern for religious and moral order in London, his alarm was also a response to social problems in London. The King's order reflected anxieties regarding uncontained and violent young men. The King and his advisors not only feared rising crime in London, but were most immediately concerned with the possibility of Jacobite uprisings or social disorder. Gangs of thieves who found sanctuary in London's streets and the public houses where they congregated threatened social order in one way, but the fear of such unruly groups of men fuelling any sort of Jacobite discontent was also very real.[99] In order to prevent disruptive youths from '[drawing] down the Vengeance of God upon this Nation', the King ordered his Lord Chancellor to call together the Justices of the Peace of Middlesex and Westminster and direct them to 'make the most diligent and careful Enquiry and Search for the Discovery of any thing like this and the like Sort, tending in any wise to the Corruption of the Principles and Manners of Men'. The Justices were to report back to the Lord Chancellor with their findings and then together they would devise a plan to suppress these activities.[100]

The Middlesex Justices placed an advertisement in the *London Gazette* asking anyone with information regarding 'Wicked Clubs' to come to one of several public meetings in order to share their knowledge. With no person 'comeing [*sic*] to make any Discovery or give any such Information', and lacking evidence of Jacobites, the justices came to their own conclusion, which they wrote to the Lord Chancellor on 26 May 1721. Their conclusion was the problem had nothing to do with Jacobites, rather:

> the Prophaneness and Debauchery which prevails and increases in the Town and County proceeds chiefly from the Mascarades [*sic*] and Gameing houses and from the increase of Play houses and Publick houses of all Sorts in all parts of the Town, and also from the difficulties which attend the presentation and Suppression of them.[101]

It is perhaps no surprise that these Justices singled out gaming and playhouses. Since the re-establishment of theatres after the Restoration, the king's Lord Chamberlain and his subordinate, the Master of Revels, worked to exercise control over dramatic entertainment. The efforts of the Lord Chamberlain varied in their success and during the early eighteenth century, and initial regulation targeted immorality in plays. By the 1730s, however, the political consequences of plays increasingly worried the government, both locally and nationally.[102] In 1735, Sir John Barnard, an independent Member of Parliament from London introduced a bill to limit numbers of playhouses. Barnard's bill reflected local and national concerns about the social and economic consequences of theatrical entertainment. Many people worried that plays contained corrupting messages and in some cases incited people to violence (most notoriously evidenced by a 1735 riot at the Haymarket theatre that occurred in the presence of the king and queen).[103] Others were concerned about the area around theatres, which became centres of prostitution and haunts for pickpockets or other criminals. Economically, playhouses were thought to take space away from more regular businesses that employed 'the industrious Poor'. The introduction of theatrical entertainments to an area raised local rents and induced owners to rent their buildings to more 'profitable Tenants', who lacked 'Innocence and Morality'.[104] The 1720s and 1730s witnessed a rise in theatrical entertainment presented at fairs and arguments against fairs and their entertainment echo those against playhouses.[105]

Playhouses and fairs plagued Middlesex and London authorities and both evaded suppression attempts throughout the early eighteenth century. Urban authorities were troubled that theatrical entertainment often spilled out of fairgrounds and onto Middlesex streets, taking place in temporary play booths as well as at licensed and unlicensed fairs. According to the Middlesex justices, booths set up to act drolls and for the 'exercise[of] unlawful Games and Plays' were one of the most dangerous consequences of fairs, but such entertainments were also dangerous on their own. Temporary, and occasionally permanent, playhouses were erected in various areas of London, including Goodman's Fields and Hampstead.[106] Similar to London's Aldermen, the Middlesex justices considered play booths and unlicensed playhouses occasions for 'vice and immorality and to the debauching and ruining of Servants Apprentices and others as well as to the disturbance of the Publique Peace'.[107] Though the justices expressed their apprehension regarding these amusements, they were rarely able to devote enough force to quell the entertainments.

Temporary playhouses dodged city and county regulation efforts as successfully as pretend fairs. Even as early as 1716, in late October, city officials targeted a booth set up in West Smithfield. The booth was located within the festival grounds of Bartholomew Fair, but this play-booth manager profited from his business long after that year's fair had ended. Inhabitants around Smithfield petitioned the court to take down this illegal play booth, arguing that 'Tollerating a shew Booth within the Rounds', subjected the inhabitants to 'many inconveniences as well by pickpockets and Lewd Persons', who frequented the area. These petitioners obviously believed the city sanctioned this booth for it to have existed for so long on its own, but they devised their own methods to suppress it. They wanted City cooperation and called for 'Four Lamp Lights set up at each corner of the Field near the Rounds', and for 'six able Watchmen at Duty there from six at night till six in the morning during the Winter season', in order to prevent such entertainment in the future. The inhabitants hoped these safety measures would not be necessary.[108]

Many fair entertainments offended and challenged London authorities' notions of what entailed a properly ordered commercial city. The court's regulation suggests their concern was with the largest population attending fairs: young men of the lower orders. Officials feared that the spectacle of London fairs detracted from these men's potential to be industrious in ways that promoted social order and benefited the city's commerce. Unlicensed theatrical entertainment seemed to particularly threaten urban order, especially during the 'heyday' (1720–1735) of fair theatre, when London's professional theatrical performers and managers participated regularly in fair-time entertainment.[109] These professionals in addition to successful strolling companies of actors, such as the company operated by Hannah Lee, had both money and talent to devote to theatrical spectacle. People attended these events for many reasons – the actors, the story, but also the elaborate scenery. Early in the century, Mrs. Mynns, for example, featured entertainments designed by Elkanah Settle, a respected theatrical designer and writer.[110] His 1707 spectacle *The Siege of Troy* featured 'scenes, machines and movements', and new stage decorations provided by Mrs. Mynns.[111]

The theme of this early spectacle was not as important as the fantastic setting, but by 1728 and 1729, play booths featured shortened versions of popular London plays such as Gay's *The Beggars Opera*, noted for its political satire and, in particular, its thinly veiled critique of the Prime Minister, Sir Robert Walpole. Walpole once attended a performance and publicly laughed at himself, even asking for an encore of a song believed to allude to him. However, his good humour remained in the theatre.[112] City officials and national authorities were alarmed not just with the increased politicization of London's theatre during the late 1720s and early 1730s, but also by its spread into summertime theatre at places such as play booths at fairs as well as unlicensed playhouses.[113] London's Aldermen were concerned especially with a playhouse erected in Goodman's Fields and run first by Thomas Odell and then by Henry Giffard. The Aldermen believed this playhouse had 'very many ill consequences', including, 'affecting morals, lessening... industry, and losing the time of those persons employed in [the silk, woollen and other manufacturers]'. Because the theatre was not within their jurisdiction, they petitioned the King to suppress the theatre before it 'may prove to be of very great prejudice to the trade of this city'. [114] Restricting the theatre of London's fairs was one aspect of a much larger movement by urban and national officials to control what they believed was a growing problem contributing to idleness.[115]

Unlicensed theatre held in all reaches of the City and county not only distracted people from their occupations, but officials feared the social implications of satirical comedies filled with political critiques, such as *The Beggar's Opera* or Fielding's 1737 *The Vision of the Golden Rump*, another attack on Walpole. Official concerns about the social and economic implications of unchecked theatrical entertainment mingled with wider fears of the implications of politicized theatre and contributed to the eventual issuance of the 1737 Licensing Act. This Act effectively put the lid on theatrical entertainment presented by performers not attached to the licensed theatres Drury Lane, Covent Garden, and the King's Theatre. Actors who performed away from these theatres risked being tried for vagrancy.[116] This act did dampen the theatre of London's fairs, though many playbooth proprietors turned towards other types of dramatic entertainment, such as puppet shows or 'pantomimes'. Dramatic entertainment provided by live actors eventually returned in creative ways, especially by the 1740s. London fair theatre, however, was never the same.[117]

The everyday dangers of fairs

City and county officials blamed fair entertainments, such as theatre, for a host of evils, but their orders against fair amusements are rarely specific about the ill consequences of fairs apart from the economic and moral threat posed by their entertainment. A search of the Old Bailey Proceedings from the period 1716–1753 reveals the extent to which London's illegal fairs actually did disrupt social order. If London authorities kept abreast of Old Bailey trials, there was much evidence to back up their claims that fairs threatened urban security. These proceedings include often vivid descriptions of the ways in which people profited from illicit activities at fairs and reveal a culture of rioting, drunkenness, pick pocketing, and pawn shops.

Tottenham Court Fair in Middlesex seemed especially dangerous. Newspapers frequently mention it as a dangerous location. On 16 August 1729, *Fog's Weekly Journal* reported that two robberies were committed in one night and that 'Several other Robberies had been committed in the ... Fields since the Beginning of that Fair'.[118] In order to get between the fair and the City, one had to cross open and dark fields, which were frequented by robbers and other criminals. Beyond being locations of criminal activity, the fair was hazardous for personal safety. A child, a woman, and a ten-year-old boy were all run over by hackney coaches on different occasions.[119] One woman even had aqua fortis, a chemical solution of nitric acid in water, thrown in her face at the fair. She later died from this injury.[120] This unlicensed fair is mentioned in four out of thirty-three cases at the Old Bailey that include references to fairs – it was the site of an attempted rape, three assaults and robberies, theft in a music booth, and counterfeiting. Elizabeth Pulwash (Pate) described explicitly a brutal assault and attempted rape, which happened after she left Tottenham Court Fair by herself.[121] Though in one trial the accused casts doubt on her, insinuating that she was a prostitute, Pulwash claims to have stayed at the fair to watch a 'clock-work' after her two friends left. She most likely explained her late and unaccompanied departure from the fair into the dark, largely rural, and hazardous fields surrounding the fair in order to appear innocent and absolve herself of any notion that she invited the sexual encounter.[122] Pulwash was brutally assaulted, stripped, and robbed of nearly all of her clothes by three men equipped with both a dagger and a pistol. After these men assaulted and attempted to rape her for nearly three hours, they tied her to the back of another man also assaulted and robbed by the criminals, and tossed them both into a ditch, where they remained until four or five the next morning.[123]

The fields surrounding Tottenham Court fair were dangerous, but so were the fair booths, particularly those providing musical entertainment. Walter Simmons had an encounter with Hannah Stuart, alias 'Yorkshire Hannah', at such a booth in 1740. While waiting to meet up with a fellow workman at the fair, Simmons entered a music booth (probably aware of the reputation of music booths as bawdy houses, he makes it seem as if he entered one only to pass time while waiting for a friend). Here, he met Stuart, who invited him to have a drink. Though he allegedly, 'called for a Pint of Beer', he received a 'Decanter of Cyder'. He did not have enough money for this beverage, but that failed to stop him from enjoying the drink with his newfound companion. He soon, sadly, discovered this woman's motive for filling him with cider – as he was drinking, he felt Stuart take his watch from his pocket, and watched as she ran into a door in the back of the booth. Simmons followed, and threatened to break down the door. The 'Drawer', asked him to stop because he was, 'making a Riot in the Booth'. Proclaiming his sobriety to the court, Simmons revealed that he then laid down on a bed in the back of the booth, because he had a 'Fear of being murder'd', if he left. He remained until Stuart's return, whereupon she told Simmons he was drunk and that she did not have his watch. In fact, she did not – she had given the watch to the booth's fiddler to hide for her. The crime was uncovered and the criminals apprehended, though Shilcock, the fiddler, was let go because he was so drunk, 'he did not know (what) one Hand (did) from the other', though this apparently did not prevent him from playing music.[124]

The Middlesex justices associated most of the disorder of fairs with entertainment taking place in the confines of temporary fair booths. In booths, actions were invisible not only to authorities, but also to clear-thinking people who might protect or warn fellow fair-goers or serve as credible witnesses should that need arise. In testimony from the Old Bailey, evidence suggests many people at fairs drank too much to be of much help to others. Defendants often blamed drunkenness as their excuse for criminal behaviour. Though juries at the Old Bailey some-times accepted this alibi, many times they did not. When accused of pickpocketing, for example, Thomas Bostock argued he was not guilty because 'he had been at Southwark Fair and was drunk'.[125] This plea was partially successful, because Bostock was declared guilty only for 10d of the 2s he was accused of stealing.

The Proceedings of the Old Bailey provide much social evidence of the danger and disorder Middlesex justices and London's Aldermen feared at fairs.[126] Cases from this court reveal how criminals manipu-lated the temporary and uncertain status of fairs as one means to cloak their criminal intent, provide alibis for themselves, or to excuse their illegal actions. Some blamed fairs for their criminal behaviour. In one case, Anthony Meagre and his accomplice explained to the victim they robbed outside of Bartholomew Fair, 'we have been gaming and need money'.[127] Some accused criminals found alibis in fair work. Christopher Murphy, for example, proved he was not guilty of horse theft because as the crime was committed, he was acting in a booth at Southwark Fair.[128] For other accused criminals, fairs provided a last-ditch explanation for their sudden acquisition of goods. John Scoon argued that he did not steal a watch chain from Samuel Wilson's shop, but that he won it at Southwark Fair, though he could not prove his claim.[129] After stealing £20 worth of sugar from the confectioner to whom he was apprenticed, William Simmons made his getaway by asking his master for time off to go to Bartholomew Fair. The confectioner, Henry Allen, who consented to his apprentice's request, did not question why he failed to return for a week – until Simmons's father brought back his son and exposed the crime. After committing theft, many prisoners took stolen goods to a fair where they sold them for quick cash, which they often spent on games or drink, as did Michael Herring, William Holbrook, and Jeremy Reynolds, who spent their spoils from selling stolen children's stockings and a wig on brandy and the Pass table at Southwark Fair.[130]

Some cases that came before the London Sessions also reveal the potential hazards of fairs. In one case, Sarah Small explained how she was 'seduced by an unknown man in Bartholomew Fair'. The man provided her with liquor and proceeded to 'debauch' her in one of the area inns. She later became his mistress and eventually conceived his child.[131] George Wilson, an apprentice, explained how William Handy 'prevailed' upon him to go out and rob with a group of men. During Bartholomew Fair, they robbed a woman of 4d. and a thimble (which they threw away).[132] Even thieves found difficulties at fairs. John Ballard, who had stolen 12 pounds from Thomas Kent in Bow Lane argued that, after he purchased clothes with 5 of the pounds, the rest was picked out of his pocket in Southwark Fair.[133]

London's many newspapers contributed to public opinion that fairs could be dangerous places – yet at the same time, they actively sold the pleasures of fair entertainment through classified advertisements and news reports. Newspapers promoted fair entertainments, which were likely a good source of advertising income during summer months. They frequently reported that incognito royalty or other notables attended fairs.[134] At the same time, disturbances at fairs were also reported and these reports helped spread the idea that fairs could be quite dangerous. In 1725, for instance, The *Daily Journal* reported that a 'Gallery at Lee's Booth in Southwark-Fair happen'd to fall: The Iron Spike penetrated the Body of a young Man so deep that he died the same Day'.[135] Another man broke his leg in the same accident. In 1729, newspapers reported that a 'Big Boy tumbled out of a flying Chair at Bartholomew Fair, and was kill'd'.[136] Such events were exceptional, but likely memorable. During the period 1695–1764, London's *Daily Post* is full of advertisements and news reports about entertainments at Bartholomew and Southwark fairs, but very few reports mention accidents, deaths, or criminal activities. Tottenham Court Fair is exceptional in its news coverage that features more about disturbances or crimes committed at the fair and less about the entertainment.

By 1746, the Middlesex justices had spent much time decrying and prohibiting illegal or disorderly fairs including May Fair, Paddington Fair, Hampstead Fair, Highgate Fair, Mile End Fair, Bow Fair, Tottenham Court Fair, and Welsh Fair (only two of which, May Fair and Bow Fair, operated with legal charters).[137] They worried about their inability to effectively suppress entertainments, which not only damaged the 'Youth', but also contributed to the 'corruption of good Manners and Detriment of Trade and Lawful Business'.[138] Lacking man power and capital to back up their regulations, justices were frustrated by their lack of progress. Since their increased efforts to curtail illegal fairs in the 1720s, fair entertainment only grew. They willingly acknowledged that '... during the greatest part of the time from the beginning of May to the End of September at some place or other within a few Miles of this Town some one or other of these fairs are held and great Resort is had to them'.[139]

Middlesex officials tried a new approach to solving the problem of both chartered and pretend fairs in 1746. Appealing to national authority, the justices spelled out their grievance in a letter to Philip, Lord Hardwicke, and Lord High Chancellor of Great Britain. Here, they listed what they believed tended, 'to the Injury of the publick and to the Ruin and Impoverishment of private persons and families'. They highlighted the danger of fairs by noting that not only had a constable once been killed at May Fair, but they claimed that the largest fairs, Tottenham Court, Welsh, and May fairs attracted, 'very near ten thousand persons many of whom stay till one, two, or three o'clock in the Morning as we have been credibly informed and verily believe'.[140] Such large numbers of men and women were distracted from their families, trade, and manners by 'common players of Interludes', as well as dancing, drinking, and gaming booths.[141] It was the presence of these booths, especially at May Fair, that the justices blamed for most of the troubles they associated with fairs. They argued that proprietors of such booths used 'every way and method taken to tempt and entice persons of both Sexes to meet and assemble together', which led, in their opinion, to 'Innocent persons' being 'debauched','All manner of Vice Immorality and Prophaness' committed in the open, and teaching innocent people the bad habits of 'Gaming, Drinking and Swearing'. Most dangerously, especially for commerce and personal safety, justices believed these occasions led, 'Servants [to] defraud their masters', and to the formation of 'Gangs of rogues and Thieves' who 'patrole about the Streets and make it dangerous to be abroad even early in the Evening'.[142]

More than a threat to property and personal safety, the Middlesex justices found fairs detrimental to the social and economic fabric of London families, particularly those of low economic means. Justices argued that fairs caused

> [t]he poor [to] grow even poorer and many families are thrown on their respective parishes by reason that the heads of such families cannot resist the Temptation of frequenting these fairs in the Summer Season where they either wantonly spend and squander away in drinking and Gaming or at these Shows and Drolls that little they had reserved for support of themselves and Children'.[143]

These fears illustrate many of metropolitan London's growing pains during this time of rapid expansion. Urban authorities from justices to constables to parish leaders were overtaxed in their attempts to provide basic services, such as charity and protection, to London inhabitants.[144]

At times, authorities found that fairs undermined charitable institutions and their efforts to counter problems attending urbanization. Fairs, like unlicensed alehouses and unlawful games, had long been blamed as temptations for 'gullible apprentices'.[145] They were viewed as a particular danger to the apprentices in London's Bridewell Hospital. Established during the mid-Tudor period as an institution to care for homeless children and discipline the urban poor charged with minor property offences or disorderly behaviour, Bridewell also housed and trained pauper apprentices.[146] Minutes of the governors' reports reveal the men's strict oversight of apprentices and their suspicion of allowing young male apprentices to attend Bartholomew Fair. The governors of Bridewell included London Aldermen as well as lay men.[147] Aldermen, especially, were acquainted with the many evils of London's late-summer fairs and saw them as a corrupting influence on apprentices. They found evidence of this, in addition to proof that fairs generally threatened London's poor, in cases they heard at Bridewell. Men and women were taken from fairs and brought before the governors for picking pockets, creating disturbances, rioting, or various other immoral activities. From 1691 to 1732, Bridewell's governors presided over five cases involving crimes or disorderly conduct committed at Bartholomew Fair. Criminal behaviour represented the spectrum of expected illegal or disorderly activities conducted at fairs. One woman, Sarah Miller, was brought before the Bridewell governors for, 'making disturbance in a house in Bartholomew Fair'.[148] A suspected pickpocket was apprehended in the fair, and a man, Stanley Edwards, was brought in at midnight after being apprehended at a gaming table and, 'not giving any good account of himself'.[149]

Most alarming for the Bridewell governors, however, were disturbances at fairs involving their own apprentices. Governors presided over the conduct of their apprentices in an effort to maintain the reputation of their apprenticeship system.[150] In 1743, newspapers reported a 'great Number of Bridewell Boys' had gathered at Tottenham-Court Fair in a 'riotous disorderly Manner, with Clubs and Staves'. They committed 'great Outrages' and wounded many people before making their escape. One of the boys later died from the injuries he received during the riot.[151] On 11 September 1755 the Bridewell governors were informed that 'several' of their apprentices had 'committed great Disorders' at

Bartholomew Fair on Thursday 4 September (by 1755, the beginning of the fair was 3 September due to the 1752 calendar conversion).[152] After examination, the governors found not only that sixteen apprentices had rioted at Bartholomew Fair, but that at least a dozen apprentices later caused a violent disturbance at Southwark Fair. In each case, informers reported that Bridewell apprentices were 'making a Riot' in the fair. At Bartholomew Fair the riot turned against the three Bridewell Beadles sent to break up the riot and 'admonish' the apprentices to return home. One unruly apprentice, Thomas Caines, 'broke Fitch the Beadle's head and Knock't him down upon his Asking him what he did with a bludgeon in his hand'.[153] Apprentices also injured a second Beadle in addition to additional bystanders. Many of the apprentices were apprehended on the spot, but most of them managed to escape – some from as far up as four stories high. Some fled after the incident and others were eventually caught. This included Francis Feilder, who had been at Bartholomew Fair 'in the Hospital Cloathing (which he said was his own)'.[154]

In 1755, the late-summer fair season disrupted and undermined the City's charitable efforts to make productive citizens out of some poor London men. Bridewell's overseers attempted to stop further damage to the training and reputation of their apprentices by 'correcting' apprentices found guilty of rioting at fairs. Corrections included sending some apprentices to the Hemp blocks while allowing no other apprentice to speak to them, some were sent to 'Matthew's Hole separate from the rest', and the worst offenders were 'corrected in the presence of the rest of the Apprentices and then Stript [and] turn'd out of the Hospital'. After delivering punishments, the oversight committee noted the blame for the rioting was 'Cheifly in the Artsmasters', who obviously neglected to enforce the Governors' orders that apprentices should be 'kept at Home on Holydays'. The governors continued to complain of the extent that masters overlooked orders. Because one master retorted that he would have abided by these laws if he 'knew 'em', the Governors agreed that the rules regarding apprentice conduct, the duty of the Beadles, and the responsibilities of artsmasters should be printed and posted in each shop and in the 'Lobby, Court Room & Dineing Room', of the Hospital. The governors also proposed new responsibilities for the Masters, including stipulating they follow their apprentices to the Chapel for services and that every artsmaster would keep his apprentices, 'in his Appartment on Holydays and he himself shall stay at home the Evenings during the time of Bartholomew and Southwark fair in Order to keep his Apprentices there'.[155]

Popular and Elite Resistance to Fair Regulation

The long and difficult struggle to curtail, or at the very least transform, a type of entertainment begun in the medieval era and still dynamically existent in eighteenth-century London reveals important issues about interactions between urban authorities and common people. Resulting struggles included popular and even elite resistance to regulatory efforts targeting fairs. Social struggles over attempts to transform traditional festivity illuminate the ways in which people's everyday use of urban space helped form London's character differently from city officials' conceptions of the ideal use of this space. Resistance to urban authorities' regulatory efforts came from business men and women, fair-goers, and criminals who continued to profit from and enjoy their customary use of urban space for amusement and their own versions of commerce. In 1735, for example, a group of London Citizens and Inhabitants of West Smithfield petitioned the Aldermen who were in the process of considering their legal rights to regulate Bartholomew and Southwark Fairs. These inhabitants asked the court to continue Bartholomew Fair for fourteen days. Their petition was denied, but it is clear that continuing this fair for longer than three days benefited many Londoners, particularly those who profited by living near the centre of fairs.[156]

Both London's Aldermen and the Middlesex justices were frustrated also by elite attempts to defy their efforts. The struggle to regulate London's fairs reveals a contest between local and traditional authority. Bartholomew Fair, for example, continued to be held at least in part because by the early eighteenth century, heirs to Richard Rich, the Earl of Warwick (and also of Holland), held partial rights to the fair. Many of the Lords Warwick seem to have enjoyed farming the profits from the fair, and a few of them actually embodied dissolute masculinity. Edward Rich, the sixth Earl of Warwick and third Earl of Holland must have horrified city fathers.[157] This particular Lord Warwick, 'grew into young manhood, without any paternal control' (his father had died when he was two).[158] His close friend was Lord Mohun, who was killed in 1712 in a famous duel with the Duke of Hamilton. The two men had many adventures together, including serving as 'volunteers in Flanders in March 1693/4'. Warwick hid Mohun after he killed 'Captain Hill at Charing Cross [in a duel]', and they were both together when Warwick mortally wounded 'Captain Coot' in a late-night duel in Leicester Square. Warwick fled to France for a short time, but eventually surrendered to the House of Lords. He was tried along with Mohun (an accomplice) in Westminster Hall. The trial in March 1699 was a spectacle attended by peers, their wives, and anyone who could obtain the highly sought tickets issued for the event. When city fathers looked to London's elite men to help curtail the disorder of fairs, they did not consider men such as Warwick and his son (another well-known rake) useful patriarchs.[159]

Later heirs to the West Smithfield manor were no more willing to serve as moral guardians for the fair. When, in 1761, the City Lands committee investigated shutting down Bartholomew Fair, the city attorney advised them against it because the current heir to the manor, William Edwards, Baron Kensington, who lived in Wales as an absentee landlord, refused to sell his rights to the fair.[160] London's Aldermen viewed this with suspicion, and thought it was more about Edwards's contempt of civic officials than the amount of profit he derived from the fair.[161] Elite male authority at this fair only confounded city officials' efforts to police urban festivity.

In Middlesex and Westminster, justices also found that their county's politically and traditionally powerful families sometimes stood in the way of abolishing the disorderly May Fair. However, a powerful resident, the Earl of Coventry, was instrumental in finally abolishing that fair in 1764, but other elite Londoners who lived in the area flouted county regulatory efforts.[162] Middlesex county officials viewed with suspicion the elite families with their London residences in the newly prestigious housing developments around May Fair (an area known collectively by that name). They believed the 'Gentlemen and others in Office and Authority within the City of Westminster', who lived near where May Fair was kept, should have been obliged 'to act with the utmost Vigour', to regulate the disorderly fair.[163] With the apparent sanction of gentlemen living in May Fair, Middlesex authorities believed regulation of fairs under their jurisdiction would be impossible. May Fair '[took] the lead every year of all the fairs which are [held] in this county' and as long as this fair 'flourished' and was 'encouraged', they would be 'charged with partiality' if they focused on the regulation of other fairs.[164] The censure Middlesex justices directed at nationally prominent gentlemen and politicians who lived in the neighbourhood of May Fair does not reveal reasons behind elite inattentiveness to the problems of the fair. It does speak volumes, however, about a split between local and national authority and antagonism between powerful middling men and the traditional elite. Justices were worried their own concerns meant little to elite men, and that common men would follow that lead. Despite the anxiety of the Justices, one elite male did step forward to assist in regulating the fair. The Earl of Coventry's authority was enough to influence the suppression of May Fair, demonstrating that it did sometimes take aristocratic authority to implement social changes that would be followed by common people.

The unsuccessful regulation of fairs should also make us question whether or not City, county, and national officials always agreed that this was an urban amusement worth regulating. Repeated orders were largely ineffective due to inconsistent enforcement. Orders were occasionally successful, but usually because they were accompanied by the efforts of reform-minded individuals who also had power to implement changes, such as the Earl of Coventry, or inhabitants who petitioned the court. A lack of collective agency on the part of individual constables and other urban enforcement authorities led to uneven enforcement.

By the 1750s, a decade prior to the successful cessation of Southwark Fair, dangerous and disorderly behaviour at fairs had become legendary. City and county attacks on these popular amusements seemed to incite those who resisted them into ever more outrageous actions. At least, this is how it appears in popular accounts of London's fairs. What may have occurred, instead, was that by the middle of the eighteenth century, fairs were solidly immortalized in the popular imagination as hazardous to public, political, and personal order. Publicity about the ways in which fairs threatened London's social order may actually reveal that they were beginning to be more successfully contained. By the 1740s, certainly, illicit theatre had been contained by national legislation. London's fair theatre was never the same after the Licensing Act. Actors and managers returned to London's theatres and found an approved permanent home for their summertime work at the newly instituted Haymarket Theatre.[165] At the same time, amusements such as commercial pleasure gardens and spas targeted at various classes, from elite to labouring, drew some patrons away from fairs and into circumscribed and more selective venues. Increasingly from the 1730s on, advertisements in London newspapers featured commercial venues competing with fair entertainment. Venues such as Cuper's Gardens, the New Wells, Sadler's Wells and others offered a variety of entertainment often featuring rope dancing, puppet shows, and singing similar to what was presented at fairs.[166] One example of the growing year-round industry for fair entertainment is that provided by Isaac Fawkes. During fairs, he advertised his 'dexterity of hand', exhibition of musical clocks and the presentation of his 'little Posture-Master' (his son).[167] Fawkes presented the same entertainments at his theatre in James Street during the regular year.[168] Gaming houses existed outside fairs, as well. Authorities were on the watch for 'gamesters' and found them in June 1731 in Cuper's Gardens, a pleasure garden located in Lambeth.[169]

Throughout the 1750s, detailed accounts of disorderly happenings at fairs signified people's agreement that such locations of public amusement were not 'safe'. At mid-century, newspapers included accounts of the 'ups and downs' (a very early and small 'Ferris wheel') at Bartholomew Fair breaking and falling to the ground.[170] Though no one was injured, the 'mob seized and burnt [the ups and downs]'.[171] In 1755, newspapers reported the Bridewell apprentice riot in Bartholomew Fair. A 1759 account described how a young woman went into a public house at Bartholomew Fair, ordered a pint and fought over the payment. During the argument, the drawer, meaning to strike the woman, struck her child instead and killed it. Some riotous behaviour was even committed in apparent support of the nation. In 1758, for example, a group of young men went around Bartholomew Fair shouting, 'King George for Ever', while knocking down everyone who came in their way and 'behav[ing] outrageously'.[172] Newspapers reported in 1760 how a pregnant woman at Bartholomew Fair had an arm broken and was so bruised in the crowd that she was not expected to survive, and how at Southwark Fair 'several couples, exhilarated with liquor, [who] fell into a deep ditch' would have been suffocated by the mud had they not received immediate assistance.[173] Such incidents reinforced notions that fairs offered Londoners very few redeeming opportunities, especially as the growing middle classes increasingly attended amusements at polite, commercial establishments. In their absence, people viewed fairs as places occupied primarily by rough and ill-mannered people. While literary depictions and legal orders had long asserted that fairs were places to which only the 'worst' people resorted, it was not until mid-century that London amusements had actually become segregated enough that fairs were not regularly attended by the emerging middle classes.

Londoners maintained an interest in the latest sensational happenings at fairs – perhaps because this was an aspect of urban life that had long been associated with London identity in literary and visual accounts. The notion that disorderly mobs threatened urban stability right under the nose of authority became a part of London's identity. Though social disorder at fairs seemed to rise to new levels of violence and danger, Southwark Fair was successfully ended in 1763. Urban authorities at last had the upper hand on some metropolitan festivity. Its suppression was relatively smooth. After an inquiry into the City of London's legal rights to suppress both Bartholomew and Southwark Fairs, the City Lands Committee found that the City had full rights to Southwark Fair. They stopped the fair in 1762. Play booth proprietors attempted to contest this suppression the following year by building their booths, but over a hundred constables assembled at Suffolk Place in Southwark and demanded that the men take the booths down.[174] The *St. James Chronicle or the British Evening Post* printed the rumour that 'Southwark Fair will be kept this Year in St. George's Fields, near the Fighting Cocks, out of the Jurisdiction of the City', but no attempt was made.[175] At last, City regulation and manpower came together. Booths were dismantled and the fair came to an end.

Middlesex authorities continued to battle both May Fair and the county's 'pretend fairs' through the early 1760s. After repeated attempts to suppress May Fair, it was finally abolished in 1764. Tottenham Court Fair in Middlesex proved much more difficult to suppress. Despite an order issued to suppress the fair in 1748, it continued until 1827.[176] Welsh (or Welch) Fair was no longer a problem for urban authorities after 1754, when it moved to a new location outside of metropolitan London. Other small fairs continued sporadically until the mid-nineteenth century, but after the mid-eighteenth century, fewer people frequented these festivals.

Bartholomew Fair did not end as easily. The City Lands Committee found that William Edwards, 1st Baron Kensington, of Johnson near Haverford West in Wales, 'was entitled to some benefits arising there from', and he was not willing to sell this right.[177] Edwards informed city officials that he had an 'Extensive Estate in and about Smithfield which would in case the fair was suppressed by greatly reduced in value'.[178] Perhaps sensing an opportunity to become wealthier, or merely not willing to part with his piece of London, Edwards would not sell without an 'Extraordinary sum' the City was not willing to pay.[179] Bartholomew Fair continued until the nineteenth century when, in 1827, William Edwards, 2nd Baron Kensington, agreed to sell the City his interest in the fair. Even with the private interest gone, smaller versions of the fair continued until it eventually died out by the 1850s.[180]

William Adams, whose story opened this chapter, experienced first-hand the cultural debate regarding changing urban conditions happening during the transition from the seventeenth to eighteenth centuries in London. Two conflicting situations played out to undermine his apprenticeship. To Adams's parents, driving a dog-drawn cart at fairs seemed a ludicrous and useless skill for a future carpenter to learn. They most likely expected him to receive the customary training of a carpenter's apprentice. William Adams's parents failed to understand the usefulness of providing amusement at fairs, though for different reasons than London's magistrates. Joseph Bidwell, the master, worked from a different understanding of the great profit to be made in providing entertainment to the city's children and anyone else with a few pence to spare for amusement. Customary fair entertainment was changing. People of all classes sought more opportunities for leisure and did not believe amusement needed to be tied to charters or licenses (proven by the numerous 'pretend fairs' emerging during this time). Through their participation in these unlicensed opportunities for urban amusement, Londoners helped create a new type of festivity. By the middle of the eighteenth century, London authorities were actually issuing licenses approving the new, controlled outdoor urban entertainment found at London's many pleasure gardens and outdoor tea rooms. In these entertainments directed at both middle- and lower-class Londoners, there emerged a new form of urban amusement that combined elements of the old fairs with new understandings of commercially confined – and polite – urban play.

Notes

1 Portions of this chapter have appeared in: T.J. Boisseau and Abigail M. Markwyn (eds), *Gendering the Fair: Histories of Women and Gender at World's Fairs* (Urbana, Chicago and Springfield: The University of Illinois Press, 2010).

2 Ilana Krausman Ben-Amos, *Adolescence and Youth in Early Modern England* (New Haven, CT and London: Yale University Press, 1994), 84; see also A.L. Beier, *Masterless Men: The Vagrancy Problem in England, 1560–1640* (London and New York: Methuen, 1985), 23–4. Beier estimates apprentices formed 15 per cent of London's population in 1600, but only 4 or 5 per cent by 1700.

3 John Rule, 'Employment and Authority: Masters and Men in Eighteenth-Century Manufacturing', in Paul Griffiths, Adam Fox and Steve Hindle (eds), *The Experience of Authority in Early Modern England* (New York: St. Martin's Press, 1996), 288.

4 Peter Earle discusses parental anxiety in helping sons choose appropriate careers: *The Making of the English Middle Class: Business, Society and Family Life in London, 1660–1730* (Berkeley and Los Angeles: University of California Press, 1989), 89–90.

5 LMA, Middlesex Sessions of the Peace, MJ/SB/B/89, No. 903, 56–7, August 1732.

6 Ben-Amos, Adolescence and Youth, 84–5.

7 Adams' petition was first brought to the court 31 August 1732 and he was discharged from his apprenticeship on 7 September 1732; Middlesex Sessions: LMA, SM/PS Sessions Papers, Justices' Working Documents, August 1732, *London Lives, 1690–1800*; (www.londonlives.org, accessed 1 December 2010).

8 Patrick Wallis, Cliff Webb, and Chris Minns, *Leaving Home and Entering Service: The Age of Apprenticeship in Early Modern London*, LSE Economic History Working Paper, No. 125/09 (London School of Economics, October, 2009), 4.

9 J.R. Kellett, 'The Breakdown of Guild and Corporation Control over the Handicraft and Retail Trade in London', *The Economic History Review*, New Series, 10, no. 3 (1958): 381–94, 381–2.

10 Peter Linebaugh, *The London Hanged: Crime and Civil Society in the Eighteenth Century* (Cambridge: Cambridge University Press, 1992), 62.

11 Rule, 'Employment and Authority', 288–9.

12 J.M. Beattie, *Policing and Punishment in London, 1660–1750* (Oxford: University Press, 2001), 55–7.

13 Bridget Hill argues, 'During the eighteenth century – if not before – the old paternalistic relationship between masters and servants was giving way to a stricter contractual one', in *Servants: English Domestics in the Eighteenth Century* (Oxford: Clarendon Press, 1996), 5.

14 Robert Shoemaker, *The London Mob, Violence and Disorder in an Eighteenth Century City* (London and New York: Hambledon and London, 2004), 17–18; See also Bridget Hill; Tim Meldrum, *Domestic Service and Gender, 1660–1750: Life and Work in the London Household* (Harlow: Pearson Education, 2000), 61–3; and Carolyn Steedman, *Master and Servant: Love and Labour in the English Industrial Age* (Cambridge: Cambridge University Press, 2007).

15 Meldrum, *Domestic Service and Gender*, 13–15.

16 Peter Earle, 'The Female Labour Market in London in the Late Seventeenth and Early Eighteenth Centuries', *Economic History Review*, New Series, Vol. 42. No. 3 (August, 1989): 339.

17 Masters sometimes provided money for their servants to attend fairs. One example is Stephen Monteage who records money given to his servant, Margaret, for at least two London fairs; *Diary of Stephen Monteage*, London Guildhall Library, MS 205, v. 7, 1746.

18 Faramerz Dabhoiwala, *The Origins of Sex* (Oxford: Oxford University Press, 2012), 64.

19 Paul Griffiths, *Lost Londons: Change, Crime, and Control in the Capital City, 1550–1660* (Cambridge: Cambridge University Press, 2008), 292.

20 Dabhoiwala, *Origins of Sex*, 64.

21 *Ibid.*

22 Beattie, *Policing and Punishment*, 468–71.

23 Elaine A. Reynolds, *Before the Bobbies: The Night Watch and Police Reform in Metropolitan London, 1720–1830* (Stanford: Stanford University Press, 1998).

24 Dabhoiwala, *Origins of Sex*, 64.

25 Andrew T. Harris, *Policing the City: Crime and Legal Authority in London, 1780–1840* (Columbus, OH: Ohio State University Press, 2004), 31–2.

26 The ways in which the 'reformation of manners campaigns' contributed to policing in London is discussed in Robert Shoemaker, *Prosecution and Punishment: Petty Crime and the Law in London and Rural Middlesex, c. 1660–1725* (Cambridge: Cambridge University Press, 1991), Chapter 9, 238–78.

27 Shoemaker, *Prosecution and Punishment*, 272.

28 The Repertories of the Court of Aldermen and Orders of Common Council include frequent orders to restrain and prevent immoral behaviour at fairs including Bartholomew and Southwark Fairs. Orders consulted for this study include those appearing between the 1690s and 1760s. Orders were most intense during 1694–1708 and 1713–17 and again from the late 1720s through the 1760s.

29 *Reasons Formerly Published for the Punctual Limiting of Bartholomew Fair* (London, 1711), 3.

30 *Ibid.*, 9.

31 'A view of the times, their principles and practices: in the third volume of *The Rehearsals*. By Philalethes'. Volume 3. London, 1708-9.

32 *Ibid.*

33 Andy Wood, *Riot, Rebellion and Popular Politics in Early Modern England* (New York: Palgrave, 2002), 119-20; see also Paul Griffiths, *Youth and Authority: Formative Experiences in England, 1560-1640* (Oxford: Clarendon Press, 1996), especially Chapter 3.

34 *Reasons for Suppressing the Yearly Fair in Brook-Field, Westminster; Commonly Called May-Fair* (London, 1709), 12-13.

35 *Ibid.*

36 *Ibid.*, 14-15.

37 *Ibid.*, 13.

38 Ordinary of Newgate's Account, *London Lives, 1690-1800*, OA170308110308110001, 11 August 1703 (www.londonlives.org, accessed 10 January 2011).

39 *Ibid.*

40 LMA, Middlesex Sessions: Sessions Papers, Justices' Working Documents SM/PS, *London Lives, 1690-1800*, LMSMPS500900044, July 1703 (www.londonlives.org, accessed 10 December 2010).

41 *Ibid.*

42 Old Bailey Proceedings: Accounts of Criminal Trials, *London Lives, 1690-1800*, t17030707-2, 7 July 1703 (www.londonlives.org, accessed 10 December 2010).

43 *Reasons for Suppressing ... May-Fair*, 8-9.

44 *Ibid.*, 9.

45 *Ibid.*

46 *Ibid.*, 7-8.

47 *Ibid.*, 10.

48 *Ibid.*, 31-2.

49 Meldrum, *Domestic Service and Gender*, Chapter 3. Works that discuss early modern English understandings of patriarchy and proper gender and familial order include: Griffiths, *Youth and Authority*; Hannah Barker and Elaine Chalus, *Gender in Eighteenth-Century England: Roles, Representations and Responsibilities* (London: Longman, 1997); Robert Shoemaker, *Gender in English Society, 1650-1850: The Emergence of Separate Spheres?* (Longman, 1998); Anthony Fletcher, *Gender, Sex and Subordination in England, 1500-1800* (New Haven, CT: Yale, 1999).

50 *Post Man and The Historical Account*, 30 November-2 December, 1708.

51 *Ibid.* and *Post Man and the Historical Account*, 13-15 January 1709.

52 *Post Man and the Historical Account*, 30 November-2 December 1708.

53 LMA, Repertories of the Court of Aldermen (hereafter 'Rep'.), 98, f. 410, 26 July 1694.

54 *Ibid.*, f. 395.

55 *Ibid.*, f. 410.

56 LMA, Court of Common Council Journals, 54, fo. 692, June 1707.

57 *The proceedings on the King's Commissions of the Peace, Oyer and Terminer, and goal delivery for the city of London; and also the goal delivery for the county of Middlesex, ... in the mayoralty of the Right Honble Henry Marshall, Esq; Lord-Mayor* (London, 1744-45), 23.

58 *Ibid.*

59 The Proceedings of the Old Bailey (OBP), 5 December 1744, trial of William Brister, James Page, Theophilus Watson, et al. (T17441205-34) (www.oldbaileyonline.org, version 6.0, accessed 17 April 2011)

60 *Proceedings on the King's Commissions of the Peace*, 23.

61 *Ibid.*, 24.

62 *Ibid.*

63 *Ibid.*; OBP, 5 December 1744.

64 For example, the riot of young men at May Fair described in *Reasons for Suppressing ... May-Fair* and the rioting Bridewell apprentices at Bartholomew Fair described below.

65 *Flying Post or the Post Master*, 6-8 September, 1698.

66 Rep., 98, f410, f 413.

67 OBP, 6 September 1732, trial T17320906-20.

68 *Ibid.*, 16 October 1734, trial T17341016-23.

69 Rep. 98, f 413. The order was originally issued on 26 August 1690.

70 This analysis is based on a review of classified advertisements placed during the period 1698-1763 in the *Evening Post*, *Post Boy*, *Daily Advertiser*, *Weekly Journal or British Gazetteer*, *Daily Journal*, and the *Daily Courant*.

71 Rep. 118, f391.

72 *Ibid.*

73 *Ibid.*

74 *Ibid.*

75 Rep. 104, f.313, May 1700.

76 The proposed 1735 Playhouse Bill would have curtailed the activities of strolling players and limited unlicensed playhouses. Christina Kiaer, 'Professional Femininity in Hogarth's *Strolling Actresses Dressing in a Barn*', in Bernadette Fort and Angela Rosenthal (eds), *The Other Hogarth: Aesthetics of Difference* (Princeton, NJ and Oxford: Princeton University Press, 2001), 80.

77 Rep. 104, f. 376, June 1700.

78 Rep. 107, f. 460, 20 July 1703.

79 Sybil Rosenfeld, *The Theatre of the London Fairs in the Eighteenth Century* (Cambridge: Cambridge University Press, 1960), Chapter 2.

80 Rep. 104, f. 375.

81 The 1737 Licensing Act extended an earlier act issued under Queen Anne, which punished 'common players of interludes' as 'rogues, vagabonds, sturdy beggars and vagrants'. By the 1737 act, the category of 'common players' was expanded to include, 'every person who shall, for hire, gain or reward, act, represent or perform, or cause to be acted, represented or performed any interlude, tragedy, comedy, opera, play, farce or other entertainment of the stage, or any part or parts therein [without a license] ... shall be deemed to be a rogue and a vagabond ... ' from 'The 1737 Licensing Act', in David Thomas (ed.), *Theatre in Europe: a Documentary History - Restoration and Georgian England, 1660-1788* (Cambridge: Cambridge University Press, 1989), 207-8.

82 Rep. 139., f. 233.

83 *Ibid.*

84 *London Evening Post*, 10-12 July 1735.

85 This incident, and Lee's petition to Parliament regarding the 1735 Playhouse Bill, is discussed in Chapter 5.
86 Collections of fair announcements are located in the British Library, British Library N. TAB. 2026/25 and Guildhall Library, MS 1514. Some of these are from newspapers, while others are copies of playbills advertising various fair entertainments. Advertisements for fair entertainment are also located in various London newspapers, including the *London Evening Post, Daily Journal, Daily Courant, London Daily Post and General Advertiser*, and others.
87 *Daily Post*, 4 September 1732.
88 See Chapter 5.
89 The Middlesex Justices issued orders against these unchartered fairs in 1718, 1725, and 1748. Orders were posted in areas surrounding fairs. Robert Shoemaker discusses the allure to the London population of fairs held at Tottenham Court, Bow, Bromley, and Hampstead in *Prosecution and Punishment*, 287.
90 Such festivity, in particular, threatened the young. See Griffiths, *Youth and Authority*, 122–4.
91 This earlier order is mentioned and reissued in the Middlesex Sessions of the Peace, Orders of Court, August 1724, MJ/o/001.
92 *Ibid.*
93 LMA, Middlesex Sessions of the Peace, Orders of Court, January 1744, MJ/o/C/004.
94 Rep. 142, f. 145, 24 Jan 1737 and 31 Jan 1737.
95 *Ibid.*
96 *Ibid.*
97 Rep 145, 1 June 1741.
98 Middlesex Sessions of the Peace, MJ/o/C/001.
99 Jeremy Black, *Eighteenth-Century Britain, 1688–1783* (Basingstoke and New York: Palgrave, 2001), 186–88; Paul Samuel Fritz, *The English Ministers and Jacobitism between the Rebellions of 1715 and 1745* (Toronto and Buffalo: University of Toronto Press, 1975); Eveline Cruickshanks and Jeremy Black (eds), *The Jacobite Challenge* (Edinburgh: J. Donald; Atlantic Highlands, NJ: Humanities Press, 1988); Douglas Hugh, *Jacobite Spy Wars: Moles, Rogues and Treachery* (Thrupp, Stroud: Sutton, 1999).
100 Middlesex Sessions of the Peace, MJ/o/C/001.
101 *Ibid.*
102 See Vincent J. Liesenfeld, *The Licensing Act of 1737* (Madison: University of Wisconsin Press, 1984), Chapter 1.
103 Liesenfeld, *Licensing Act*, 24–5.
104 *The Universal Spectator and Weekly Journal.*
105 Rosenfeld, *Theatre of the London Fairs*, Chapter 2. Lawrence Manley has written a recent article which examines the tradition of theatre at London's Inns during the sixteenth and early seventeenth centuries. Theatre at London fairs was similar in some ways to this earlier tradition because some performances at fairs were held in inns or their courtyards. Lawrence Manley, 'Why Did London Inns Function as Theatres?', *Huntington Library Quarterly* 71, no. 1 (March 2008): 181–97.
106 Arnold Hare and David Thomas, *Theatre in Europe: A Documentary History, Restoration and Georgian England, 1660–1788* (Cambridge: Cambridge University Press, 1989), 194.

107 Middlesex Sessions of the Peace, MJ/o/C/oo3.
108 Rep. 121, f. 429.
109 This is how Rosenfeld refers to London fair theatre during the 1720s and 1730s – prior to its being curtailed by the Licensing Act.
110 Rosenfeld, *Theatre of the London Fairs*, 19–20.
111 Copy of advertisement found in Henry Morley, *Memoirs of Bartholomew Fair* (1880; reprint Detroit, MI: Singing Tree Press, 1968), 284.
112 Hare and Thomas, *Theatre in Europe*, 195.
113 See William J. Burling, *Summer Theatre in London, 1661–1820* (London: Associated University Press, 2000).
114 Hare and Thomas, *Theatre in Europe*, 206.
115 Not all city officials were opposed to this particular theatre. Norma Landau demonstrates that a Middlesex justice, Sir Samuel Gower, profited from granting a license to sell alcoholic beverages to the playhouse in Goodmans Fields: he owned a house in the area that his tenant ran as a 'respectable' public house. 'The Trading Justices Trade', in Norma Landau (ed.), *Law, Crime and English Society, 1660–1830* (Cambridge: Cambridge University Press, 2002), 53–4.
116 *Ibid.*, 206–7.
117 This is Rosenfeld's argument in *Theatre of the London Fairs*.
118 *Fog's Weekly Journal*, 16 August 1729.
119 *Weekly Journal or British Gazetteer*, 17 October 1724; Daily Courant, 10 August 1732; *Country Journal or The Craftsman*, 19 August 1738.
120 *London Evening Post*, 19 August 1742.
121 She is called Elizabeth Pervish in the *London Evening Post*, 22 February 1737.
122 The fields around London were popularly known as locations in which illicit sex could be expected, and a woman crossing the fields alone at night may have appeared to be open to sexual encounters. See Laura Gowing, '"The Freedom of the Streets": Women and Social Space, 1560–1640', in Mark S.R. Jenner and Paul Griffiths (eds), *Londinopolis: Essays in the Cultural and Social History of Early Modern London* (Manchester and New York: Manchester University Press, 2000), 144.
123 OBP, 13 October 1736 and 20 April 1737, REF: T17361013–4, REF: T17370420–59.
124 OBP, 3 September 1740, REF: T17400903–55.
125 OBP, 12 October 1720, REF: T17201012–2.
126 'The first published collection of trials at the Old Bailey dates from 1674, and from 1678 accounts of the trials at each session (meeting of the Court) at the Old Bailey were regularly published. Inexpensive, and targeted initially at a popular rather than a legal audience, the *Proceedings* were produced shortly after the conclusion of each session and were a commercial success. With few exceptions, this periodical was regularly published each time the sessions met (eight times a year) for 160 years. In 1834 it changed its name, but publication continued until 1913'. From Clive Emsley, Tim Hitchcock and Robert Shoemaker, 'Historical Background', Old Bailey Proceedings online (www.oldbaileyonline.org/).
127 OBP, 16 October 1728, REF: T17281016–13.
128 OBP, 15 October 1718, REF: T17181015–2.
129 OBP, 6 December 1721, REF: T17211206–3.
130 OBP, 4 December 1724, REF: T17241204–53.

131 LMA, City of London Sessions: Sessions Papers – Justices' Working Documents SL/
PS, 11 December–16 February 1732, www.londonlives.org, LMSLPS150420064, 15 June
1731.

132 *Ibid.*, 22 July 1754, www.londonlives.org, LMSLPS150650070.

133 *Ibid.* 2 October 1698, www.londonlives.org, LMSSLPS150090051.

134 Examples are: 'his Royal Highness, the Prince came *incognito* to Southwark Fair,
and saw the Play at Bullock and Leigh's Booth', 28 September 1717, *Original Weekly
Journal*; in 1719, the Prince again went *incognito*, and with 'only one Nobleman and a
Footman attending him', to see performances at Bartholomew Fair. 29 August 1719,
Weekly Journal or Saturday's Post; and in 1725, 'his Royal Highness the Prince of
Wales came *Incognito* by Water from Richmond, attended by the Earl of Deloraine
… and went to see the Humours of Bartholomew Fair'. 4 September 1725, *British
Journal*.

135 *Daily Journal*, 11 September 1725.

136 *British Journal or The Censor*, 30 August 1729.

137 Rosenfeld, *Theatre of the London Fairs*, 131.

138 LMA, 1746 Order against Welsh Fair, Middlesex Sessions of the Peace, 11 July,
MJ/o/C/005.

139 *Ibid.*, 8 May 1746, MJ/o/C/005.

140 *Ibid.*

141 *Ibid.*

142 *Ibid.*

143 LMA, MJ/o/C/0058, May 1746.

144 Beattie, *Policing and Punishment*; Robert Shoemaker, 'Reforming the City: The
Reformation of Manners Campaign in London, 1690–1738', in Lee Davison, Tim
Hitchcock, et al., *Stilling the Grumbling Hive: the Response to Social and Economic
Problems in England, 1689–1750* (New York: St. Martin's Press, 1992).

145 Ian Archer, *The Pursuit of Stability: Social Relations in Elizabethan London*
(Cambridge: Cambridge University Press, 1991), 207.

146 *Ibid.*, 243; Beattie, *Policing and Punishment*, 27. See also, William G. Hinkle, *A History
of Bridewell Prison, 1553–1700* (Lampeter: Mellen Press, 2006), especially Chapter 10.

147 Faramerz Dabhoiwala, 'Summary Justice in Early Modern London', *English Historical
Review* (June 2006), 800.

148 Bridewell and Bethlem Archives, Bridewell Royal Hospital: Minutes of the Court of
Governors, 4 September 1696, BR/M: BB, LL ref: BBBRMG202020084.

149 *Ibid.*, 6th January 1689–8th August 1695, Currently Held: BB LL ref:
BBBRMG202010170, 20 August 1691; Bridewell Royal Hospital: Minutes of the Court
of Governors BR/MG, 26th June 1713–2nd August 1722, 13 September 1717, LL ref:
BBBRMG202040321.

150 Tim Hitchcock, *Down and Out in Eighteenth Century London* (London: Hambledon
Continuum, 2007), Chapter 6.

151 *Daily Advertiser*, 9 August 1743; *General Evening Post*, 4 October 1743.

152 Bridewell and Bethlem Archives, Bridewell Royal Hospital: Minutes of the Court of
Governors, 22 May 1751–1 December 1761. London Lives, BBBRMG202070230, 11
September 1755. Morley addresses reactions to the calendar conversion, 350–1.

153 *Ibid.*

REGULATION AND RESISTANCE AT LONDON'S FAIRS

155 Bridewell and Bethlem Archives, Bridewell Minutes, 22 May 1751–1 Dec. 1761, 13 November 1755.

156 Rep 139. Petitioners against the limitation of Bartholomew Fair also appeared in court in 1744, Rep 148, f385.

157 E.A. Webb, *The Records of St. Bartholomew's Priory and of the Church and Parish of St. Bartholomew the Great, West Smithfield*, Volume II (Oxford University Press, 1921), 294.

158 Arthur L. Cooke, 'Addison's Aristocratic Wife', *PMLA* 72, no. 3 (June, 1957): 376.

160 LMA, 19 August 1761, Journal of the City Lands Committee, Vol. 53, 162. The Warwick title had, by this time, passed to another branch of the Rich family.

166 Newspapers feature advertisements for such entertainment occurring outside the bounds of fairs.

168 See for examples his advertisements in *Daily Advertiser*, 1 April 1731, *Daily Post*, 15 January 1731.

169 *London Evening Post*, 22–23 June 1731. In another incident, a well-dressed 'Sharper' picked pockets in Cuper's Gardens. *London Evening Post*, 17–19 May 1743.

170 Norman Anderson, *Ferris Wheels: An Illustrated History* (Bowling Green, OH: Bowling Green State University Press, 1992), 9.

173 *Lloyd's Evening Post and British Chronicle*, 8–10 September 1760; *Ibid.*, 19–20 September 1760.

4

'Dirty Molly' and 'The Greasier Kate':
The feminine threat to urban order

Cheap-side Cits come to [Bartholomew Fair to] see horned Beasts
brought hither from all Parts of the World, when they might behold
the very same Monsters at home, if they wou'd but be at the pains of
consulting their own Looking-glasses: The pious Reformers of the City
have been long endeavouring to put down this Nursery of Wickedness
and Irreligion, as they call it; but the beloved Wives of their own
Bosoms, and their virtuous Daughters, better understand their own
Interest, than to lose any Opportunity of getting abroad and planting
Cuckoldom and Fornication, as their Mothers did before 'em.
'Mr. Brown' in *Familiar and Courtly Letters to persons of honour and
quality, by Mons. Voiture*

Late Stuart urban reformers hoped to regulate London's summertime
urban festivals out of existence, but the city's fairs intrigued foreign
visitors to London. One visitor revelled in the seasonal disorder of
London's 'Long Vacation'. Writing in late August, 'Mr. Brown' described
local Londoners weary of seasonal festivity happy to be near the end of
the summer. As a tourist, however, Mr. Brown, 'could heartily wish, as a
Soldier does by the Wars, or a Woman by Enjoyment, it would last much
longer'. [1] Implicit in his analogy was a gendered understanding – women
seek out 'enjoyment' in every sense, and were one of the main attractions
of London's summertime festival, Bartholomew Fair. Brown explained
to his readers that Smithfield had 'always the Reputation of being a Place
of Persecution', which his readers would have known referred to the
area's past as a location for punishing heretics, traitors, and common
criminals.

Before the gallows were located at Tyburn, Smithfield was a place
of public execution. Executions had taken place there as late as 1652. The
area was particularly associated with the Protestant executions during
the reign of Queen Mary.[2] At the turn of the eighteenth century, Brown

argued Smithfield remained a place of persecution, 'with the difference, that the Women do that in this Age which the Priests did in the last, and make as many poor Sinners suffer as by Fire'.[3] Sexually transmitted disease was only one means by which women contaminated male revellers – even wives and daughters of London's citizens threatened to 'cuckold' husbands and fathers and uproot the sexual and familial order of the city with their sexual play.

Commentary on London's fairs seems paradoxical: printed descriptions of fairs warn men against their imminent dangers, while at the same time enticing male readers by equating such dangers with public and alluring women. Commentary against fairs repeats the familiar trope that equated disorderly streets with sexually available urban women who frequented them. Eighteenth-century descriptions of the types of women found at London's fairs reveal understandings of the 'dangers and the pleasures of urban femininity' in this early modern city.[4] Sexualized depictions of women who attended or worked at fairs reveal how gender was employed in negotiations over the use of urban space.[5] As people re-imagined London, they imposed their own conceptions of how eighteenth-century cities should look and function.[6] Thinking about gender and, in particular, women's place within the metropolis was central to re-conceptualizing the use of urban space. However, as Laura Gowing demonstrates, early modern uses of urban space also determined gender relations. Examining ideas about gender and sexuality in literature about fairs reveals the complex interaction between 'imagined and actual space', and demonstrates how, and to what extent, this configuration shaped women's everyday use of urban space as well as the construction of individual gendered identities.[7] Gendered prescriptions of women at fairs do not necessarily reveal practice, but they do allow us insight into the means by which social commentators employed particular gendered understandings in their attempts to explain, critique, or fantasize about London's fairs.[8] This commentary further reveals how the gendered meanings attached to urban space fluctuated in the early modern city.

Clearly, in late-Stuart and early-Georgian London, there existed understandings that public, urban spaces did not suit reputable and chaste women. Urban space was sexualized as London grew from the sixteenth through eighteenth centuries, and gender provided social commentators a means to communicate anxieties about urban life.[9] Fairgoers were frequently warned in literature about the dangers men faced when encountering disorderly women at fairs. Women also knew this and understood their own risk of being perceived as sexually available while at fairs. At fairs there were plenty of deceptive women who looked outwardly like 'angels' or may have seemed 'helpless' and in need of assistance.[10] In reality, literary descriptions of such women repeated the idea that men tempted by outward appearances might soon unmask these women's true, destructive natures. Men misled by deceptive women at fairs faced various types of ruin – financial, physical, and moral. At the same time, however, cultural representations commonly presented prominent and sexually available women as one of the most alluring (to the heterosexual male reader or viewer) attractions of fairs. Sexually available women were only a portion of the women present at fairs, yet such women were singled out in commentary on fairs as representing all women found there.[11]

From the late seventeenth century, sexualized women, especially of the lower orders, were increasingly viewed as threatening good order in London. This perception was based on the types of changes occurring in the city. Public concerns about women at fairs were certainly shaped by a growing belief that women, particularly single women, could turn to criminal activity as a means to 'make ends meet in London'.[12] Many young women migrated to London looking for work, and once there, competed with each other for low-paid and unskilled or low-skilled employment. In London, many women worked for their own livelihood and were not dependant on husbands or fathers.[13] Ian Archer demonstrates that, during the 1620s, London's high mortality resulted in many female-headed households. Overall, visitors to the city commented on the public and unsupervised presence of women in venues where they interacted freely with members of the opposite sex.[14] Lacking support from a family network, women who depended upon their own work for survival may have turned to theft, prostitution, charity, or begging – and all of these activities made women a more visible nuisance in London.[15] Beattie demonstrates that during the late seventeenth century, the benefit of clergy was removed from shoplifting and servant's theft. These were largely considered women's offences, and making them capital crimes was one means by which authorities addressed anxieties about women's criminal behaviour.[16] This legal change was likely shaped by the demographic reality that increasing numbers of both migrant and native-born women turned to criminal activity, influencing public views that women could threaten urban stability. Women who turned to criminal activity as a means of economic support were certainly present in London's fairgrounds.

Anxieties about the threat underemployed women posed to a well-running metropolis were elaborated in fair literature that emphasized their status as sexualized female subjects. Women featured in this literature were curious *because* of their sexual difference and because that difference was on display in a public setting. Reflecting understandings that appropriate male lust ought to be directed at women, printed representations of women at fairs acknowledged (and helped construct) heterosexual male desire as 'natural' – but then warned men that their lust might lead them into risky situations.[17] Popular depictions repeat a warning to men that women at fairs were not always what they seemed, and, in particular, that they might be conduits of sexually transmitted disease.[18] Women depicted in fair literature play upon men's lust, but they were also depicted as threatening to the urban environment, despite (or perhaps because of) their appeal to male desire. Using their sexuality, women in cultural representations of London fairs were powerful figures who used their appeal to bring down urban order, production, and commerce.[19]

Sexualized representations of London's poor women reveal emerging and contested middling ideas about gender and sexuality. Therefore, it is important to recognize that moral categories imposed by the middling and upper ranks of society likely do not reflect actual behaviour.[20] Rather, such understandings of sexual immorality reveal emerging elite assumptions regarding female sexuality. Loose women at fairs may have evoked lustful thoughts in men, but middling readers certainly understood such representations as contrary to respectful femininity. By the early eighteenth century, new ideas that as the 'fair' sex, women had potential to serve as moral examples for middling and elite society were constructed and reinforced in conduct literature and moral drama.[21] This discourse targeted specific groups of polite and economically advantaged women. Such views, however, did not apply to all orders of women and they did not replace older views that any woman's sexual nature (if unchecked) could lead to social disruption. Women who attended or performed at urban fairs seemed the antithesis of the genteel and chaste women celebrated in eighteenth-century conduct literature and fiction written for women.[22]

Women frequenting city spaces such as fairs opened themselves up to suspicion regarding their sexual nature.[23] Chastity was central to conceptions of elite women's femininity and women had to mind their behaviour at places such as fairs in order to maintain polite reputations. The Marquis of Halifax wrote that women who 'continually seek diversion' at fairs or similar locations made 'themselves cheap' because they were so often seen in public. References to the economy of femininity are repeated in the Marquis's advice: elite women should recognize themselves as embodying value that was degraded by their presence at fairs.

Not only did an elite woman potentially devalue her reputation at fairs, but a woman overly concerned with diversion could become 'engaged in a circle of idleness', and thereby squander the value of her femininity on a non-productive pursuit. Proof, during the summer months, that a woman wasted her industry on idleness was revealed if a woman might 'know all the players names, and [was] intimately acquainted with all the booths in Bartholomew-fair'.[24] The Marquis clearly conveys that fair entertainment had power over women. Such urban amusement could make women become like soldiers who were 'obedient' to the sound of their captain's trumpet. While soldiers were summoned to battle, the trumpet call of a fair summoned such women to, 'a puppet play or a monster'.[25] Ladies were advised, instead, to avoid becoming overly associated with seasonal diversions. If they were, the consequences were 'not to be endured'. Elite women known to be 'gamesters' exposed themselves to 'ill-mixed company', and began to 'neglect ... civilities abroad', as well as their proper place of work, their 'business at home'.[26]

A woman's age was also singled out as making fair-going all the more inappropriate. In *The Ladies New-Year's-Gift: Or, Advice to a Daughter*, the author advises daughters to 'every seven years' make an effort to become 'Graver'. This is preferable to becoming, 'like the *Girls of Fifty*, who resolved to be always Young, whatever Time ... hath determined to the contrary'.[27] Such women behave as if going to a play is a chore, though they secretly enjoy it. Likewise, such a woman pretends to need to go to Bartholomew Fair to 'look after the young folks' when in reality 'she taketh them for her excuse'.[28] Daughters are advised that this type of woman is 'of all Creatures the most ridiculous' and her attempts to appear young, though old, look like 'a new patch upon an old gown'.[29] This sentiment was echoed by the Marquis of Halifax, who put it this way: 'To be too eager in the pursuit of pleasure whilst you are young, is dangerous: to catch at it in riper years is grasping a shadow; it will not be held: besides that by being less natural, it groweth to be indecent'.[30]

Compared with the ideals presented in prescriptive literature targeting elite women, the sexual liberty of lower-order women at London's fairs shocked or titillated readers becoming used to new understandings of polite femininity. Literary and artistic portrayals of sexual or disorderly public women were the needed foil for contemporary portraits of respectable and elite women. Sexual women at fairs were the antithesis to images of moral women espoused in conduct literature. During the eighteenth century, elite women were increasingly viewed as essential to social settings because they had a 'superior morality'. This developed sense of refinement had the potential to encourage the elevation of male manners.[31] Such views had limits, however. In particular, representations of illicit women reminded people that the presence of polite women in some contexts had little influence. Elite women were as susceptible as men to the temptations of fairs. An elite woman's mannered example simply could not improve her surroundings at an urban fair – especially as long as women from all social backgrounds were visible and active there.[32]

A popular 'Dialogue Song' sung at Bartholomew Fair, supposedly for the Prince of Wales, and printed in a collection called *The Curiosity: or, the Gentleman and Lady's General Library*, depicts the type of woman men imagined (and perhaps hoped) were present at Bartholomew Fair. The dialogue is between a man and woman who meet at the fair. The man is smitten by the 'dearest Maiden fair' and he asks her to stay with him because her glance, 'has sent a Dart Quite thro' [his] glowing Heart'. No doubt aware that she is being perceived as a young, attractive, and available woman, the maiden warns, 'Dear Sir, I'm none of the Town, That will – for Half a Crown – Obligingly lie down, To please you'. Nevertheless, the man continues his plea, asking the woman to come 'Away to the Fair, [to] taste the Delight of e'ery fine Sight, Inviting'. He reveals his true intentions in the next verse, when he suggests once in the fair, 'We'll thence to the Tavern, Where, in a fly Cavern, We'll toy and be frisky!' The woman counters with what seems to be concern about her reputation: 'What if the Sport shou'd Inflame my young Blood? While wanton Desire, To quench Love's Fire, Directs me'. Her worries, as revealed in the next stanza, however, do not concern her virtue. Rather, her concern is that her lover should prove to be 'a fumbling Beginner, a worn-out, old Sinner, With Mumbling and Grumbling, A Flash in the Pan, Sir, And nothing of Man, Sir'.[33] Songs like this, performed in London fairs and then published for a wider audience, reinforced London officials' fears that fair booths 'erected for plays, shows, lotteries, musick [and] Taverns' were places to which the 'Worst and Lewdest of both sexes resort'.[34] This fair ballad portrays one 'lewd' couple as they plan a retreat to a tavern. The song plays with ideas about gender and proper expressions of sexuality. Seeming to present a woman concerned with protecting her sexual reputation at the fair, the song ends by celebrating a sexually experienced woman seeking an equally experienced male partner. The twist in this ballad humorously reinforced the idea that sexually loose women were not only present at fairs, but they also thoroughly enjoyed them. The song presented a worldly woman employing a guise of innocence to succinctly embody the debauchery of fairs.

Male writers reinforced the notion that bawdy women epitomized urban disorder and commonly associated promiscuous and some-times deceitful women with fairs. In Edward Ward's satirical peri-odical piece *The London Spy* (1698–1700), the two central protagonists visit Bartholomew Fair. While there, one of the main characters spies a woman 'labouring in the Crowd, like a *Fly* in a Cobweb'. Compelled by his manners to protect this seemingly vulnerable woman, one of the men escorts her out of the crowd, defending her from 'the rude Squeezes and Jostles of the careless Multitude'.[35] Feeling proud of his conduct, it is only after safely guiding the woman from the crowd that the 'London spy' realizes he has been duped. As the woman 'Shuffl'd [back] into the Crowd', he discovers the extent of her ploy – hardly a helpless woman at all, she had deliberately used her femininity as a decoy. Her reward to the civil protagonist was an empty pocket. Embarrassed by his 'over-care of [the] Lady, and carelessness of [him] self', the man uses this incident to instruct his companion (and all male readers) about the potential haz-ards of women in Bartholomew Fair. One had to be as mindful of these ladies and their unpredictable nature 'as Country people are of Stags in Rutting-time; for their accustomary ways of Rewarding Kindnesses, are either to take something from you, you would unwillingly part with; or give you … that which you would be glad to be without'.[36] Reinforcing and naturalizing an idea about the manipulative character and sexual threat of women from lower orders, male readers undoubtedly learned rules regarding which types of women were appropriate recipients of civility, but such tales would have only increased their uncertainty about who did deserve protection. Readers received a strong message warn-ing them about hidden dangers of such things as sexually transmitted disease. The danger of joining the multitudes at fairs was the complexity of navigating the crowd and properly identifying reputable women – especially when among the crowd could be women from all walks of life.

Disorderly women and a confused gender order were depicted as part and parcel of popular amusements at London fairs, especially Bartholomew Fair. When Ward wrote the *London Spy*, City and county officials were beginning their long campaign to suppress metropolitan fairs. Yearly, urban officials braced for the summer months by issuing orders against these disorderly events. Urban officials and social reform-ers spent good amounts of time attempting to quell these urban festivals, and through this process they aroused people's interest in what made them particularly disorderly. While legal authorities tackled fair regula-tion, they became frequent settings in didactic or satirical literature and print depictions, which illustrated the ill effect of fairs on London and wider Britain's society and commerce. Central to these portraits, as the tempting and distracting female drummer in Hogarth's *Southwark Fair*, were depictions of unruly public women who attended, performed or provided goods and services at fairs. While London's authorities frequently mentioned that fairs could potentially ruin both sexes, cultural evidence demonstrates that women, in particular, were portrayed as key to propagating urban disorder.

The problem of women's work at fairs

Fairs upset cultural understandings of public gender roles, but they also provided a forum for examining women and commerce in the city. Orders against fairs, as shown in Chapter 3, commonly expressed anxiety that these gatherings disrupted business and threatened male productivity. London elite's changing understandings of 'proper' commerce had implications for women's work at fairs. New conceptions that urban work space should be regular and orderly contradicted the temporary (though increasingly permanent) and mobile commerce of fairs, which were work spaces in which labouring men and women profited seasonally by providing goods, food, entertainment, and housing.[37] Commentaries on London fairs frequently singled out women's behaviour as most representative of the broader threat of such commerce. Women continued to work at fairs, however, in the face of both legal efforts to restrict urban festivity and popular literature and prints condemning women at fairs by featuring unruly female characters who worked at or attended them.[38] Though negative representations had little impact on women's continued work at fairs, they did contribute to middling and elite readers' own notions of which spaces and what activities were appropriate for women.[39] In fact, as is explored in Chapter 5, women's continued work at fairs in the many entertainment venues there – acting, fair-booth management, acrobatics, and food service, for example – made them instrumental to the formation of commercialized leisure. Nevertheless, debates regarding women's work at fairs reflect gendered ideas regarding appropriate zones within the city for female labour as well as safe locations for men's leisure.

Regulating gender order in public (or, to borrow a term from Michèle Cohen, 'social') spaces was a vital concern of middling men and city officials interested in policing and reforming their city and enforcing ordered masculine commerce.[40] With diminishing commercial value, city fathers thought festivity interfered with working men's productivity, morality, and financial security. One reason fairs invited so much criticism may have been that these spaces were perceived as particular spaces for female labour.[41] Early-modern European work conditions had transformed since the 1500s, reflecting new understandings of gender-specific labour that emerged as occupations became more specialized. The medieval craft system under which masters trained journeymen apprentices declined and in its place emerged a guild system made up of wage labourers. Merry Wiesner argues there were more important work roles for women under the old apprentice system. For example, masters' wives and daughters were often present in shops working alongside men. When competition among journeymen for wages intensified, women were slowly excluded from work opportunities in guilds.[42] While there was certainly no 'golden age' for women's work opportunities prior to 1650, opportunities did decline after this date.[43] Women continued to work in occupations deemed gender-appropriate, including domestic service, which seemed to be an extension of their work at home. One such occupation included selling goods and services at urban markets or fairs, where labouring women found opportunities.[44] Many times such work contributed to a family economy, but we can imagine, also, that such a space provided job opportunities for single women.[45] In diverse European urban areas, it was the same – women were excluded from some types of labour because they lacked access to the same types of education of business networks as men, but they remained active workers in such places as urban fairs and markets.[46]

By the early eighteenth century, a time when proto-industrialization prompted new notions that labour ought to be focused on production and free of idleness, many social observers and urban authorities increasingly viewed fairs and their marketing opportunities and entertainment as distracting from productive commerce. Many fair workers were temporary labourers, who pieced together work from a variety of sources – and many of these mobile and flexible workers were women.[47] Women who sold goods at markets were 'visible, talkative, and competent', labourers, who challenged notions of what was 'female work'.[48] Working outdoors without the obvious supervision of husbands or fathers, female fair workers challenged dominant understandings about proper commerce and gendered work roles, which Protestant Europe defined as occurring within the 'godly commonwealth' of a male-headed household. According to this configuration, women were ideally responsible for running the household on the inside, while men were responsible for external family affairs.[49] The presence of women working openly at fairs, not always visibly attached to men, challenged gendered notions of proper work and alerted readers to urban women who were not supervised by male authority.[50] London authorities, who were aware that large numbers of those who migrated to London for work opportunities were women, may have been alarmed at the comparative freedom of urban women, who lacked the 'constraints that hedged in the lives of most women, married and single, in the villages and small towns in which most of the population lived'.[51]

Women worked at fairs in great numbers – as performers, itinerant pedlars, and booth managers. Because a reconfiguration of masculinity also had implications for the ways in which people understood femininity and appropriate female behaviour, women's business was eventually affected by new understandings of appropriate urban commerce. However, for a time in the late seventeenth through mid-eighteenth centuries, women's business at fairs continued as usual. Though urban authorities made great attempts to curtail fair theatricality, which some associated with unruly femininity, their true focus was on curtailing non-productive male behaviour.[52] If city officials did not directly legislate against women, their attempted regulations of fairs had implications for their female workforce, just as it did for men who worked at fairs. With the gradual suppression of the duration and quantity of London fairs, a work space slowly contracted for any men and women who used them to support their livelihood, yet through at least the mid-eighteenth century, women remained active workers at fairs.

Representing unruly women at fairs

As writers and artists debated the urban behaviour of men, they implicated women as responsible for men's attraction to non-productive activities, particularly fair amusements. In many tracts, women are particularly singled out as undermining men and male labour at fairs. Popular literature was one means through which Londoners expressed their anxieties about living and working in a rapidly expanding metropolis. Writers of popular works on fairs often evoked negative representations of unruly women to encapsulate their fears that London's patriarchal authority ineffectively quelled potentially disorderly urban amusements. Such writings employed symbols of unchecked female power and 'topsy-turvy' gender order at fairs as shorthand for the general threat festivity posed to London's social order and safety.[53] Descriptions of fair visual culture 'developed and transmitted' ideas about gender to Londoners, as well as to wider reading audiences.[54] Gendered ideas transmitted via such representations were largely misogynist, painting women as disorderly. Yet, while men were advised in periodical literature to avoid specific entertainments or women at fairs, women in the late seventeenth and early eighteenth centuries were not explicitly advised in social commentary to discontinue their work.

London city officials never singled out the presence of women at fairs as especially destructive, yet they implied that London's commercial spaces should be devoted to mannered and masculine commerce, not seasonal festivity in which women were actively involved. In orders regulating fairs and their attending entertainments such as drama, gaming, and drinking, city officials voiced their concerns in terms of the amusement's impact on men. Women visibly working in a variety of occupations at fairs interfered with men's ability to remain industrious faced with the temptations of public, feminine spectacles at the capital's fairs. Literary and print culture implicated public women, from food sellers to rope dancers, for contributing to fair disorder and danger. This commentary reveals that the regulation of fairs was informed by understandings of gender-appropriate behaviour: both because it sought to earmark and preserve specific areas of London as spaces that should be devoted to orderly and male commerce and because the informal campaign against fairs in print culture utilized gendered imagery in its depictions of the danger of fairs.

Representing the fair sex at work and at play

In the *London Spy*, Ward's two main characters equate public unruliness with the presence of bold female street performers on more than one occasion. These characters reveal their own middling gender expectations when they observe female acrobats at Bartholomew Fair, where they join a crowd observing two women walking on their hands. These women's performance becomes, for them, symbolic of women's 'true' usefulness. The London spy is 'pleas'd to see the Women at this sport, it make 'em seem to have a due Sense of the Ills done by their Tongues, to degrade which, they turn'd 'em downwards, giving the Preheminency [sic] to their more deserving Parts; for which Reason they practic'd to walk with their Arses upwards'.[55] Women inverting the 'natural' condition of men by standing on their hands enhanced what these men felt was their appropriate female function. Their 'tongues' were de-emphasized while their reproductive capability and sexual difference were accentuated. After witnessing these women, the urban spectators conclude 'a Woman is a meer Receptacle' and standing on legs should be considered an unnatural posture for a woman.[56] In this account, female acrobats become more than performers. Their sexual difference, not just their skills, made them a public distraction while at the same time it reinforced notions of gender hierarchy.

In traditional social hierarchy, women represented a potential threat to social order if they lived outside the authority of their families, as many women who performed at London fairs did. Years of misogynist discourse dating to early Christianity represented women as synonymous with 'nature'. Gender historians argue that women have often been viewed as closer to natural forces and less civilized and disciplined than men. As the benefactresses of Eve, the original temptress and sinner, women were seen as potentially disruptive members of society.[57] In response to this discourse, early modern England's social order situated women within families. Here, their dangerous potential could be contained and directed to their other 'natural' qualities which benefited society – such as childrearing.[58] While not all women actually fulfilled these expectations, such ideas informed interpretations of women's public behaviour. Women who lived apart from traditional sources of authority were potentially disruptive members of society, a fact not lost on Ned Ward or other writers or artists who depicted sexual women in their work as a means to represent the overall chaos of the city streets.[59]

In literary and artistic representations of summertime festivity, prominent female fair workers became symbols communicating the overall disorder associated with urban fairs. A popular song about Bartholomew Fair portrayed the surprising mix of people one might find at the fair, including 'Milliners, Barrow-Wenches, and Mantua-Makers' among the list of people including, 'sneaking Pick-pockets, City Coquets, [and] Kept-Mistresses'.[60] In 1738, John Bancks wrote a poem inspired by Hogarth's depiction of Southwark Fair (discussed in Chapter 1), which featured dangerous public femininity. In his painting, Hogarth echoes the theme of man's fall related to the temptation of a woman throughout. Above the crowd, he places a placard advertising a dramatic presentation of the fall of man. While the title is not readily apparent, the viewer can just make out a man and woman, whom we assume to be Adam and Eve, standing on either side of a tree. In the midst of the crowd below, Hogarth centrally depicts a female drummer, who has been the subject of much speculation by art historians.[61] This woman draws attention to herself with her pleasing appearance and the noise she makes on the drum. Bancks views this female drummer in the context of concern with fair disorder, and presents her seemingly innocent beauty as the catalyst for the danger which all around her befalls Southwark Fair and its patrons:

> See how the Louts, with eager Stare,
> Own Cupid's Reign, ev'n in a Fair!

Smit with the painted Drummer's Face,
They long to try the leud Embrace.
Ah Lads! 'tis Poison all within;
To 'scape the Pain, avoid the Sin![62]

Meanwhile, as attention is focused on this siren of Southwark Fair, the balcony of a booth collapses and threatens the female performers above as well as the goods, trades people, and fair-goers below. What, specifically, is the poison Bancks mentions? Certainly, sexually transmitted disease – the subject of tracts describing prostitution at London fairs – but also love sickness, distraction, and the slow down of the city's production.[63] It is not surprising that the only respectable commerce present at Hogarth's Southwark Fair, the sale of fine porcelain, is the most visibly and imminently threatened. These fine goods, central to polite and orderly households, will be certainly shattered. The only upstanding female salesperson flees, while a disreputable woman overseeing a gambling operation continues her work despite the danger. It is clear in Hogarth's representation that the fine China booth most likely had little traffic: the temporary gaming set-up, a piper, and a dancing dog block access to it.

According to popular representations of fairs, men who braved the crowds knowingly risked their vitality and earning potential. If tempted by the delicious smells of cooking food at fairs, they had to ignore possible contamination by un-hygienic female servers such as 'dirty *Molly*, or the greasier *Kate*'.[64] Spoiled or diseased food represented a potent threat, which was underscored by depicting unclean servers as women.[65] Male fair-goers might also lose themselves as they witnessed feminine spectacles overhead, especially if they happened to observe the rope dancer 'Lady Mary'. At Bartholomew Fair in 1703, this seductress intrigued viewers including an 'old gentleman' who admired her performance. A witness to this man's fascination exclaimed, 'look upon the old gentleman; his eyes are fixed upon my Lady Mary: Cupid has shot him as dead as a robin'. The man observing the impact of the rope dancer's performance on audience members remembered how a different rope dancer once infatuated him. Comparing Lady Mary to his own favourite, his comment reveals that part of the satisfaction of watching female performers at fairs was an expectation of bawdiness: 'those roguish eyes [of Mary] have brought her more admirers than ever Jenny Bolton had; it is a pity, says I, she has no more manners, and less ill-nature'.[66]

Popular representations of women enjoying fairs typically featured at least one encounter inside a fair booth, which begins to shed light on why urban authorities worried about the entertainments offered there. Though only temporary wooden structures, fair booths shielded men from the gaze of authorities as well as from social expectations regarding their behaviour. A favourite location for constructing booths was within the open yards of inns. These booths were enclosed wooden structures resembling barns that varied in size.[67] Within booths, female performers and a host of immoral activities, including gambling or prostitution, were shielded from the outside world. Mr. Brown, who visited Bartholomew Fair and described it for his foreign audience, wrote a letter describing the fair from the confines of the 'Gun-Musick-Booth'. Having only entered the booth because he sought a place apart from the crowd to sit and conduct his correspondence, Brown found as much noise inside the booth as outside. Within this booth, he was 'distracted with a thousand Noises and Objects, as a Maid whirling round with a dozen Rapiers at her Neck, a Dance of Chimney-Sweepers, and a Fellow standing on his Head on the top of a Quart-pot'.[68] Brown, being appropriately inhibited, managed to continue his letter despite the distractions.

Within the confines of temporary play booths, male characters in fair literature were not only intrigued by performers or actresses in roles in which they had plenty of agency and often had opportunities to cross-dress,[69] but they also faced advances by the women seated next to them. In *A Walk to Smithfield*, the male protagonist is surrounded by forward and sexually suggestive women both while observing the various delights of 'Fawkes' Medley' – a popular sleight-of-hand entertainment frequently attended by respectable people – and while seated in the audience of *Jepthah's Rash Vow*, which was aptly subtitled: *or the Virgin Sacrifice*. In the play booth, he describes being 'nestled in between the soft Hips', of two citizen's wives. These London women enjoy having a man wedged between them while he, in turn, takes pleasure in being seated in such close quarters next to sexually forward women. Not only does he enjoy the physical contact, but also the women's flirtatious advances – the 'blowsabellas'[70] whisper to him that they are 'both cut Loaves [and] therefore, much safer to trade with than Virgins'. These 'citizen's wives' have more than commerce on their minds, yet they use references to trade (what they and author know *ought* to be happening at a fair) to imply the sexual commerce in which they are truly invested. In Fawkes's booth, the protagonist alternates watching the intended show of a vaulting horse and a ladder dance with the unintended show of the audience, many who are female. Among the women present, he observes 'the old game going forwards, all over the Booth'. This 'old game' included both the disguised and blatant sexuality of 'the pretty Females' seated next to him. Some of these women appeared 'coy and precise', while others, '[appeared] otherwise tho when all came to all, there was little difference, for the first said nay and took it, and the other took it without saying anything, so that nothing but love's Harmony could be seen from one side of the Booth to the other'.[71]

Depictions of London's women from trading families at the fairs reveal elite scepticism about respectability among the lower orders. Such literature provided one means for some middling readers to distance themselves from London's trading families, while middling readers from trading backgrounds may have been instructed in proper conduct within their own families. Polite readers of *A Walk to Smithfield* recognized the sexually forward behaviour of these citizen's wives as inappropriate according to the notions of chastity and female behaviour espoused in didactic works. Depictions of unruly trading women at fairs reveal, also, how the public behaviour of a woman increasingly became associated with how outsiders viewed the overall commercial activity of her family. Margaret Hunt explores ways in which late-Stuart religious writing increasingly compared one's spiritual life to well-ordered private business. Works representing sexualized trading women at fairs reveal a converse, but related, understanding. If one ought to 'cast up one's spiritual accounts in the same way a shopkeeper does his earthly goods', a shopkeeper also ought to be sure that his family represented his good business sense in orderly public morality and conduct.[72] When literature about London's fairs was read by middling people striving to be 'polite' and further the status of their business, it may have taught lessons about the power female family members had while representing the overall quality and soundness of a family business in public.

Sexually forward female fair patrons who enjoyed festivities presented one threat to their male counterparts – but illicit women who worked in the same spaces represented the true danger of fairs. Should men experience encounters with female performers and fair-goers and still emerge unscathed at the end of the day, they had one last temptation to withstand. When night fell, men negotiated their most dangerous obstacle in the darkened alleys or cloisters of fairs. Their virtue, honour, physical and financial well-being were all in danger should they succumb to the apparent pleasures of female flesh or gaming. At Bartholomew Fair, these activities were held in the cloisters of Bartholomew Hospital, separated from the fair by the hospital gate.[73] When men entered this area, they encountered women such as one poet described as the 'lewd Matron', with a 'red Brandy Face' sitting at the entrance to a bawdy house in the cloisters.[74] The reputation of the cloisters in Bartholomew

Fair is clear in a 1707 poem *The Cloyster in Bartholomew Fair; or, the Town-Mistress Disguis'd*. The poem is a treatise on the various types of prostitutes found throughout London. The author swears that no 'sad mishap, Of swelling Groin, or weeping Clap, Or Bubo, or Venereal Shanker, Occasion'd [his] Poetick Anger'.[75] Rather, he asserts that his friend, 'Young, Airy, Witty, Rich, Gallant, well Belov'd, and Pretty', was ruined, 'in two Years time, by Punks in London'. The result of his sexual adventure was that he was 'Clapt, and Pox'd, and clearly Undone, Diseas'd and miserably Poor'. After his London adventure, he returned to the country for 'relief', only to die within two months. The poem targets young men, offering them advice so that they might avoid similar ruin. It demonstrates the 'Arts of the Prostituted Whore' and warns that prostitutes look fine to 'outward View', but:

> Tho' Angels they may seem in Dress, and Mein,
> But could you View the frightful Fiends within …
> No Canibals upon the Indian-Coast,
> Nor Desart Shores to Men by Shipwrack Tost,
> Can be so dangerous, as are the Wiles,
> The treacherous Kisses, and bewitching Smiles,
> Of Mercenary Jilts; whose only Trade,
> Is daily acting Love in Mascarade:
> True Canibals, who can with Ease devour,
> A dozen Men while Time shapes out an hour'.[76]

'Lewd' women did not confine themselves to the cloisters and likely worked throughout the fair. In one poem, a woman suspected of 'lewdness' incites a riot when apprehended by the constable in Bartholomew Fair. Threatening to take her to Bridewell, the Constable was interrupted in his task by people witnessing the arrest. The woman was 'Fine dress'd [and] by all admir'd'. Her 'Beauties soon the num'rous Mob had fir'd'. The crowd rioted, undermined the authority of the constable, and freed the 'lovely Female'. Soon, people's 'Sunday Cloths' were bloodied and members of the crowd rioted without knowing why. Meanwhile, the 'unconcern'd' woman was 'carry'd off' away from being apprehended and brought to Bridewell.[77] Prostitutes worked throughout London at all times of the year, but at urban fairs men were particularly vulnerable – especially those who came to town only for the seasonal festivity. Literature that described the types of women one encountered at fairs helped warn men of the sexual, physical, and spiritual threats to their reputation they could encounter at fairs. Depictions of unruly or sexual women at fairs most likely compounded the problem, however. The promise of visible and sexual women likely became one feature that drew men to fairs in the first place, but as is revealed in the above poem, their presence at fairs also threatened to utterly disturb the festivities.

From breeches-wearing and thigh-exposing rope dancers and greasy female servers in food stalls, to the prostitutes in the darkened cloisters of St Bartholomew's Hospital, women at fairs were depicted as the conduits of distraction, disease, and overall social disorder. This singling out of women at fairs as destructive to every aspect of commerce and men's lives leaves us with the impression that their work opportunities at fairs may have diminished in the face of negative views of their presence there. While this commentary combined with the legal efforts of London's city officials defined London's streets as appropriate space only for controlled, orderly, and masculine commerce, such an idealized work space did not emerge quickly, if at all. Over the long eighteenth century, women continued to work at fairs, and some were even quite successful and influential. Gendered representations from the late seventeenth and early eighteenth centuries denote urban streets as locations of male commerce, and portray women who worked in the same locations as suspicious – but recorded evidence of women's working lives in London reveals that this configuration was contested, ignored, or both, and not easily imposed by city officials and social critics.

London's Aldermen worried about fair booths of 'Extraordinary Largeness' erected during Bartholomew fair for 'Stage Plays Musick and Tipling'. Their concerns were not only over how such booths increased traffic and 'interupted and Diminished' trade. They were also concerned that such locations had become 'Receptacles of vicious and disorderly Persons/Lewdness – and Debauchery'.[78] Placing official commentary in the context of cultural representations of fairs demonstrates that urban authorities likely believed significant numbers of lewd or disorderly individuals at fairs were women. City officials did not discuss in detail what happened within fair booths intended for music, gambling, or dramatic presentations, but they recognized that the events occurring in these secluded locations helped spread 'Wickedness and Vice'. Cultural commentary reveals that those familiar with fairs believed these undesirable qualities in men were promoted and encouraged by the sexually forward women they encountered at fairs.

Depictions of unruly public women are central to almost all popular representations of fair entertainment from the late seventeenth through mid-eighteenth centuries. Though gendered imagery contributed to an eventual re-definition of what constituted suitable work for women, as Deborah Valenze, Bridget Hill, and others have shown, it is important to remember that these ubiquitous images present a lopsided view of the ways in which women participated in and profited from London's fairs.[79] Behind satirical depictions of working women at fairs are the actual experiences of women. These women's available work opportunities were certainly shaped or influenced by their own, their family members', and working men's ideas of appropriate female occupations. However, their understandings of what was appropriate differed from beliefs held by London's middling male journalists and artists. Satirical commentary on women's behaviour at fairs was informed more by artists' and writers' own notions of how women ought to contribute to society and the economy rather than by the needs and beliefs motivating women's choices to undertake work at fairs.

Cultural representations of women at fairs and men's response to those women demonstrated the sexual possibility of festive urban spaces. In print, London's fairs became spaces where sexual women drew men in despite their better understanding. As the danger of fairs was equated with sexualized women, fairs gained reputations as spaces in which productive men were ruined. However, this configuration also made fairs more alluring and helped naturalize heterosexual understandings that sexually available or interesting women drew men to fairs. Male fair-goers were assumed to be heterosexual and their masculinity was underscored by the occasional depiction of effeminate men at fairs. The masculinity of men who failed to enjoy the dirt, crowding, and spectacle of the fair was suspect. This was the case for the easily fatigued man in fine stockings depicted in a 1750 song called, 'Bartholomew Fair'. He wished for some 'sturdy Fellow [to] take [him] in his Arms, and gently lift [him] over this extravagant wide Channel', in order to get to the other side of the fair – not for a feminine spectacle, but to see the 'Turk's Booth'.[80] The author of the song emphasized that this man was 'passionately fond' of the man's performance.

Discourse regarding sexual danger in early-eighteenth century London constructed an urban environment full of sexually-charged heterosexual men. Fears that male heterosexual desire could not be predictably contained are frequently echoed in cultural representations of fairs. Women featured in fair literature tempt men to abandon productivity and, like Adam before them, men choose to fall. A solution to this urban threat was to remove the temptation. No orders were issued against women, but all sexualized festive spaces were targeted. As London's fairs were sexualized, women present in these venues became susceptible to attacks on their reputation. Wives and daughters of 'Cheapside Cits' who attended London fairs entered '[nurseries] of Wickedness and

Irreligion'. 'Mr. Brown' likely recognized this motivation for the City's 'pious Reformers' when he points out what he perceives as an irony: while targeting licentiousness at fairs, urban reformers' own wives participated in the sexual liberty of such occasions.[81] While there is not evidence that any Alderman's wife actually cuckolded her husband at a fair, there existed certainly an understanding that fairs presented even seemingly respectable citizens' wives opportunities to test sexual boundaries and urban order. Their presence at fairs simultaneously supported and challenged urban reform efforts: even if women at fairs were not sexual or immoral themselves, they risked being perceived as such. Because citizens' wives and daughters were at fairs, urban reformers were compelled to protect them.

In the disorderly spaces of urban fairs women's reputations were at risk. Fair literature demonstrated that it was difficult to discern virtuous from immoral women at fairs. A reputable woman in a fair booth or crowd ran as much risk as any other of being 'squeezed' inappropriately. Though urban reformers never explicitly mentioned their concern for their own wives or daughters, the gendered notions espoused in fair literature informed their reform efforts. From the beginning of the eighteenth century, a concerted legal attack on London's fairs was accompanied by an increase in cultural representations of men enticed into fairs and ruined there because of various temptations offered by women. Such printed representations informed urban reformers' perceptions of London's festivity, which they felt compelled to regulate; in the meantime, wives and daughters continued to attend and work at London's fairs.

Notes

1 *Familiar and Courtly Letters to persons of honour and quality, by Mons. Voiture*, Vol. 1. London, 1700, 184.

2 Peter Whitfield, *London: A Life in Maps* (London: British Library, 2006), 41.

3 *Ibid.*

4 Laura Gowing, '"The Freedom of the Streets": Women and Social Space, 1560–1640', in Paul Griffiths and Mark S.R. Jenner, *Londinopolis: Essays in the Cultural and Social History of Early Modern London* (Manchester and New York: Manchester University Press, 2000), 130.

5 Popular literature featuring sexualized descriptions of women are a product of the 'media revolution of the Enlightenment' in which sex, and in particular the lives of 'low-born whores' was more frequently a subject of mass culture. See Chapter 6 in Faramerz Dabhoiwala, *The Origins of Sex: A History of the First Sexual Revolution* (Oxford: Oxford University Press, 2012).

6 Jean E. Howard's recent study examines how the 'city' in early-modern London plays was 'a place where both status and gender relations were constantly being renegotiated': *Theater of a City: The Places of London Comedy, 1598–1642* (Philadelphia: University of Pennsylvania Press, 2007), 27.

7 *Ibid.*, 130–1.

8 Helen Berry discusses the 'distance between prescription and practice', in *Gender, Society and Print Culture in Late-Stuart England: The Cultural World of the Athenian Mercury* (Burlington, VT: Ashgate, 2003), 3.

9 Gowing, '"Freedom of the Streets"', 132.

10 Such women are presented in works such as *The Cloyster in Bartholomew Fair*, *The London Spy*, and *A Walk to Smithfield*, discussed below.

11 Randolph Trumbach argues that a 'decided minority of London's women [appeared] in stories of prostitution, illegitimacy, and adultery', in *Sex and the Gender Revolution*, Vol. 1: *Heterosexuality and the Third Gender in Enlightenment London* (Chicago: University of Chicago Press, 1998), 13. See also Tim Hitchcock, *English Sexualities, 1700–1800* (New York: St. Martin's Press, 1997).

12 J.M. Beattie, *Policing and Punishment in London, 1660–1750: Urban Crime and the Limits of Terror* (Oxford: Oxford University Press, 2001), 67–8. The idea that innocent women could be tempted into criminal and immoral activity is famously represented in Hogarth's 1731 series, *A Harlot's Progress*. This series is also explored in Dabhoiwala, *Origins of Sex*, 282–96.

13 Out of his sample of women who appeared in the London church courts from 1695–1725, Peter Earle finds that over 83 per cent of 'spinsters' and about 85 per cent of widows were either 'wholly' or 'partly' maintained by their own employment. The vast majority fall in the category 'wholly maintained'. Peter Earle, 'The Female Labour Market in the Late Seventeenth and Early Eighteenth Centuries', *Economic History Review* 42, no. 3 (August 1989), 337.

14 Ian Archer, 'Material Londoners?', in Lena Cowen Orlin (ed.), *Material London ca. 1600* (Philadelphia: University of Pennsylvania Press, 2000), 184–5.

15 Beattie, *Policing and Punishment*, 68–9.

16 *Ibid.*

17 This idea is elaborated in Trumbach, *Sex and the Gender Revolution* and Hitchcock, *English Sexualities*. Helen Berry examines how the *Athenian Mercury* negotiated notions of same-sex and heterosexual desire, 212–16.

18 Illicit sex was discouraged in early modern England for a number of socially destructive reasons beyond disease, including the fact that it frequently produced bastard children, ruined families, often involved drinking, and could lead to infanticide. See Dabhoiwala, *Origins of Sex*, 27–8.

19 Joy Wiltenburg demonstrates that English female characters use sexual attractiveness as a source of power in seventeenth-century street literature, in *Disorderly Women and Female Power in the Street Literature of Early Modern England and Germany* (Charlottesville and London: University of Virginia Press, 1992), 144.

20 Faramerz Dabhoiwala, 'The Pattern of Sexual Immorality in Seventeenth and Eighteenth-Century London', in Mark S.R. Jenner and Paul Griffiths (eds), *Londinopolis: Essays in the Cultural and Social History of Early Modern London*, (Manchester: Manchester University Press, 2000), 87.

21 Ingrid H. Tague, *Women of Quality: Accepting and Contesting Ideals of Femininity in England, 1690–1760* (Rochester, NY: Boydell Press, 2002), 19–20.

22 *Ibid.*, 22–3; Actresses and other women who performed in public were frequently equated with prostitutes. See Kimberly Crouch, 'The Public Life of Actresses: Prostitutes or Ladies?' in Hannah Barker and Elaine Chalus (eds), *Gender in Eighteenth-Century England: Roles, Representations and Responsibilities* (London and New York: Longman, 1997).

23 Robert B. Shoemaker, *Gender in English Society, 1650–1850: The Emergence of Separate Spheres?* (London and New York: Longman, 1998), 270–2.

24 George Saville, *Miscellanies*. Glasgow, 1751, 79–80.

25 *Ibid.*

26 *Ibid,* 80–1.

27 'The lady's new-year's-gift: or, advice to a daughter ...' London, 1701. *Eighteenth Century Collections Online.* Gale. Huntington Library & Art Gallery. 24 July 2009, 115.

28 *Ibid.*, 115–16.

29 *Ibid.*

30 Saville, *Miscellanies*, 79.

31 Dabhoiwala, *The Origins of Sex*, 181–2.

32 Elite women who embodied new ideas of polite femininity were thought to have a 'civilizing influence' on men with whom they mixed at social gatherings. See Lawrence Klein, 'Gender, Conversation and the Public Sphere in Early Eighteenth-Century England', in J. Still and M. Worton, *Textuality and Sexuality: Reading Theories and Practices* (Manchester: Manchester University Press, 1993), 106–11.

33 *The Curiosity: or, the Gentleman and Lady's General Library* (York, 1738), 25–8.

34 Rep. 98, 410. 26 July 1694.

35 Edward Ward, *The London Spy*, 4th edn (London: J. How, 1709), in Randolph Trumbach (ed.), *Marriage, Sex and the Family in England 1660–1800* (New York and London: Garland Publishing, 1985), 248.

36 *Ibid.*, 248–9.

37 See Neil McKendrick, John Brewer, and J. H. Plumb (eds), *The Birth of a Consumer Society: The Commercialization of Eighteenth-Century England* (London: Europa Publications, 1982); Paul Langford, *A Polite and Commercial People: England, 1727–1783* (Oxford: Clarendon Press, 1989).

38 Michael Roberts discusses attitudes about early modern English working women in his analysis of representations of women in 'characters', and pastoral poetry, '"Words they are Women, and Deeds they are Men": Images of Work and Gender in Early Modern England', in Lindsey Charles and Lorna Duffin, *Women and Work in Pre-Industrial England* (London, Sydney and Dover, NH: Croom Helm, 1985), 145–51; See also Wiltenburg, *Disorderly Women*; and Dianne Dugaw, *Warrior Women and Popular Balladry, 1650–1850* (Cambridge: University of Cambridge Press, 1989).

39 For an examination of representations of women in periodical literature and novels consumed by middle-class audiences, see Rosalind Ballaster et al., *Women's Worlds: Ideology, Femininity and the Woman's Magazine* (Houndmills: Macmillan, 1991); G.J. Barker-Benefield, *Culture of Sensibility: Sex and Society in Eighteenth-Century Britain* (Chicago: University of Chicago Press, 1992); Katharine Rogers, *Feminism in Eighteenth-Century England* (Urbana, IL: University of Illinois Press, 1982);

Kathryn Shevelow, *Women and Print Culture: The Construction of Femininity in the Early Periodical* (London and New York: Routledge, 1989); Janet Todd, *The Sign of Angellica: Women, Writing and Fiction, 1660–1800* (London: Virago, 1989); Vivien Jones (ed.), Women *in the Eighteenth Century: Constructions of Femininity* (London and New York: Routledge, 1990); and Vivien Jones (ed.), *Women and Literature in Britain, 1700–1800* (Cambridge and New York: Cambridge University Press, 2000).

40 Although the work of scholars such as Michèle Cohen and Peter Borsay focuses primarily on spaces of 'polite' leisure, this chapter broadens the scope of recent work on the gendered regulation of social space to include middling attention to spaces of popular amusement. See Cohen, 'Manliness, Effeminacy and the French: Gender and the Construction of National Character in Eighteenth-Century England', in Hitchcock and Cohen, *English Masculinities, 1660–1800* (London and New York: Longman, 1999); Borsay, *The English Urban Renaissance: Culture and Society in the Provincial Town 1660–1770* (Oxford University Press, 1989), 37; Miles Ogborn, *Spaces of Modernity, London's Geographies, 1680–1780* (New York: Guilford Press, 1998).

41 The prevalence of women workers in urban markets is explored in a number of important studies of the nature of women's work in early modern Europe. See for example Merry Wiesner, *Working Women in Renaissance Germany* (New Brunswick, NJ: Princeton University Press, 1986). Paul Griffiths examines magistrates' criticism of women street sellers in sixteenth and seventeenth-century London in Chapter 3 of *Lost Londons: Change, Crime, and Control in the Capital City, 1550–1660* (Cambridge: Cambridge University Press, 2008).

42 Wiesner, *Working Women.*

43 Amanda Vickery, 'Golden Age to Separate Spheres? A Review of the Categories and Chronology of English Women's History', *Historical Journal* 36 (1993), 383–414.

44 Wiesner, *Working Women*; Shoemaker, *Gender in English Society*, 174–5.

45 Our knowledge of single women's work at urban markets is limited by archival sources in which it is easiest to find historical evidence of married women's experiences. Wiesner begins to explore evidence of single women's work in early modern Germany in 'Having Her Own Smoke: Employment and Independence in Germany, 1400–1750', in Judith M. Bennett and Amy M. Froide (eds), *Singlewomen in the European Past, 1250–1800* (Philadelphia: University of Pennsylvania Press, 1999), 192–216. Here, she discusses suspicions of single women who peddled or sold in markets. In Frankfurt, for example, city fathers viewed street selling as a type of poor relief for widows or soldier's wives, not an occupation for single women, 207. For an analysis of 'never-married' women's work in the early modern English urban economy, see Chapter 4 in Amy M. Froide, *Never Married: Singlewomen in Early Modern England* (Oxford: Oxford University Press, 2005).

46 See Alice Clark, *Working Life of Women in the Seventeenth Century* (1919; reprint New York: A.M. Kelley, 1968); Ivy Pinchbeck, *Women Workers and The Industrial Revolution, 1750–1850* (New York: A.M. Kelley, 1930 and reprint 1969); Bridget Hill, *Women, Work, and Sexual Politics in Eighteenth-Century England* (Oxford and New York: Basil Blackwell, 1989); Mary Prior, 'Women and the Urban Economy, Oxford 1500–1800', in Prior (ed.), *Women in English Society 1500–1800* (London and New York: Methuen, 1985); Peter Earle, *A City Full of People, Men and Women of London, 1650–1750* (London and New York: Methuen, 1994).

47 Roberts, '"Words they are Women"', 134–6.

48 *Ibid.*, 153.

49 Susan Dwyer Amussen, *An Ordered Society: Gender and Class in Early Modern England* (New York: Columbia University Press, 1988), 43–7; See also David Underdown, 'The Taming of the Scold: The Enforcement of Patriarchal Authority in Early Modern England', in Anthony Fletcher, *Order and Disorder in England* (Cambridge: Cambridge University Press, 1985), 116–36; Patricia Crawford, *Women and Religion in England, 1500–1720* (London and New York: Routledge, 1993). The ways in which families existed as an important aspect of social order in early modern Germany is explored in Lyndal Roper, *The Holy Household: Women and Morals in Reformation Augsburg* (Oxford: Oxford University Press, 1989); and Wiesner, *Working Women*; Heide Wunder, *He is the Sun, She is the Moon: Women in Early Modern Germany*. Trans. Thomas Dunlap (Cambridge, MA: Harvard University Press, 1998).

50 See Chapter 5, especially Hannah Lee, who worked as a successful strolling company manager.

51 Beattie, *Policing and Punishment*, 71.

52 See Kristina Straub for the ways in which unchecked femininity was associated with disorderly spectacles in theatrical entertainment; *Sexual Suspects: Eighteenth-Century Players and Sexual Ideology* (Princeton, NJ: Princeton University Press, 1992).

53 Joy Wiltenburg, *Disorderly Women*, 7–9. For an analysis of the idea of 'topsy turvey' gender order in popular culture, see Natalie Davis, 'Women on Top', in *Society and Culture in Early Modern France* (Stanford, CA: Stanford University Press, 1975).

54 Susan Dwyer Amussen, 'The Gendering of Popular Culture in England', in Tim Harris (ed.), *Popular Culture in England, c. 1500–1850* (New York: St. Martin's Press, 1995), 67.

55 Ward, *London Spy*, 240.

56 *Ibid.*

57 Wiltenburg, *Disorderly Women*, 8. For an in-depth analysis of ideas regarding women, see Constance Jordan, *Renaissance Feminism: Literary Texts and Political Models* (Ithaca and London: Cornell University Press, 1990).

58 See Amussen, *An Ordered Society*; Crawford, *Women and Religion*.

59 Women's urban mobility was frequently equated with London's disorder in print. See Gowing, '"Freedom of the Streets"', 139.

60 'Bartholomew-Fair', in *An Entire New Collection of Humourous Songs, Never Exhibited in any Joyous Company Whatever* (London, 1750), 11.

61 See Henry Wheatley, *Hogarth's London* (London: Constable and Company, 1909), 427; E.D.H. Johnson, *Paintings of the British Social Scene from Hogarth to Sickert* (London: Weidenfeld & Nicolson, 1986), 25–7; Bernadette Fort and Angela Rosenthal (eds), *The Other Hogarth, Aesthetics of Difference* (Princeton and Oxford: Princeton University Press, 2001), 83.

62 John Bancks. *Miscellaneous works, in verse and prose, of John Bancks* (London, 1738).

63 The threat of venereal disease is discussed in Tony Henderson, *Disorderly Women in Eighteenth-Century London: Prostitution and Control in the Metropolis, 1730–1830* (London and New York: Longman, 1999), 38–41; 168–9.

64 *Bartholomew Fair: An Heroi-Comical Poem* (London, 1717).

65 Paul Griffiths discusses London magistrates' concern with spoiled food sold by street sellers and, in particular, how fears of contaminated street goods increased during plague years, in *Lost Londons*, 132–3.

66 *An Historical Account of Bartholomew Fair: containing a view of its origin, and the purposes it was first instituted for. Together with a concise detail of the changes it hath undergone in its traffic, amusements, &c.* (London: John Arliss, 1810), 11–12. BL 11644 c 55.

67 Sybil Rosenfeld, *The Theatre of the London Fairs* (Cambridge: Cambridge University Press, 1960), 150–1.

68 Voiture, *Familiar and Courtly Letters*, 186.

69 Cross-dressing or powerfully seductive female characters were featured in plays such as *The Unnatural Parents, or the Fair Maid of the West, The Book of the Play of John of Gaunt in Love, The Ship-Wreck'd Lovers; or French Perfidy Punished*. In the later play, an English lady and captain stranded on an island find 'a Part of the Island governed only by Women' and have a 'Punishment inflicted on them by the Female Government'. *Public Advertiser*, 3 September 1759, quoted in Rosenfeld, 143.

70 This term has several meanings and connotations. The most applicable in this case is that it refers to 'red faced' women with loosened hair – as red-faced as if they had been using bellows to blow a fire. These women's red faces and dishevelled appearance might also stem from having been in the crowd at Bartholomew fair during the summer, from drinking, from sexual activity, or all three. Readers of this work might have imagined any of the above. The 'Blowsabella' was also a country dance, as Don Bewley has pointed out to me.

71 *A Walk to Smithfield*, 2–3. For a description of middling and elite opportunities to behave licentiously at amusements such as masquerades, see Terry Castle, *Masquerade and Civilization: the Carnivalesque in Eighteenth-Century English Culture and Fiction* (Stanford, CA: Stanford University Press, 1986).

72 Margaret R. Hunt, *The Middling Sort: Commerce, Gender, and the Family in England, 1680–1780* (Berkeley and Los Angeles: University of California Press, 1996), 174.

73 Farringdon Without had the 'great majority of [disorderly] houses' in London between 1710–1749. Henderson, *Disorderly Women*, 64–5.

74 *Bartholomew Fair: An Heroi-Comical Poem* (London, 1717), 28.

75 *The Cloyster in Bartholomew Fair; or, the Town-Mistress Disguis'd* (London, 1707), A2.

76 *Ibid.*, 6.

77 *Bartholomew Fair: An Heroi-Comical Poem* (London, 1717), 28–9. Dabhoiwala examines the 'rise of popular resistance to the arrest of street-walkers', in *Origins of Sex*, 71–2.

78 Rep. 139, 234.

79 Deborah Valenze, *The First Industrial Woman* (New York and Oxford: Oxford University Press, 1995); and Hill, *Women, Work, and Sexual Politics*.

80 'Bartholomew Fair' in *An Entire New Collection of Humourous Songs, never exhibited in any joyous company whatever* (London, 1750).

81 Voiture, *Familiar and Courtly Letters*, 184.

5

Locating the fair sex at work[1]

He. Town Follies and Collies, and Mollys and Dollys,
   for ever adieu and for ever.
She. And Beaus that in Boxes; Lie smuggling their Doxeys,
   With Wigs that hang down to their Bums.

From 'The Country Dialogue'

'The Country Dialogue' appeared in a 1714 book of 'the newest play-house songs'. The ballad featured a familiar narrative of a couple yearning to leave the noise and amenities of London for the simplicity of the country, to feast on nothing 'but what we do breed, and wear on our Backs, The Wool of our Flocks'. The song is not remarkable for either innovative poetry or musical styling, but rather is made notable by the context in which it was performed. Though featured in a book of 'play-house' songs, which the reader would interpret to mean theatres, 'The Country Dialogue' was actually performed at a much less formal venue: 'Mrs. Mynn's [sic] Booth in Bartholomew-Fair'.[2] Such ballads were popular and frequently published. Many existing printed copies of 'drolls' (short plays) and songs performed at fairs originated in Anne Mynns's and later her daughters, Elizabeth Leigh and Hannah Lee's, fair booths.[3] Mynns and her daughters made a good livelihood operating play booths and overseeing a company of players at both Bartholomew and Southwark Fairs throughout the early eighteenth century. Their names were well known as among the best providers of fair entertainment – and they used that recognition not only to advertise their play-booth business, but also to sell pamphlets featuring the theatrical and musical entertainment they managed.

From the perspective of the twenty-first century, the fact that two women operated a thriving business in the heart of a city fast becoming a global centre is surprising. Are we incorrect, though, in assuming these women were notable? This chapter investigates how fairgrounds provided a space for working women of all income levels. Some were as respected and renowned as Mrs. Mynns and her daughter, and others worked in lesser capacities selling goods from baskets. This diversity of working women is depicted in a souvenir fan sold at Bartholomew Fair (see Figure 5.1). Women who worked at fairs were visible. Their presence did not alert London fair-goers; rather, their service in many capacities was expected. As discussed in Chapter 4, working women at London's fairs were increasingly satirized and blamed for gender order gone awry in eighteenth-century cultural discourse. This discourse, however, reflects merely expectations and assumptions of polite middling under-standings as they took shape during the eighteenth century. Satirical depictions reveal how efforts to modernize London revolved around emerging class-specific understandings of appropriate gender hierarchy.

Historical evidence demonstrates that women who worked at fairs were much less colourful than depicted in popular literature and that such portrayals had little impact on female fair workers. In fact, marginal economies thrived in London suburbs, and within these marginal mar-ketplaces, labouring and poor women found ways to supplement meagre resources to meet their household needs.[4] An examination of women's actual work at fairs cautions us against interpreting cultural representa-tions of female fair workers as evidence that their workspaces constricted during the late seventeenth through mid-eighteenth centuries.[5] Though there was a sexual division of labour in the early eighteenth century, it did not entail the type of rigidly defined separate work spheres associated with the nineteenth-century middle class, who increasingly associated women's work with the domestic sphere and men's work with the world beyond the home.[6] Early modern men and women did have understand-ings of their usual, separate work spheres. Within families, husbands were responsible for the world outside of the home, and women had responsibilities within the domestic realm.[7] Early modern women's pres-ence in great numbers as street pedlars, in fact, reflects a certain sexual division of labour, but at the same time this work occurred away from their homes.[8] More urban early modern European women may have worked in street trades such as itinerant peddling, and fairs were a space in which women were welcome as workers.[9] This type of casual labour usually required little capital and could be done to supplement the family economy.[10] Historians of women's work understand such labour to be an especially attractive occupation for early modern women, especially urban women, who were increasingly excluded from skilled occupations available to guild members.[11]

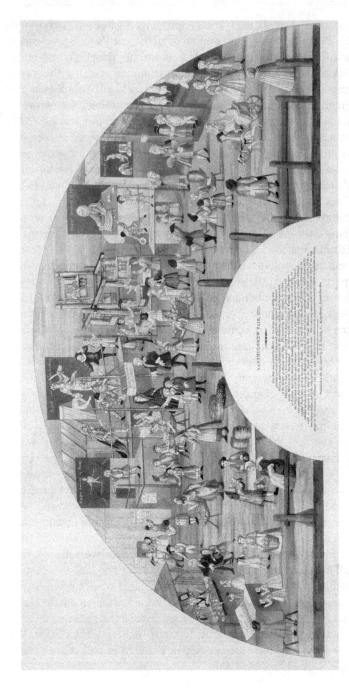

5.1 Bartholomew Fair Fan, published J. Setchel, c. 1721. Guildhall Library, City of London/The Bridgeman Art Library.

Fair records enrich our understanding of early modern gender and work and reveal that women by no means solely performed exclusively low-skilled labour. Though in some cases women dominated urban markets, London fair records reveal that large numbers of men joined women as workers participating in this form of part-time and seasonal occupation. In any event, fair records contest notions of a strict sexual division of labour among the types of jobs men and women undertook at fairs. At late seventeenth- and early eighteenth-century fairs, women often worked in managerial positions usually considered 'male', especially as fair-booth proprietors.[12] It is clear that while this cultural discourse painted fairs as a disorderly type of commerce dominated by women, male workers actually constituted the majority of workers at fairs. At the same time, women found work beyond casual peddling – they were visible and successful as managers in fairground commerce and its supporting industry of inn- and tavern-keeping.

Most of London's chartered fairs were established primarily for market purposes during the Middle Ages, but as consumer goods became more widely available in London's network of shops, urban authorities perceived the commercial function of fairs as overshadowed by their entertainment.[13] Nevertheless, there were many itinerant traders and pedlars, food-service workers, and entertainers who continued to supplement their living with seasonal employment at fairs, which took place alongside permanent London businesses. During the early stages of industrialization, the growth in manufacture of consumer goods benefited not only shopkeepers, but hawkers and street sellers as well.[14] Women found the most opportunities for this type of work in cities, where both goods and customers were widely available and regularly held fairs provided a reliable workspace. Women who found work at fairs sold food and drink and goods ranging from trinkets such as dolls or ribbons to porcelain. They were also involved in the entertainment industry of fairs and worked as dancers, actresses, or singers and even as play-booth managers. In short, women worked in the same jobs as men. Certainly, many women took advantage of the crowds at fairs and worked as prostitutes or pickpockets. At all levels, women visibly contributed to the commerce of fairs.

One 'women's' occupation (because it happened within the domestic realm) that profited during fairs was victualling or inn-keeping. Rooms in houses surrounding fair grounds were leased to those who attended and worked at fairs. This was a seasonal source of income for many, and traditionally women made up a majority of those running businesses providing food and lodging. Peter Earle demonstrates that among a sample of working London women, wives who ran businesses devoted to food, drink, and entertainment made up three-quarters of his total sample.[15] Though usually operated as family businesses, these occupations were considered well-suited for women's domestic skills, and women were active in daily operations.[16] Whether or not these were occupations considered 'male' or 'female', they were vital to the smooth running of London's fairs, and stood to lose much income should fairs be successfully curtailed.

Women working in family inn-keeping businesses sometimes influenced urban policies by resisting orders regulating fairs and continuing their business. These women also had clout when representing their businesses to the outside world. Records from the Old Bailey, for instance, reveal that married women who ran taverns and inns often testified in lieu of their husbands when their family businesses were robbed. These testimonies reveal, also, the many roles women filled in tavern-keeping. In 1732, Elizabeth Davil testified that she 'kept a Victualling House', just to the west of Bartholomew Fair in the Parish of St. Sepulchres. In early September, while most likely recovering from her busy season in late August, Elizabeth sought relief from her swelling legs and asked her new servant, Elizabeth Pardoe, to assist in 'rolling' her legs with cloth. During Bartholomew Fair, Davil earned well above her usual income. In 1732, she stashed £18 of extra earnings in her dresser drawer, near the rolls of cloth fetched by the servant. £6 of Davil's money was missing after Pardoe helped wrap her employers legs. Davil's son later discovered Pardoe with the money. In recounting the theft, Davil revealed how she oversaw her family's business, supervising the cook and servants and also interrogating a servant her son suspected committed a theft.[17] Similarly, Anne Chapman ran an inn near West Smithfield. It is not clear if she was widowed, but from all appearances, she ran this business alone. Chapman appeared in court when tenants (a husband and wife) stole a bottle of gin, which they in turn sold in the fair, and failed to pay their rent according to their lease agreement.[18]

Though recorded evidence of women's work as street sellers and itinerate pedlars is scarce, their applications for licences to 'show' (*monstrare*) wares or performances or to sell food or drink at fairs are recorded in surviving records from Bartholomew Fair's Pie Powder Court.[19] Pie Powder courts were held in fairs and markets for the duration of those occasions and had jurisdiction in commercial matters.[20] During the early eighteenth century, the City judges of the Sheriffs' Court, and one representative of the Lady Warwick, Lady of the Manor, oversaw the Pie Powder Court in Bartholomew Fair.[21] The early Pie Powder Court records provide an untapped resource that sheds new light on women's working lives in early modern England. Scholars examining London fairs have typically analysed only Pie Powder Court records from the late eighteenth century, but these records usually only record the last names of those seeking licences to exhibit goods or shows at the fair. The following discussion is based instead on the rolls from the period 1709–1732.[22]

Bartholomew Fair's Pie Powder Court rolls contain very little detail other than brief records of disputes and listings of those who acquired licences to trade or exhibit entertainment at the fair. The advantage of the earlier rolls is that they record both the first and last name of licensees; making it easy to uncover trends such as the numbers of people advertising shows at the fair versus those who actually acquired licences as well as the percentages of women acquiring licences to work in the fair. Though later records from Bartholomew Fair lack full names, they do specify which goods or type of entertainment each individual was licensed to show, though they do not contain much detail beyond this.[23] Records from the early eighteenth century merely state which type of licence each individual purchased – *pro venditione esculent* (for the sale of food), *pro venditione poculent* (for the sale of drink), *pro venditione gingerbredd* and, the most common licence, *pro venditione monstrare* (to 'show' – wares or performances).

The Pie Powder Court records provide an important glimpse into women's participation as legitimate labourers in eighteenth-century London. These records support historiography arguing that large numbers of women in the seventeenth and early eighteenth centuries supplemented their family income through itinerate work such as selling goods at markets or fairs.[24] They reveal, also, that at Bartholomew Fair many women sought licences to legally sell their goods and services at fairs. Though it is not always easy to determine what goods or services women provided, in some cases additional information about them is available in other sources. For example, some women who purchased licences also took out advertisements in newspapers in which their entertainment is described.[25] Actresses or play-booth managers are particularly easy to locate; however, the trade of the large majority of these women is presently unknown.

It was possible for fair traders to evade the legal process of obtaining a licence. This is clear if the names of those who advertised shows are compared to the names of people who obtained licences. In some cases, people were brought into the fair's court and fined for failing to obtain a proper licence.[26] Since it was possible to evade licensing, the Pie Powder Court records are not an entirely precise record of the numbers of men and women who worked at fairs, and, in the case of women, we must consider whether or not these records reflect accurately their numbers. Though such labour required a low level of capital investment, the economic status of these women varied and some may not have afforded fair licences.[27] The most successful hawkers possessed the expendable capital required to pay the licensing fee of London's chartered fairs, while others may have attempted to circumvent licensing and sell their goods illegally.

Women's ubiquitous and active work at London fairs is represented in a print from a fan sold at Bartholomew Fair during the 1720s [see Figure 5.1]. Completed as a souvenir of one's visit to the fair, the fan does not satirize the activities as Hogarth's *Southwark Fair* [Figure 1.1] does for that fair. Though the fair's activities seem almost too orderly, it does depict a number of women at work in various capacities. Women are portrayed preparing and selling sausages, taking admission to play booths, hawking fruit from a basket, selling food from a wheelbarrow, offering toys and other trinkets in a stall, and, of course, acting in performances. These women represent various economic positions. A woman who has leased a space for a stall or booth has paid considerably more than a mobile woman with a basket or wheelbarrow, who might have more easily evaded paying a licence. A woman engaged in either performing or taking admission at a play booth may have been a member of a larger London theatre company, may have been working with her husband, or may have operated this business alone. Even Hogarth's more unruly depiction of a fair gives us some idea of women's work. Fleeing from beneath a falling play-booth balcony is a nicely dressed woman who had been hawking fine porcelain dishes. This saleswoman can be immediately compared to the less-finely attired woman on the ground in front of her booth running what looks to be a portable gaming table.[28] The fact that Hogarth chose to depict his most reputable female trader in the most immediate peril reveals his notions of respectable women's suitability for an occupation such as fair-trading.

If we examine the numbers of women who acquired licences at fairs between 1702 and 1732, even accounting for variations in record-keeping and keeping in mind people's evasion of licensing, it is clear that women were consistently present in noticeable numbers. During the 1720s, an overall increase occurred in the number of licences issued, from 80 in 1719 to a peak of 129 in 1724, and the percentage of licences issued to women increased slightly, from 23 per cent in 1719 to 31 per cent in 1721. Increases and decreases in the numbers of licences issued coincide with city efforts to limit the fair to the original three days stipulated in its

Licences Issued in Bartholomew Fair's Pie Powder Court 1709–1732[29]

Year	Number of licences issued	Number of licences issued to women	Percentage of total licences issued to women*
1709	10	2	20%
1710	15	4	26%
1711	18	4	22%
1712	17	3	18%
1713	29	3	10%
1714	45	8	18%
1715	46	12	26%
1716	52	10	19%
1717	10	2	20%
1718 (no record)			
1719	80	18	23%
1720	105	25	24%
1721	145	45	31%
1722	113	27	24%
1723	100	21	21%
1724	129	31	24%
1725	125	28	22%
1726	120	28	23%
1727**	70	15	21%
1728	19	3	16%
1729	28	3	11%
1730	37	3	8%
1731	39	9	23%
1732	25	3	12%

*Percentages are rounded to the nearest hundredth
**This year Thomas Carbonell, English Sword Bearer and Thomas Elderton, Common Cryer of the City of London, 'came in person to this Court and individually petitioned that the aforesaid licences be revoked and monies received for them should be restored, and that no such licences should be granted again in the future. And in return, of their own free will, they offered and undertook to pay £20 paid annually, revoked the licences and restored the money received for them. And [the Court] also concede that no more licences of this sort would be granted in the future, saving the rights of this liberty'.

charter. The London Swordbearer's lease, which entitled him to farm profits from fair licences, expired in 1708 and the city officials saw this as their opportunity to finally restrict the tenure of an occasion they considered a growing nuisance. In this year, London's Court of Common Council issued an order restricting the fair to its original three days.[30] Lower numbers of licences in 1709 reflect the city's early vigilance in carrying out this order. By 1715, however, the court was obliged to issue yet another order reminding Londoners of the fair's regulation. The steady increase in licences issued in the period 1709–1715 reveals the fair's renewed growth. Only seven years after the court's order, the number of licences issued by Bartholomew Fair's Pie Powder Court more than quadrupled from 10 to 46. Clearly, enforcement had abated. The prospect of trading for fourteen days instead of three attracted more pedlars and 'showmen' to the fair. This increase of licences occurs, also, during what Sybil Rosenfeld calls Bartholomew Fair's 'theatrical heyday'.[31] Not only did London's established companies of 'strollers' continue to present dramatic entertainment at fairs, but actors, actresses, and managers from London's theatres joined them. This influx of 'professional' actors eventually declined with the imposition of the 1737 Licensing Act, which limited dramatic (spoken) entertainments to London's patent theatres.[32] We are not able to witness, however, the impact of this decline in the records of Bartholomew Fair's Pie Powder Court because existing records end in 1732, only to begin again in 1790.

Rising or falling numbers of leases could also correspond with oversight of the fair by the heirs to the Rich family, who held the rights to the manor in which the fair took place. Bestowed by King Henry VIII on Richard Rich at the Dissolution, by the eighteenth century, the old priory and the attending fair profits belonged to his heirs, the Lords Warwick. In early August 1701, Edward Rich, the Sixth Earl of Warwick and Third Earl of Holland, died. At his death, his titles and property fell to his 4-year-old son. Warwick's widow, Charlotte Middleton Rich, the Lady Warwick, represented her minor son in overseeing the fair.[33] Evidence does not reveal that Lady Warwick spent much effort attending to Bartholomew Fair. Numbers of licences issued in the period 1709–1717 are low compared to those issued after 1719. Perhaps not coincidentally, the young Lord Warwick came of age in 1719. When Lord Warwick reached his majority, he may have stepped up efforts to collect fees for licences at the fair. At the same time, City efforts to curtail the fair slowed, signifying either hesitance or decreased ability to successfully regulate the fair under him. City authorities appear to have taken advantage of a lapse in male authority over Bartholomew Fair, using the Lord's minority as an opportunity to finally curtail the prolonged festival. Such fears were justifiable in light of the symbolic message the public may have taken from having a young (widowed at 21), and by all reports, pleasant looking woman overseeing the fair. In this context, London's authorities stepped up as the city's 'patriarchs'. As such, they would have understood their role to ensure orderly regulation of Bartholomew Fair. While concerned with an increase in disturbances at all London area fairs, Bartholomew Fair may have especially concerned them because it lacked a symbolic authority figure. During the everyday happenings of the fair, the Lords of the manor did very little (besides profit); however, the lack of male over-sight at the fair would have troubled authorities who operated according to their era's gender hierarchy in which unruly adult men were control-led by orderly male authority. The regulation attempts of City authorities reveal their willingness to take advantage of the absence of elite, male oversight of the fair. City officials likely perceived the widowed Lady Warwick as vulnerable and not able to confront city attempts to curtail the fair. At the same time, those who profited from the fair may have viewed Lady Warwick's oversight of the fair as an opportunity to evade legal fair procedures.

A different possibility is that the young widow manifested changes she actually wanted. After enduring a marriage to a husband consid-ered to be one of the 'Roaring Boys' of the late Restoration (he was tried for manslaughter in 1699 and eventually died young at 28), Lady Warwick perhaps supported endeavours to quell unchecked frivolity in West Smithfield.[34] She may have invited the City's increased regula-tion of the fair, viewing City officials as appropriate male overseers of Bartholomew Fair. On the other hand, her son – known to take after his father – may have encouraged more people to attend and profit from the fair. Coming into his majority, the profits of Bartholomew Fair would have been attractive. Considering this complexity, we can only specu-late about the connections between female oversight of Bartholomew Fair, reduced licence fees collected, and increased City regulation during these years. No records address Lady Warwick other than to say she attended the opening of the fair or that her representative was appointed to Pie Powder Court. Nevertheless, despite fluctuations in numbers of licences issued for selling items or services at the fair, Bartholomew Fair continued and the percentage of licences issued to women remained stable, suggesting their continued use of this fair as a reliable work space.

Throughout these developments, the number of licences issued to women hovers around 20 per cent, with occasional drops below this number and a peak of 31 per cent in 1721. The continued presence of women as pedlars or exhibitors demonstrates they remained active workers at fairs. This number reveals, also, that women did not make up the bulk of trade at London's fairs (at least officially licensed trade). While many women did obviously find work at urban festivals, it was by no means a venue dominated by working women. Depictions of London fairs, which portray dangerous female performers or sellers, exaggerate the presence of women. They equate women with this work at fairs even as it is officially dominated by their male contemporaries. Literary and print depictions of fair disorder hinge on representations of disruptive women because this gendered deployment backed up by traditional understandings of women's place in social and spiritual order enabled artists and writers to underscore the imminent threat fairs posed to urban order. Of course, the most infamous group of unlicensed women at fairs not represented in the records of Bartholomew Fair's Pie Powder Court – pick-pockets and prostitutes – provided these writers with the best metaphors of the female threat to male industry and commerce.

Widows, whores, and masterless women at London's fairs

Unemployed, unmarried urban women or recent female migrants to London often turned to crime or prostitution. This happened especially if women were cut off from their familial or community support systems.[35] Middling men, represented in print culture by Ned Ward's 'London Spies', viewed female pickpockets and prostitutes as especially dangerous threats to social order. Societies for reformation of manners devoted much time prosecuting prostitutes, especially in London's most fashionable neighbourhoods (primarily the West End).[36] Richard Steele reinforced concern about London's prostitutes at popular evening resorts in his London 20 May 1712 *Spectator*. In this issue, he describes a visit to London's Spring Garden (later commercialized as Vauxhall pleasure garden). Accompanied by a knight, 'Sir Roger', Steele visits Spring Garden for an evening walk beneath the moonlit, nightingale-inhabited trees. To his companion's dismay, a 'Masque … came up behind him, gave him a gentle Tap upon the Shoulder, and asked him if he would drink a Bottle of Mead with her'. Sir Roger was, 'startled at so unexpected a Familiarity' (while not enough so that he immediately left the gardens). Upon leaving, the knight remarked to the 'Mistress of the House' that 'he should be a better Customer to her Garden, if there were more Nightingales, and fewer Strumpets'.[37]

While most certainly presented as a prostitute, the woman who interrupts Sir Roger's reverie is merely an unescorted woman. To the early eighteenth-century reader, however, she represented the potential social disorder stemming from women living outside traditional gender order. London's informers found urban women suspicious, especially if unmarried and outside the control of men. Middling urban dwellers viewed such women as potential prostitutes, pickpockets, or bearers of bastard children, who might, in turn, become dependent on poor relief (if they did not become criminals themselves).[38] Streetwalkers freely inhabited urban streets as masterless women. In literary accounts, such women symbolized fair disorder because they obviously, 'flouted patriarchal rules for women's occupation of space'.[39] Written descriptions of fairs commonly depict them as known work space for prostitutes. They especially associate the cloisters of St Bartholomew's Hospital with prostitutes, one reason why a 1707 poem about the varieties of prostitutes working in London is titled, *A Cloyster in Bartholomew Fair*.[40]

Much evidence suggests that thieves frequented fairgrounds and the areas around them, and many of them were women. Some people found legitimate work at fairs, while maintaining illegitimate work on the side. For instance, Anne Braseby and William Goodspeed, a boy of 15, were caught stealing goods from a gentleman's home. Goodspeed was found in Bartholomew Fair, Braseby under a bench in Moorefield. Both 'belong[ed] to the Poppet Shews in Bartholomew Fair'.[41] Ann Rutt, 'Wife of Richard Rutt', testified that Mary Jingen picked her pocket of 12s. during Southwark Fair.[42] Sarah Dawson took advantage of two men who had been drinking in a booth. Once the men passed out, she relieved them of their silver watches.[43] Popular accounts of women who stole goods inside rooms or music booths suggested they were prostitutes. The Old Bailey records do not always make these connections, but victims of such crimes likely did not admit publicly to all events that transpired behind closed doors.

Though they were by no means respected, as prostitutes, early eighteenth century women did not operate outside the law. The policing of 'streetwalking' was undertaken by local watch committees, constables, and beadles – there was no uniform London-wide approach to dealing with prostitution, and its treatment varied from parish to parish.[44] During the early eighteenth century, prostitution was erratically prosecuted.[45] Views of prostitution shifted from the late seventeenth through mid-eighteenth centuries. In the earlier period, social reformers viewed prostitution, or 'Whoring' as one aspect of a larger problem of 'Lewdness', or 'sexual acts' including 'adultery, fornication, uncleanness [that is, masturbation], lasciviousness, sodomy, obscene talk, lewd books of pictures, procuring, concubinage, incest, rape and polygamy'.[46] In the late seventeenth century through early eighteenth century, labelling a woman a whore said more about her sexual immorality than about an economic exchange or cash payment for sexual services.[47] During this period, societies for reformation of manners nevertheless focused on regulating 'streetwalking', and found much of this behaviour at London's fairs. Some social critics, however, viewed it as a necessary evil, including Bernard Mandeville, who made the case for public brothels in his 1724, *A Modest Defence of Public Stews*.[48] By the mid-eighteenth century, the reformation of manners campaign had declined in influence and newer conceptions of prostitutes as victims of male desire and economic circumstances gained credence.[49] This is a period of time in which there was a gradual 'separation of personal morality and public affairs', and some sexual licence, such as that proposed by Mandeville, was increasingly debated.[50]

While meanings associated with prostitution were debated throughout the late seventeenth through early eighteenth centuries, many women undertook this occupation at London's fairs. Areas associated with prostitution were often also considered especially dangerous for male fair-goers. In popular accounts of fairs, prostitutes specifically embody fair disorder, but even outside the fair prostitutes were a visible presence. These women worked the same London streets becoming a growing space for middle-class promenading and display.[51] What made fairs unique, especially Bartholomew Fair, were the number of areas closed off from view of the street in which one might procure a prostitute. It is not clear whether or not city officials feared this relative seclusion would make men more willing to solicit a prostitute, but being away from open public scrutiny made cloisters and the insides of fair booths similar to brothel spaces (or 'bawdy houses'). Bartholomew Fair was especially associated with a wide availability of prostitutes because of the ward in which it was located, Farringdon Without. This ward had long been 'the most trouble-prone' of the London wards.[52] The largest majority of bawdy houses known to have existed in London between 1710 and 1749 were here. Tony Henderson demonstrates that 70 of the total 110 known houses were located in Farringdon Without.[53] Just as London's theatre community took advantage of moneymaking opportunities at fairs, prostitutes from Farringdon Without's bawdy houses likely profited in the nearby cloisters and booths of Bartholomew Fair.

Prostitution is never mentioned specifically as a concern of city officials who attempted to regulate fairs, however. Their focus instead was on dangerous venues found at fairs (many of which would have been work spaces for prostitutes). When, in 1735, city officials re-launched their campaign to stamp out illicit entertainment at fairs, they focused not on prostitution, but on booths intended for plays, gambling, or music.[54] This year they issued an order based on one made originally in 1708. They hoped to restore Bartholomew and Southwark Fair to three days, but they specifically targeted any booths 'not set up for Dealers in Goods and Merchandizes proper for a fair', or those featuring 'stage plays, musick and Tipling'. The order targeting Southwark Fair gave bailiffs permission to pull down any 'nuisance' booths.[55] Again, there is no specific definition of what constituted a nuisance booth, but there are clues in the cultural discourse discussed in Chapter 4. For example, the description of the play booth featured in *A Walk to Smithfield* suggests such activities may have been associated with notions of sexual immorality.[56] An anonymous 'Earl' finds a suitable 'courtezan [*sic*]' in 'Madam Crisp', who had been 'shewing her Activity [dancing]' in a music booth at Bartholomew Fair. This pretty woman beckoned the Earl while he was passing the booth and before he knew it, he was 'persuaded to enter the Place of iniquity'.[57] There are also clues about disturbances and dangers of fair booths in narratives from the Old Bailey court proceedings. Fair booths were mentioned in the proceedings as sites of illicit activities and were locations at which one expected to find criminals. Booths in which illegal activities occurred featured in more than one witness's narrative at the Old Bailey – for example, William Shilcock was robbed by 'Yorkshire Hannah' in a Tottenham-Court fair booth, and in a different year, two fair-booth musicians were accused of robbing and assaulting Richard Coates.[58]

The London Alderman's 1735 order was directed at all music, gaming, drinking or play-booth managers; however, the only individual targeted by this legislation was Hannah Lee, a long-time resident of Southwark and respectable manager of a strolling company and fair play booths. Lee entered the play-booth business as her mother's partner. She joined her mother, Anne Mynns, in operating a successful business, which she assumed upon her mother's death.[59] Mynns had been a successful fairbooth proprietor at London's fairs during the late seventeenth and early eighteenth centuries. Her booth featured music and theatrical entertainment and was especially popular at both Bartholomew and Southwark Fairs. Together, Mrs Mynns and her daughter Hannah produced some of the most popular fair entertainments, including *The Siege of Troy*, which Mynns commissioned Elkanah Settle to write in 1705. Settle's drolls were, according to the well-known actor Theophilus Cibber 'generally so well contrived, that they exceeded those of their opponents in the same profession'.[60] This droll had a typical dramatic narrative, but what made it attractive to audiences was its overabundance of spectacle. Drolls at Lee's booth were always popular, and a number of them were printed and sold at the booth.

Hannah Lee enjoyed much success as a fair-booth proprietor and strolling acting company manager. Her career at London's fairs extended over 40 years. During that time she operated her booths alone and in partnership with other booth proprietors. For a time, she was an active operator of two booths in Southwark Fair, which seems to have been her base. A news report in 1737 mentions that her house 'on the Bowling Green near the Borough', had been robbed of 'divers Things of Value'.[61] By 1749 (despite various obstacles to her success, including a death at her booth and concerted regulation attempts), Lee operated a semi-permanent 'tiled' booth with the showmen Yeates and Warner.[62] Newspapers reported in 1739 that Lee married Yeates, but this is the only evidence that the partnership extended to marriage.[63] It certainly made sense that these two would have consolidated their interests by making their fair entertainment a family business.

Despite her success, Lee could not afford to have her business curtailed by social-reforming City fathers or members of Parliament. In 1735, the City issued its latest warning regarding the length of fairs and the inappropriateness of play-booth entertainment. Their admonishment coincided with the proposal of a bill in Parliament, which would curtail strolling companies of actors and impose limits on dramatic entertainments. Lee took action in the face of each threatened regulation, realizing the detrimental impact such legal changes would have on her livelihood. She took her objections to Parliament where, on 21 April 1735, she submitted a petition against the Playhouse Bill and argued that her business and all of the funds she had invested in it were in danger. She estimated her investment to be approximately £2,000 or above in 'Two Booths ... Buildings, Cloaths, Scenes, Decorations, and other necessaries'. Her strolling company had by then become 'her whole Substance ... on which she subsists', and she feared that 'being now infirm in Body, and old, she must be ruined, if the Bill should pass into Law'. In operating her business, she hoped she carried on her mother's intention in running a respectable company. She argued to Parliament that she presented 'innocent and amusing' entertainments that were patronized by many notable people. She also claimed: 'her and her late Mother's Companies have always been Nurseries for the greatest Performers that ever acted on the *British* Stage, particularly the celebrated Mr. *Powell* and Mr. *Booth*, as well as great Numbers of the present Actors at the Theatres of *Drury Lane* and *Covent Garden*'.[64] Though Lee's petition to have her counsel speak against the Bill was rejected, the Bill was eventually withdrawn.[65] Her business was safe from national regulation (at least until the passage of the 1737 Licensing Act), but the obstacle presented by the City remained.

Five months after petitioning Parliament and probably relieved at the stalling of the Playhouse Bill, Hannah Lee's business was interrupted by the City. After issuing their warning that 'nuisance booths' would be torn down by bailiffs, Mrs Lee, apparently ignoring this legislation, was targeted. On 23 September 1735, London's Court of Aldermen and Common Council met and recorded that Mrs Lee had 'erected a Booth in or near Southwark wherin [sic] she continues to Act Plays and Interludes in defiance of the law'.[66] It is difficult to imagine that this woman who, only five months before, petitioned Parliament about the future of her business was not aware of the City's latest attempts at legal regulation of fair booths. Perhaps her defiance reveals her belief that this legislation, as many previous orders, would not be enforced. She may have continued her business three weeks beyond the chartered time allocated to Southwark Fair in previous years, though this year she was aware that no national laws prohibited her dramatic entertainment. Whether knowing or not, Lee entered a contest between local and national authorities. With the apparent sanction of Parliament, she challenged the authority of local officials to limit her business. Here was a woman who had publicly denounced national legislation that would have assisted the City in its efforts to abolish play-booth entertainment at fairs. Though her voice was of little legal consequence to Parliament, City officials nonetheless would have been aware of her participation in petitioning against the Bill.

Hannah Lee's 1735 dismissal of city legislation and the continuation of her business were poorly timed. Not only did her appearance in Parliament make her a target as far as local officials were concerned, but her sex certainly did not help matters. What remains unclear is if Lee was singled out due to city officials' gendered understandings of work and urban space. As a female play-booth proprietor, she exemplified the threat to the commercial (and masculine) space London's officials wanted to create. Not only did she provide entertainment London's officials called a 'growing evil with mischievous consequences', but also she did this as a woman. A thriving female play-booth operator represented a double threat – she was the ultimate temptress luring men away from productive labour, using both femininity and spectacle and overseeing a sheltered space for this amusement. We can only suppose the extent to which visual and literary depictions of disorderly women at fairs influenced how City fathers perceived Hannah Lee. Though she had, indeed, run a respectable and popular family business throughout the early eighteenth century, it was during this time that many vivid and misogynist depictions of women who worked at fairs – particularly as performers – were produced.

Southwark's bailiff informed on Hannah Lee in late September 1735.[67] The court summoned Lee and, though the record is not clear, her entertainment most likely ceased. While this incident can be read as evidence that certain occupations made women more susceptible to legal or social sanction, it also demonstrates how one woman continued her business despite notions about women's work at fairs. Here we have a strong businesswoman, carrying on her mother's business and doing so without consideration of or appealing to her sex. In the historical record, there is no evidence that Lee found her sex an impediment to her rights or success as a business owner. She believed her livelihood was worthy of government protection despite the fact that she was a woman. As a business owner, she petitioned Parliament, never showing any indication that she believed her sex might hinder her appeal. As a resident and business owner within the jurisdiction of London, she only hoped to profit from the public demand for entertainment. By flouting city legislation inhibiting her business, she acted as did many other play-booth proprietors who also extended their shows long after fairs had ended.

There is other evidence that women who worked in managerial positions at fairs did not see themselves as participating in a 'male' profession. In most cases, they merely continued a family-run business. As in other family businesses, widows frequently assumed the operation of a business upon a husband's death. The 'Widow Barnes' operated a booth along with 'Mr. Evans and Mr. Finlay' during May Fair in 1706 – and she had apparently provided entertainment at Bartholomew Fair the previous year as well.[68] Another Leigh, widow of the play-booth proprietor Francis Leigh, continued her husband's business after his death in 1719.[69] In the five years prior to his death, Leigh purchased a licence to show at Bartholomew Fair in 1714 and jointly in 1715 with Jacob Spiller. In 1719, we know his wife continued his partnership with William Bullock, which the two men had established in 1717. When Leigh assumed her husband's business, however, she did not purchase a licence (neither did Bullock, this year, though he did in 1720).[70] We can only speculate as to why, but it may perhaps have been due to the expenses related to the death of Francis Leigh influencing Leigh and Bullock's ability to purchase a licence. In Bartholomew Fair's Pie Powder Court rolls, it is apparent that both men and women evaded licensing. This gender-neutral aversion to the legal process of obtaining a licence makes it difficult to determine whether or not having access to ready capital impacted decisions to acquire a licence and if having enough funds for licences always related to gender.

Access to ready capital was not the main motivating factor behind a fair exhibitor's decision to legally obtain a licence. In particular, Timothy

Fielding, an actor and prosperous play-booth proprietor, was called into court for 'showing an interlude called a Droll without licence [*sic*] from the court, and for words spoken in the same, in contempt of the court'.[71] What this reveals is that in most years, licensing violations went unnoticed. Fielding was apparently prosecuted more for the 'words spoken' in his droll (which had supposedly been attended by the Prince and Princesses of Wales) than for his initial evasion of the licensing process. Along with his partner John Hippisley, Fielding presented *The Envious Statesman or The fall of Essex* and *Humours of the Forced Physician*, which was taken from Molière's *Le Médecin malgré lui*. This year's entertainment was particularly elaborate, including a large acting company of eleven men and seven women, as well as three dancers, and an extra band.[72] While Fielding and Hippisley may have been overextended from hiring so many performers, it seems more likely they did not believe obtaining a licence was mandatory (unless brought into court, after which Fielding did purchase a licence and promised to 'act lawfully in the future'.). Something about their entertainment stood out, attracting the attention of the constable. From an examination of the limited evidence pertaining to licensing at Bartholomew Fair in the early eighteenth century, purchasing a licence to show at the fair does not appear to have been more likely for male over female play-booth proprietors, though when men ran businesses with their wives, it seems that they and not their wives have sought the licence.

In some cases, historians' own expectations of women's work identities at fairs lead them to misinterpret evidence. When the famous conjuror Isaac Fawkes died in 1731, Sybil Rosenfeld assumes that 'Fawkes's son set up a rival show [to his main competitor Yeates] next to Lee and Harper's'.[73] In fact, while Fawkes's son did carry on one part of the family business, the Pie Powder Court register for that year lists an 'Alicia Fawkes', Fawkes's widow Alice, who purchased a licence on the feast day of St Bartholomew.[74] Performing at fairs does appear to have been a family industry, with parents handing down performance styles, skills, and materials required for shows to their children. Mynns and Lee are one such family, but showmen also trained sons to carry on particular performance styles after their death, which was the case with Isaac Fawkes. While Fawkes's wife continued operating the family business, her son maintained his father's showmanship style and reputation for engaging and superior entertainment. The younger Fawkes had performed with his father from at least the age of 12 (or so a 1722 advertisement stated), when he was called 'Fawkes's famous Boy'.[75] When the elder Fawkes died unexpectedly of an 'Ague and Fever' in May 1731, he was at the top of his career. That year he had performed at his own theatre in James Street near the Haymarket Theatre in front of many 'Persons of Quality and Distinction'.[76] Notable audience members included the 'Algerine Embassadors', and 'The Turk of Distinction, who lately came over with his Excellency Mr. Stanyan from Constantinople'.[77] Upon his death, Fawkes was reportedly worth ten thousand pounds, which he left to his wife.[78] Alice not only continued his business, but maintained her late husband's partnership with the celebrated Pinchbeck family of clockmakers. Fawkes's shows continued to feature mechanical pictures created by Edward Pinchbeck, son of the renowned clockmaker, Christopher Pinchbeck, who died in 1732. Alice Fawkes cemented this relationship by marrying the younger Pinchbeck in November 1732.[79] The younger Fawkes remained an active showman at fairs through the 1730s and 1740s.

This chapter reveals that London women who profited from their work at fairs managed to stay in business despite assaults on their character as fair workers and in the face of City officials' and middling men's new notions of commerce and the city. On the ground, women tested the bounds of their representative confinement and found them much more flexible than literary and print depictions suggest. We must consider historical occasions of women's own response to unflattering representations of their work or regulatory efforts to curtail their labour. As notions of women's proper urban work space shifted in the early eighteenth century, female fair-workers responded to, ignored, or reconfigured themselves in the face of efforts to regulate their available occupations. Without institutionalized or uniform understandings of *all* women's appropriate work, and in the absence of economic conditions which would allow working women to vacate the streets of London, women remained active participants in the city's work force.

Notes

1 Portions of this chapter appeared in Anne Wohlcke, 'The Fair Sex: Working Women at London's Fairs, 1698–1732', in *Journal of Interdisciplinary Feminist Thought* 1, Issue 1 (2005), 1–34.

2 *The compleat English secretary, and newest academy of complements. Containing the true art of indicting letters, suitable to the capacity of youth and age. ... To which is added. 1. The art of good breeding and behaviour, ... 6. The comical humours of the jovial London gossips, ... With a collection of the newest play-house songs.* London, 1714.

3 Philip H. Highfill, Jr., Kalman A. Burnim, and Edward Langhans (eds), *A Biographical*

Dictionary of Actors, Actresses, Musicians, Dancers, Managers and Other Stage Personnel in London, 1660–1800, Vol. 10 (Carbondale and Edwardsville: Southern Illinois University Press, 1984), 409. Mrs. Mynns's obituary appeared in the *Weekly Journal or British Gazetteer* on 4 January 1718.

4 Beverly Lemire, *The Business of Everyday Life: Gender, Practice and Social Politics in England, c. 1600–1900* (Manchester and New York: Manchester University Press, 2005), 28.

5 Amanda Vickery began a productive interrogation of such categories as 'separate spheres' and 'domesticity' as it has been understood by women's historians in her 'Golden Age to Separate Spheres? A Review of the Categories and Chronology of English Women's History', *Historical Journal* 36, 2 (1993), 383–414.

6 See especially Leonore Davidoff and Catherine Hall, *Family Fortunes: Men and Women of the English Middle Class 1780–1850* (London: Hutchinson Education, 1987); Catherine Hall (ed.), *White, Male and Middle Class: Explorations in Feminism and History* (Oxford: Oxford University Press, 1992); Anna Clark has examined the ways in which women and men of the working class understood and responded to notions of 'separate spheres' in her *The Struggle for the Breeches: Gender and the Making of the British Working Class* (Berkeley: University of California Press, 1995).

7 Christine Peters, *Women in Early Modern Britain, 1450–1640* (Houndmills, Basingstoke: Palgrave Macmillan, 2004), 49.

8 See Alice Clark, *Working Life of Women in the Seventeenth Century* (1919; reprint, New York: A.M. Kelley, 1968) and Ivy Pinchbeck, *Women Workers and the Industrial Revolution, 1750–1850* (New York: Augustus M. Kelley Publishers, 1930; Reprint, New York: A.M. Kelley, 1969); Merry Wiesner argues that early modern Polish women, for example, constituted more than three-quarters of traders at urban markets, in *Women and Gender in Early Modern Europe* (Cambridge: Cambridge University Press, reprint, 2000 [1993]), 117.

9 Laura Gowing, '"The Freedom of the Streets": Women and Social Space, 1560–1640' in Paul Griffiths and Mark S.R. Jenner, *Londinopolis: Essays in the Cultural and Social History of Early Modern London* (Manchester and New York: Manchester University Press, 2000); Olwen Hufton, *The Prospect Before Her, A History of Women in Western Europe, 1500–1800* (New York: Alfred A. Knopf, 1996), 77.

10 Pinchbeck's discussion of female pedlars remains valuable: *Women Workers*, 300.

11 Merry Wiesner, *Working Women in Renaissance Germany* (New Brunswick, NJ: Princeton University Press, 1986); Alice Clark, *Working Life*.

12 Women who worked in managerial positions included Hannah Lee and her mother, Anne Mynns, proprietors of a London company of strolling actors, and Alicia Fawkes, who continued her husband's booth after his death.

13 Robert W. Malcolmson, *Popular Recreations in English Society, 1700–1850* (Cambridge: Cambridge University Press, 1973); and Peter Earle, *A City Full of People: Men and Women of London, 1650–1750* (London: Methuen, 1994).

14 Robert B. Shoemaker, *Gender in English Society, 1650–1850* (London and New York: Longman, 1998), 171–2.

15 Earle, *City Full of People*, 149.

16 *Ibid.*, 147.

17 Proceedings of the Old Bailey (OBP), 6 September 1732, Ref: t17320906-20.

18 *Ibid.*, 16 October 1734, Ref: t17341016–23.

19 St Bartholomew's Fair: Piepowder Court Rolls, Ref. HB. C6, Highclere Castle Archive. Thank you to Lord Carnarvon and his archivist, Jennifer Thorp, for making these documents accessible to me. I am especially indebted to Jennifer Thorp both for realizing the richness of this historical source, cataloguing the court rolls with the National Register of Archives, and for her transcription of these rolls.

20 The exact origins of the term 'Pie Powder' is unknown. Scholars have argued either that it comes from the French for 'dusty feet' because fairs were usually held during the dusty summer months, or that it comes from the old French name for a pedlar, 'pied puldreaux'. Henry Morley, *Memoirs of Bartholomew Fair* (1880; Detroit, MI: Singing Tree Press, 1968), 76–9.

21 *A New View of London, or an ample account of that city, in two volumes, or eight sections*, Vol. 2, London, 1708, 714.

22 These earlier court rolls from Bartholomew Fair's pie powder court are held at Highclere Castle.

23 Smithfield Court Book Proceedings in Court of Piepowder, 1790–1854. Guildhall Library, MS 95.

24 See above.

25 The best example is the successful play-booth proprietor Hannah Lee, who is discussed in more detail below.

26 As was Timothy Fielding in Ref. HB C7 (St Bartholomew's Fair, Middlesex: Piepowder Court Roll 1723–1732), Membr. 10r.

27 See Margaret Spufford, *The Great Reclothing of Rural England: Petty Chapmen and Their Wares in the Seventeenth Century* (London: Hambledon Press, 1984). Spufford argues that though the government began taxing street traders by the late-seventeenth century, many women traded without licences. See also Alice Clark and Pinchbeck – both have demonstrated that this occupation was dominated by women. Bridget Hill sees increasing numbers of hawkers in London during the late eighteenth century.

28 William Hogarth, *Southwark Fair*, 1733.

29 St. Bartholomew's Fair: Piepowder Court Rolls, Ref. HB. C6 and C7, Highclere Castle Archive.

30 Morley, *Memoirs*, 297.

31 Sybil Rosenfeld, *The Theatre of the London Fairs in the Eighteenth Century* (Cambridge: Cambridge University Press, 1960), Chapter 2.

32 *Ibid.*, 44.

33 Lady Warwick married Joseph Addison, the well-known essayist, in August, 1716. Samuel Johnson, *Lives of the Most Eminent English Poets* (New York: Derby and Jackson, 1857), 556.

34 Arthur L. Cooke, 'Addison's Aristocratic Wife', *PMLA* 72, no. 3 (June 1957), 373–89.

35 J.M. Beattie, 'The Criminality of Women in Eighteenth-Century England', *Journal of Social History* 8 (1975), 80–116, 95–7; Tony Henderson, *Disorderly Women in Eighteenth-Century London: Prostitution and Control in the Metropolis, 1730–1830* (London and New York: Longman, 1999); J.M. Beattie, *Policing and Punishment in London, 1660–1750: Urban Crime and the Limits of Terror* (Oxford, 2001), 67–71.

36 Shoemaker, *Gender in English Society*, 109.

37 Richard Steele, *The Spectator* (No. 383, 20 May 1712) in Donald F. Bond (ed.), *The Spectator* (Oxford: Clarendon Press, 1965), 438–9.
38 Shoemaker, *Gender in English Society*, 302.
39 Jane Rendell, 'The Pursuit of Pleasure: London Rambling', in Neil Leach (ed.), *The Hieroglyphics of Space: Reading and Experiencing the Modern Metropolis* (London and New York: Routledge, 2002), 107.
40 *The Cloyster in Bartholomew Fair* (London, 1707).
41 OBP, 15 October 1690, ref. number t16901015-20.
42 *Ibid.*, 20 September 1693, ref. number t16930906–64.
43 *Ibid.*, 14 October 1724, ref. number t17241014-28.
44 Henderson, *Disorderly Women*, 104–5.
45 Robert Shoemaker, *Prosecution and Punishment: Petty crime and the law in London and rural Middlesex, c. 1660-1725* (Cambridge: Cambridge University Press, 1991) 7.
46 Henderson, *Disorderly Women*, 180.
47 *Ibid.*
48 Shoemaker, *Prosecution and Punishment*, 76–7.
49 Henderson, *Disorderly Women*, 180–6.
50 Faramerz Dabhoiwala, *The Origins of Sex* (Oxford: Oxford University Press, 2012), 112–14.
51 Henderson, *Disorderly Women*, 107–8.
52 Paul Griffiths, *Lost Londons: Change, Crime, and Control in the Capital City 1550–1660* (Cambridge: Cambridge University Press, 2008), 85. Griffiths discusses the reputation of Farringdon Without on pages 84–6. He says no 'other ward had as many brothels on the eve of the Reformation or three centuries later'.
53 Henderson, *Disorderly Women*, 64.
54 Music booths were especially known as places to procure prostitutes.
55 Rep. 139, 233 and 240.
56 *A Walk to Smithfield*, 2–3. See Chapter 4.
57 *Authentick memoirs relating to the lives and adventures of the most eminent gamesters and sharpers, from the Restoration of King Charles.* London, 1744.
58 OBP, 3 September 1740, ref. number t17400903-55; *Ibid.*, 6 September 1732, t17320906-32.
59 The Mynns/Lee partnership supports Beverly Lemire's findings for late seventeenth-century Southwark. Her evidence from one ledger demonstrates that businesswomen formed a 'disproportionately large number of alliances with other women, and over 70 percent of women active in partnerships ... relied on other women to assist them'. Lemire, *Business of Everyday Life*, 27.
60 Great Britain, Parliament, House of Commons. Journals of the House of Commons (1735; rpt. 1803–1813), 470.
61 *Old Whig or the Consistent Protestant*, 7 July 1737.
62 *General Advertiser*, 7 September 1749.
63 The report reads: 'A few Days since the ... noted Mr. Yeates, Master of the Puppit-Shews and Slight [sic] of Hand, was married to Mrs. Lee, so well known for her agreeably entertaining the Town with Drolls at Bartholomew and Southwark Fairs ... on which occasion a considerable Fortune in South-Sea Stock was made over to the Bridegroom'. *Read's Weekly Journal or British Gazetteer*, 14 April 1739.

64 Great Britain, Parliament, House of Commons, Journals of the House of Commons (1735; rpt. 1803–1813), 470.

65 *Ibid.*

66 Rep 139, 233.

67 *Ibid.*

68 *Daily Courant*, 1 May 1706; Rosenfeld, *Theatre of the London Fairs*, 17.

69 Highfill et al., *Biographical Dictionary*, Vol. 9, 231.

70 Ref. HB. C6 (St. Bartholomew's Fair, Middlesex: Piepowder Court Roll, 1709–1722).

71 Ref. HB C7 (St. Bartholomew's Fair, Middlesex: Piepowder Court Roll 1723–1732), Membr. 10r.

72 Rosenfeld, *Theatre of the London Fairs*, 37.

73 *Ibid.*

74 Ref. HB C7 (St. Bartholomew's Fair, Middlesex: Piepowder Court Roll 1723–1732), Membr. 10r.

75 Highfill et al., *Biographical Dictionary*, Vol. 5, 206.

76 *London Evening Post*, 13–16 February 1731.

77 *Ibid.* and *British Journal, or The Traveller*, 27 February 1731.

78 Highfill, et. al., *Biographical Dictionary*, Vol. 5, 207.

79 *Ibid.*, 208.

6

Clocks, monsters, and drolls: Gender, race, nation, and the amusements of London fairs

'Freaks', 'Monsters', and other curious people and objects were always popular early modern fair exhibits. Since the late nineteenth century, attention given to such shows has been justified by authors' interest in uncovering past 'tastes' less refined than their own era's more 'respectable' views of shows featuring people embodying difference.[1] This perspective was common in nineteenth-century portraits of fairs, including Henry Morley's *Memoirs of Bartholomew Fair*. In his study, Morley analyses English interest in curiosities from the perspective of his own era, the late-Victorian period, a time he sees as a pinnacle moment in British history.[2] In a chapter on fair monsters, Morley juxtaposes his own notions of Victorian civility and scientific understanding against what he believes is the inferior understanding of his seventeenth- and eighteenth-century predecessors.[3]

Though Morley condemns London's Bartholomew Fair for being a disorderly and juvenile festival that no longer belongs in the heart of the British nation, he also mourns its passing. His 'memory' – personal and historical – of the fair immortalizes it as a uniquely English festival and with a nostalgic tone he argues to the reader that Bartholomew Fair *is* England. Though the fair had effectively 'died' in 1849, due to lack of commerce and entertainment, Morley keeps the fair alive in this eulogy to it. 'Earth to Earth', he proclaims in his final chapter, and he conveys a sense of longing for an English tradition 'maintained for seven centuries'.[4] When Morley wrote his testament of Bartholomew Fair, the fair had ceased to exist in London. Though he condemns this childish and base festival, he mourns its loss because for all of its faults, the fair appealed to Victorians living in a much more regulated and topographically defined metropolis.[5] Morley's personal memory of the fair was shaped not only by his personal experience attending the fair in its last days, but also by myths about the fair and its social significance.

Compared to that of the early eighteenth century, Morley's world was structured and shaped by rigid enforcement of the urban environment as well as strict understandings of what constituted knowledge, appropriate gender systems, and clear notions of class boundaries. The unruly world of eighteenth-century fairs was, for Morley, arrested in its scientific understanding; yet, early modern fairs nevertheless appealed to Victorian folklorists, such as Morley, looking for less-evolved historical stages against which to compare their own progress.

Morley and other nineteenth-century historians interested in popular recreation created 'snapshots' of fairs and their entertainment that continue to shape how we view these festivals today.[6] Such views, however, focus our attention on such festivals in comparison to modern entertainments that may have evolved out of these earlier festivals. The ordinary people who attended and worked at late seventeenth- and early eighteenth-century fairs are lost in such depictions, despite the fact that their participation at fairs is what constructed that culture. The emphasis on exploring fairs as curious institutions that featured entertainments and practices unlike those found in modern entertainment obscures the everyday meanings of festivity, the messages created and communicated through fair entertainment, and the use of festive city streets to support or contest civic or national events. Through their production and consumption of late seventeenth- and early eighteenth-century fair entertainment, ordinary people contributed to popular understandings of the local London community, helped define gendered and social understandings of who belonged, and connected that collectivity to the wider British nation and world. An analysis of the popular memory of fairs reminds us that visual culture is as important as print culture in communicating to wide audiences common understandings of 'imagined' national communities.[7]

Fairs visually and aurally communicated ideas of national consciousness to a popular audience. They disseminated knowledge, notions of local and national belonging, and ideas of gendered and racial difference among Britons and against 'others' from Europe and the world. Some fair entertainments helped produce 'enduring images' of people marked as outsiders to a popular audience.[8] They also celebrated and commemorated military victories and familiarized fair-goers with the goods and people of Britain's growing colonial holdings. In short, on a much more local level than newspapers (singled out by Benedict Anderson as instrumental to national identity construction) fairs consolidated and disseminated local and national identities.[9] Though fairs were temporary events limited by the numbers of people who could be physically present at them, the everyday happenings there were represented in both print and visual culture to spatially and temporally wider audiences. Fairs are important, however, not only because they were represented in literature consumed by literate audiences, many of whom were in the process of constructing images of themselves as 'middle-class', but also because they were an arena in which a much broader spectrum of labouring and otherwise invisible Londoners and Britons contributed to, or consumed notions of 'nation' and belonging. Unlike the one-directional nature of newspapers, which audiences read, and may have discussed with fellow readers or listeners – with the exception of the literate few who took the time to write to editors and contest or support ideas – fairs were a particular site at which national imaginings could be applauded or directly contested. This was especially possible at fairs where men and women had the opportunity to participate in activities in support of dominant local and national powers, but also because they could contest them through activities authorities deemed illicit, immoral, or disruptive – gaming, prostitution, excessive drinking, and rioting, for example.

For individuals such as Henry Morley, what seventeenth- and eighteenth-century people found interesting represented their infantile understanding, and he did not wonder about the social and cultural influences that shaped popular recreation. For example, interest in 'monsters' represents to Morley an arrested stage in British national consciousness, a time during which people did not yet scientifically understand the natural history of difference.[10] This fascination with monsters occurred in 'the nation destined for a world-wide rule [just encountering] the mysteries of distant regions of the world'. He equates early English fascination with such objects to the wonder of a child just beginning to explore his or her world, and says 'however absurd in many of its forms', seeing monsters appealed to adults as if they were children '[coming] to [their] first acquaintance with the life outside the nursery'.[11] Though Morley sees Elizabethan fascination with monsters as an innocent pursuit through which 'child-like' English men and women examined the wonders of the world at home, anything beneficial about this exercise was 'degraded' by the court of Charles II. During the Restoration and after, Morley argues there was 'a strange stagnation over nearly the whole mind of Europe, and … the disposition of the rich in England continued to be throughout the whole eighteenth century indolent and trifling'. During this period '[the] taste for Monsters became a disease; of which the nation has in our own day recovered with a wonderful rapidity in presence of events that force on the development of all its powers'. Even

British children of the 1880s were more morally and intellectually developed than these forebears, including a past king – '[with] Bartholomew Fair … gone, … there are few English boys who now would care to see the giant, under whose arm it pleased Charles the Second to walk'.[12] It is interesting that Morley so harshly criticizes as morally 'stunted' Britons who enjoyed fair exhibits during the foundational period of British colonialism, without which his own British Empire would not exist. Though he views the fascination of monsters as an illness, his focus on monsters as a significant and sensational aspect of his work reveals that in his own time they had not, in fact, lost their appeal. While British Victorians purported to value exhibits from the Empire as a demonstration of British resources or industry abroad, those showcased products of the British imperial project were enabled by racialized and proto-scientific understandings apparent in the earlier wide appeal of 'monsters'.[13] Morley's condemnation of seventeenth- and eighteenth-century tastes helps the twenty-first-century reader locate a culturally defining moment underpinning the British Empire in the eighteenth-century 'disease' of loving monsters.[14]

Morley's study was written at the peak of British imperialism and scientific professionalism. He traced the origins of Britain's current might to a tradition begun during the Elizabethan Renaissance – a time during which political focus was on naval might and colonization. His Whiggish perspective of Elizabethan glory in politics and society followed by a gradual decline of English stability and morality (reaching its lowest ebb under Charles II) with eventual redemption in Victorian Britain reduces the eighteenth century to a degenerate stage in the development of the respectable 'English mind'. The cultural practices, traditions, and social organization of the Restoration and Hanoverian eras are only interesting for their 'difference' from his own period. Morley casts the entire period as 'freakish', and, with his own 'respectable' and finely developed perspective, proceeds to put it and its curiosities on display for his audience of readers. Morley becomes a respectable Victorian showman because he qualifies anything that might shock bourgeois sensibility in long passages in which he assures his audience that though fascination with such things as monsters 'still lingers among uncultivated people in the highest and lowest ranks of life', the late nineteenth century differs from this earlier period because people know better. Late nineteenth-century British men and women understood that hermaphrodites, dwarfs, giants or 'scaly boys', were, if anything, objects for scientific study and would not be awed by the spectacle of merely looking at them. On the other hand, 'in the reigns of William and Mary, or Queen Anne', people's taste for what Morley would consider to be simple amusements was 'almost universal'.[15]

A similar distancing from fair amusements continues in twentieth-century and contemporary studies of fairs. In a study which otherwise seriously considers fair theatre an object of historical inquiry, Sybil Rosenfeld dismisses the theatre of fairs as of 'no literary or intrinsic merit', though valuable for studies of 'expression of popular taste and as folk drama'.[16] This statement reasserts mid-twentieth-century notions of which works (the Western canon) merited academic study of literary form. David Kerr Cameron qualifies his portrayal of fair amusements from a twenty-first-century view in which displays of monsters or the 'grotesque' is 'sad', but 'the sad truth' remains that 'freaks were fun and endlessly fascinating', and people including the normally 'sedate' and 'deeply pious' John Evelyn were 'much taken by such oddities'.[17]

This chapter seeks to understand the popularity of monsters, freaks, machines, people, and objects from around the world in terms of why they interested men and women who saw them in the late seventeenth and eighteenth centuries. The focus is less on our own notions of what constitutes a fascinating spectacle today, or how notions of what shocks have changed from era to era. Certainly, a curiosity about the wider world and England/Britain's growing colonial endeavours sparked fair-goers' interest in viewing objects and people from around the world. However, at the same time, interest in curious displays was informed less by base or juvenile interests in the unknown and more by broadening engagement with the British Empire.[18] Elite and popular questioning driven by widening exposure to methods of scientific inquiry also fuelled interest in objects and people from around Europe and the world. The fairground was a typical arena, along with coffee houses, private homes, or other exhibition places at which objects with scientific interest were shown to the public.[19] Wax figures exhibited at fairs, for example, might be shown also to anatomy students or to artistic societies, such as the Royal Academy of the Society of Artists.[20] That people from the seventeenth-century Evelyn to a shopkeeper living in 1720s London to a regular fair-goer shared an interest in curious objects speaks to a widening 'scientific' culture and should cause us to re-evaluate our notions of who encountered such new understandings and the technologies informed by them.[21] Fairgrounds allow us to broaden our conceptualization of who participated in, or at least viewed, scientific culture and provides a means for us to examine how fair exhibits sustained or shaped understandings about cultural and social hierarchies within Britain and around the world.

The proto-science of clocks and wax works

In 1725, Isaac Fawkes, a sleight-of-hand artist, featured 'several curiosities' at his booth in Southwark Fair, including a 'miracle of nature … a woman with a horn on the back part of her head ten inches long', who had been called a 'surprising curiosity' by none other than the famous collector Sir Hans Sloane.[22] Fawkes's exhibition featured also a 'Spring Musical Clock of a new Invention', which performed music on various instruments also with 'an Aviary of Birds to such perfection as hardly to be distinguished from life itself'.[23] Evoking Sloane's words in his advertisement, Fawkes associated his products with the prestige of the great collector's own objects. We can view Sloane's participation in the European-wide activity of collecting and arranging natural specimens as a means by which he constructed his own identity as a powerful and well connected man.[24] Whether or not Fawkes's prestige was enhanced similarly is unclear, but men such as Fawkes who collected curious items to exhibit for a profit were vital to broadening popular understanding of emerging scientific culture. Fawkes's exhibits conveyed knowledge about the wider world and technologically interesting instruments to fairgoers. While Fawkes's collection did not originate with his own journeys to faraway places, it did demonstrate that he knew how to tap into and profit from the commodity culture associated with this wider world.

As Fawkes mined a global culture for his exhibits he also pulled from England's home-grown culture of expert craftsmanship. The clocks he and others exhibited represented the finest male workmanship of England, and in particular London, where clock- and instrument-makers had created a prestigious reputation for themselves as the world's finest since the Elizabethan era.[25] The ingenuity of clockmakers was on display at London's fairs for the men and women of England. Thus, 'curious' exhibits were more than items over which a fair-goer would marvel – they disseminated to popular audiences notions about the uniqueness of English men's superior craftsmanship and intellect. Barbara Maria Stafford argues that eighteenth-century science was fuelled by a belief that images 'possessed a unique capacity to teach, to uncover the relation of known parts to an unknown whole'.[26] Fair exhibitions often made such visual statements and were deliberately intended to teach those who viewed them.

Fairgrounds presented shifting and disorderly cabinets of curiosity in which people viewed, made sense of, and presumably learned something from a variety of global and local items. The popular amusements of fairs belong to a wider culture of public fascination with natural philosophy, collecting, and a general curiosity about England's place in relation to other European nations, as well as its own growing colonial empire. Such amusements also reflect the English elite's involvement in a European-wide intellectual movement devoted to early proto-scientific pursuit. At fairs, audiences paid small fees to view some of the same exhibits also displayed at court or exhibited (also for a fee) in Fleet Street coffee houses or the Royal Society.[27] The author of *Bartholomew-Fair, an Heroi-Comical Poem* celebrated technological marvels, such as the 'famous clock ... By Artists finish'd with best Work-mens Hands ...'.[28] This clock, which presented various mechanical imitations of nature, allowed fair-goers to 'pursue' the work of 'famous Newton', and from 'The Globes, and Spheres, and Mathematicks learn, And Worlds unknown with Ease you may discern'.[29] Though fair audiences viewed monsters, clocks, and wax figures for amusement purposes, these objects nevertheless exposed wide audiences to new technologies, natural philosophy, and even music performed at court. Technological advance was not the solitary focus of fair exhibits, however. The workings of clocks, mechanical pictures, peep shows, and the anatomy of monsters represented only one draw for audiences, who also consumed the political, moral, local, and national themes around which such exhibitions were shaped.

In pursuit of customers, exhibitors displayed natural and man-made curiosities including everything from live rattlesnakes to mechanical clocks. Fascinating and uncommon objects were popular with both collectors and spectators from the early sixteenth century and before (Richard Altick aptly calls the medieval church the 'common man's first museum' with its 'stock of holy relics').[30] During the Renaissance, wealthy and aristocratic European collectors influenced by natural philosophy used access to emerging networks of a trade and gathered artefacts from around the world. Such natural and man-made objects were displayed in '*wunderkammern*' or '*cabinets des curieux*'.[31] This was an expensive exercise through which collected objects supported a Neo-Platonic, hermetic world-view reinforced by displaying objects as a means to demonstrate connections between them.[32] Such collecting was popular among the continental European elite and took longer to arrive in England, where in the late sixteenth century 'scientific and artistic amateurs' of the aristocracy and gentry began participating in this wider European craze for collecting.[33] Men such as Sir Walter Cope, John Tradescant, and John Evelyn participated in the culture of collecting as either collectors or viewers of objects of natural philosophical interest.[34] As the seventeenth century progressed, Londoners from diverse backgrounds participated, also, in a less formal version of natural philosophy as they encountered growing opportunities to collect and view curiosities from around the world. A small industry of curious London shows was launched by growing interest in both natural and man-made wonders coupled with an abundance of venues in which to show them – inns, coffee houses, fairs, and streets – as well as entrepreneurs with enough surplus funds to acquire interesting objects.

The automated world of fairs

By the late seventeenth century, London's fairgrounds featured a host of mechanical pictures, clocks, and automated wax works. The availability of and people's interest in such clock-driven fairground curiosities was driven by the convergence of various political, cultural, and social movements. The quest for a reliable means to determine longitude as well as an Enlightenment-era fascination with precision, mathematics, and man-made duplication of nature all contributed to the creation of a scientific commodity culture that included many clockwork-based objects. The creation of state of the art time-keeping equipment was, in part, driven by national interest in naval developments – both the French Académie and English Royal Society sponsored campaigns for the development of a reliable time-keeping device that might be used for long periods of time at sea as an aid to navigation.[35] While circles of Europe's scholarly elite debated mechanical philosophy and searched for evidence of a universal driving force, instruments modelling new understandings of the wonder of the universe became popular.[36] Interested Londoners hoping to join in this scientific community attended public lectures held in coffee houses at which they could view mechanical instruments and observe experiments.[37] With scientific commodities in high demand and a concentration of skilled clockmakers and savvy entrepreneurs in London, it was a matter of time before mechanized shows turned up in fair booths.

Two London showmen competed to bring elaborate and marvellous mechanical displays to fair patrons. William Pinkethman was a celebrated comedian who yearly provided fair-booth entertainment at the capital's largest fairs. He, along with Christopher Pinchbeck, a clockmaker and showman, were instrumental in combining mechanization with baroque artistic representation.[38] Their mechanical presentations bridged scientific, elite, and popular culture, combining clockwork with classical music and automation with landscape and classical imagery. As savvy businessmen, they realized the appeal of mechanical representation to middling and elite audiences familiar with mechanical philosophy as

To all Lovers of Art.

THE *Wonderful Machin*, or the *Aftronomical* and *Mu-fical* C L O C K, made by Mr. *CHRISTOPHER PINCHBECK*, (who made that which His Grace the Duke of *Newcaftle* made a prefent of to the *French* Ambaffador, the *Abbot du Bois*) is to be feen during the time of *Bartholomew-Fair*, at the *Barbers* the Corner of *Hofier-Lane*, in *Weft-Smith-Field*, *London*.

6.1 Christopher Pinchbeck advertisement, *The Weekly Journal or British Gazetteer*, 23 August 1718. © The British Library Board.

well as to fair-goers merely looking to be amazed. Their advertisements especially pitched entertainments to those who wanted to emulate elite society or just stay on top of the novelties of the fair. One advertisement for Pinchbeck's astronomical and musical clock announced that this clock, valued at one thousand guineas, was 'never shown before' though it was similar to one shown the previous year that had been 'purchas'd by a Noble peer of this Realm'.[39] In the previous year's advertisement for Pinchbeck's 1716 musical clock at Southwark Fair, the exhibitor announced that the clock – not the same as one shown previously in Fleet Street – might be purchased by impressed and wealthy spectators for 700 Guineas.[40]

Pinkethman and Pinchbeck's fair exhibits attracted all types of fair-goers, not only because they appealed to diverse crowds, but also because they also told stories and represented events people wanted to see. Patrons who viewed mechanized spectacles participated in a visual culture that reinforced their notions of what it meant to be English while presenting, also, idealized representations of the landscape and people's place within that landscape.[41] Fair-goers who viewed a 'Most curious and surprising picture invented by Mr. Penkethman [*sic*] and painted by Telleman of Antwerp and others', could be satisfied to know that in their patronage of this exhibit, they joined 'their Royal Highnesses the Prince and Princess of Wales', who had lately viewed the same picture at Richmond. Spectators watching this clockwork may have imagined themselves partaking in royal culture, not only because they viewed the same picture as their future king, but because this particular picture invited them to view, and appreciate, the entire royal lineage 'from the King of Bohemia to this Time'.[42] Viewers who witnessed the spectacle were educated in the heritage of their Hanoverian (and foreign) royal family. Pinkethman's clock featured metaphoric imagery intended to encourage patriotism and to quell any doubts viewers might have had about the power or loyalty of the German Hanoverians. The 'August Assembly' of Hanoverians portrayed on the clock was attended by the nine muses and incorporated next to mythic representations of Hercules killing the Hydra and 'the famous champion of England', St George, killing the dragon. The classical Roman and foundational English mythologies evoked by this display artistically reinforced the legitimacy of the Hanoverian ascendancy. Conveying that their new ruling family was both mighty and dedicated to defending the best interests of England, this clockwork did its part to ensure acceptance on the part of Londoners who lived in proximity to the still acclimating and not unchallenged rulers. According to the English world-view presented by this clock, the Hanoverians were positioned within a lineage of powerful rulers of England, from the Romans to legendary English heroes. The clock's message is particularly meaningful when understood in the context of the events of 1722, a year during which the Jacobean 'hydra' threatened to raise its head and seize London in the exposed and 'slain' Atterbury Plot.[43]

Mechanical clocks effectively communicated notions of political order with their combined metaphors of artistic representation and technology. Once wound, clocks kept measured time in predictable increments. If properly maintained, they would continue to drive themselves and the workings tied to the inner clock mechanism. This combination of technology and art underscored a political message that the current ruling family would similarly oversee Britain on its own measured path, keeping it strong and prosperous, as long as it had popular support. In

1728, Fawkes returned to Southwark Fair where he showed a 'musical temple of arts', consisting of 'two moving pictures'. One picture featured a concert of music, and the other more patriotic depiction featured a 'view of the city and bay of Gibraltar with the Spanish troops marching and countermarching, as tho in real action'. Viewers, of course, knew of and celebrated past British success against Spain at Gibraltar. A second machine with three moving pictures showed classical figures playing on instruments and a 'beautiful view of a river with swans and other fowls and fish sporting as tho alive'. Next to this idyllic and harmonic landscape was a 'prospect of the new Palace yard Westminster with the whole procession of the late Coronation of their present majesties walking from the Hall to the Abbey'.[44] Again, a popular exhibition reinforced the strength of England and its monarchs within a pleasing English landscape, demonstrating how the nation moved like clockwork.[45] The ruling family was incorporated as an instrumental piece of the workings that maintained British strength – both at home in its natural beauty and traditions and in its military success in the wider world.

The appeal of clocks to broad audiences is not entirely clear. While popular at fairs, they were accessible to anyone who chose to spend a few pence to see them. One case at the Old Bailey provides an intriguing glimpse into classed and gendered perceptions of mechanical clocks. When Elizabeth Pullwash (Pate) testified about her brutal assault and attempted rape outside Tottenham Court Fair in 1736, she realized how essential it was for her to explain why, at the time of her assault, she was unescorted outside the fair. As an unescorted woman, she left herself open for the accused to cast doubt on her sexuality and claim she invited his and his accomplice's advances. Pullwash defended her actions, describing how she encountered the perpetrators as she 'was … coming from the Fair'. Her sister and 'some other Company were with me', at the fair but she explained that, unlike them, she had 'stay'd a little longer than ordinary to see the Clock-work, so my Company was just gone before me', and continued, ' I staid a little behind them too, to tye up my Garter'.[46] Defending her modesty, Pullwash shared how she physically protected it by ensuring that her leg stayed properly covered and mentally assured it by attending such an innocent and instructive diversion as a clock. According to the public record, her mistake was keeping company with friends who deserted her at a dangerous time rather than staying behind to watch the clock display with her. While Elizabeth Pullwash may have been accurate or stretched the truth is not as important as what she chose to tell the court. While she might have stayed alone and after dark at the fair to watch or participate in a number of entertainments, she specifically mentioned to the court that she watched a clockwork display. A gendered understanding regarding the appropriateness of a respectable woman attending clockwork after dark (in lieu of other entertainments) may have prompted her to include this fact in her statement. One validation of her explanation is confirmed by newspaper advertisements – Pinchbeck mentioned in his 1729 Southwark Fair advertisement that his 'Grand Theatre of the Muses' could be seen 'any Time of the Day, till 11 at night', so it was possible to see them at a late hour.[47] Pullwash's testimony reveals her understanding of which types of entertainments were particularly suited for modest and discreet women. The clockwork contained only messages that supported the English nation accompanied by classical music, and did nothing to ignite female sexual desire. By explaining that she had just left a clockwork, tied up her garter and left Tottenham Court Fair, Pullwash created a pre-attack sober image of herself leaving the fair, caught up in thoughts of the beauty and majesty of England.

There were many opportunities for fair-goers to consume spectacles including national discourses about England's strength and military power versus those of other European powers. Military victories were often celebrated in popular fair amusements and such displays popularized patriotic views of Britain. British victories of The War of Spanish Succession, fought from 1702 to 1713, were repeatedly commemorated in fair entertainment and exhibits. At the 1706 Bartholomew Fair, William Pinkethman presented a new droll called, *The Siege of Barcelona or the Soldier's Fortune. With the taking of Fort Montjouy. Containing the Pleasant and Comical Exploits of that Renown'd Hero, Captain Blunderbuss and his Man Squib.*[48] The droll celebrated the pivotal capture of the Spanish Fort Montjuic in Barcelona by the Earl of Peterborough in 1705, yet in a manner suited to a fair. Some of the best-known London comedic actors, including William Bullock and 'Jubilee Dicky' Norris performed the central roles of common soldiers Blunderbuss and Squib.[49] The celebratory droll contained dramatic elements and as a means to engage all members of the audience, included a romantic hero 'Captain Lovewell' as well as, for the first time at Pinkethman's booth, two actresses, Mrs. Baxter and Mrs. Willis, playing 'Maria the Governor's Daughter' and the 'Dame of Honour'.[50]

During the War of Spanish Succession, Mr. Heatly's booth in Bartholomew Fair also capitalized by presenting a 'little Opera, called, The Old Creation of the World New Revived', which included an afterpiece featuring 'the Glorious Battle Obtained over the French and Spaniards by his grace the Duke of Marlbourough'.[51] In this mechanical

display, political events were presumably shown after biblical representations of Adam and Eve, Abraham and Isaac, the wise men worship-
ping Christ, and Dives and Lazarus. Such religious representations were
always popular subjects, but combined with a celebration of British
victory they connected Britain's political victories with divine sanction,
especially when presented in 'machines descending in a throne guarded
with multitudes of angels ...'.[52] It is difficult for us to reconstruct exactly
how such political and religious messages were understood. Audiences
who witnessed spectacles with these lofty themes also watched Heatly's
'large figures, which dance jigs, Sara bands, anticks, and country dancers
between every act', and the 'merry humours' of Punchinello.[53] Heatly
presented an amalgam of amusements at his booth hoping to reach
spectators with varied interests, as did Pinkethman, whose presentation
featured music, songs, and dances and was followed by 'Mr. Simpson,
the famous Vaulter'.[54] Such diverse entertainment mentioned in advertisements reveals that fair-booth proprietors expected audiences from
varied backgrounds: men and women, common and elite. Pinkethman
appealed to 'Quality' people in his advertisement, and we know that
Ladies, Gentlemen and, on occasion, nobility, did make up audiences
for fair entertainment.[55] Showmen did not envision their patrons
dichotomously – they either expected their entertainments to reach *both*
elite and popular audiences, or they believed individual audience members capable of understanding all messages in their entertainment, or
at least enough to want to stay. Heatly imagined people from all backgrounds would share an interest in important political events while also
knowing something about country dances and 'merry humours'.

Current or recent political affairs found their way into fair amusements in the form of musical clocks, peep shows, and dramatic entertainments. After the Siege of Gibraltar in 1727, an important victory for
Britain as it withstood Spanish challenges to the Peace of Utrecht, this
event became a popular theme of fair amusements. The siege was represented both in a peep show (depicted in the Bartholomew Fair fan)
and in 1728 when it was a subject in Fawkes's 'moving temple of arts'.[56]
Anti-Spanish sentiment obviously continued at London fairs in 1738, just
prior to the onset of the War of Jenkins' Ear (1739), when *The London
Evening Post* reported a humorous account of how during a puppet
show, a 'Punch stalking before the spectators in a Spanish Habit, gave
such Disgust to an English Dog Unmuzzled ... that he leap'd upon the
stage [and] seiz'd poor Punchenello'.[57] All of these shows helped consolidate notions of Britishness by supporting the legitimacy of monarchs
and depicting and celebrating British victories against European rivals.

Fair amusements provided Londoners from various income levels occasions to participate in this national dialogue – popular consumption of fair amusements was an accessible means through which national identity was forged.[58]

Local and metropolitan identity was celebrated and consolidated at fairs, as well. At his 1730 Southwark Fair booth, Fawkes displayed a mechanical clock representing an 'artificial view of the world'. This musical clock included representations of Windsor Castle, a 'Curious Prospect of the University and City of Oxford', and the 'famous City of London' along with a prospect of 'the Ancient City of Venice'.[59] Here, England's glory in majesty, learning, and commerce was celebrated as comparable to that of the great city of Venice. Shown in London, this exhibit particularly communicated to Londoners that they resided in a city similar to very few other European cities, past and present. Ordinary fair-goers who viewed these exhibits acquired a new perspective on urban life. It would have been rare for most viewers to travel to Venice, though those who travelled with the commerce of fairs had likely been to Oxford. This representation provided fair-goers the opportunity to consider England's greatest cities not only in relation to another legendary, commercial city; this image may also have provided viewers with a different perspective on their own urban environment. Walking the city streets likely did not provide people the opportunity to imagine what the environment looked like as a whole, from a distance. Landscapes such as these provided idealized, organic depictions of urban environments. These were the predecessors to later, and much larger, landscape exhibits presented in the late eighteenth and early nineteenth centuries.[60]

Londoners also found opportunities to celebrate their metropolitan history and identities in dramatic entertainment presented at fairs. Plays both critiqued and celebrated life in this expanding city and in the process participated in the construction of people's shared understandings of living, working, and playing in London. The inhabitants and city officials of London are depicted as loyal English subjects in *Wat Tyler and Jack Straw: or, the Mob Reformers*. This droll was performed at Giffard's Great Theatrical Booth during the 1730 Bartholomew Fair and was accompanied by an exhibition of what was purported to be the dagger that killed Wat Tyler.[61] In this show, the Lord Mayor of London, Sir William Walworth, and his son, Young Walworth, are depicted as loyal heroes who save not only the City, but also their monarch, Richard II, from a Kentish rebellion led by Wat Tyler and Jack Straw during the 1381 Peasant's Rebellion. Tyler was killed in Smithfield, making Bartholomew Fair an appropriate location for this dramatic presentation. Watching this droll in its historic setting, Londoners learned the history of their city's allegiance to England.

In the prologue to the play, audiences were reminded that though heroic acts were popular themes, play-booth proprietors need not look to ancient history for inspiration – English history had its share of heroic adventurers. The prologue's actor asked:

> Why shou'd the Muse for Foreign Actions roam,
> When she can find Heroick ones at home;
> Our English Annal nobler Feats displays,
> Than e'er were told of antient Roman Days;
> In the bright Page immortal Walworth shines,
> And stands recorded in the fairest Lines.[62]

Audiences obviously agreed, and *Wat Tyler* was popular enough that it replaced a portion of the entertainments planned at the booth – it was also printed and sold for 6d. As part of the show, Giffard and Pinkethman (his business partner that year) presented a replica performance of that year's Lord Mayor's pageant, a yearly event following the election of a new Lord Mayor in which civic pride was showcased by individual guilds who created and displayed floats representing the goods and status of their companies.[63] This combination of entertainments leaves us little doubt that the play-booth proprietors wanted their audience to sympathize with the Lord Mayor's perspective in the dramatic presentation.

The characters of important Londoners in this droll, including the Lord Mayor, his son, and citizens, are constructed as urban, strong, controlled (though sometimes made a bit blind by love, as in the case of young Walworth) and, above all, loyal to the King. These upstanding citizens are opposed to a 'mob' of Kentish peasants, portrayed as lacking both common sense and formal education. This juxtaposition reinforced eighteenth-century notions of the distance between rural and urban manners. The peasants follow Tyler unquestioningly – or, if they question, their inquiries are too ignorant to be meaningful. In one scene Tyler, drunk from brandy, sleeps while his 'chancellor' Zekiel Pease-Stack rallies the rebels. Pease-Stack rouses the rebels by simultaneously invoking and dismissing religion. He claims that the rebellion does not need the 'Cloak of Religion', though after examining scripture, he finds that 'it does not encourage us (that I can find) to undertake this Rebellion, yet this I am positively assur'd of, that it does not say one Word against it', and though it asks subjects to be loyal to their kings, it 'sure does not mention *Richard,* [and] *England* is not once mentioned in the whole Bible'. To this statement, a Kentish man argues, 'but I am sure that in the latter End of the first Side of my Bible at home, I read – London, printed by…'.[64] In this droll, being a Londoner makes one knowledgeable and loyal. Those who come from regions surrounding London, not even a great distance away, are portrayed as less-educated, not able to think for themselves, and easily misled into becoming disloyal subjects.

As depicted in *Wat Tyler*, the character of Londoners consists of both local and national loyalty and pride. The underlying message is that Londoners have the unique historical responsibility to stop rebellions and disorderly activities within their city for the immediate threat they posed to the national institutions – King and Parliament – housed in the metropolis. The threat of Jacobite rebellions haunted both local and national government throughout the late seventeenth and early eighteenth centuries, which most likely accounts for the retelling of the Wat Tyler and the Peasant's Rebellion legend. Londoners were familiar with needing to remain vigilant against political plots. *Wat Tyler* communicated to London audiences that their citizens' allegiance to the monarch had a long heritage in English history and never questioned that Londoners would support their ruler. In the droll, the Lord Mayor of London assures the King of London citizens' loyalty and might, saying: 'Think not we citizens can only Trade: our Arms, great Sir, can lift the Sword as well, and know when Justice and our King wou'd strike'.[65] At the conclusion of the play, the Lord Mayor and his son heroically prove this to be true as they strike down the rebel Wat Tyler in Smithfield, Young Walworth stabbing him, and the Lord Mayor '[sending a] loyal Dagger to [his] Heart'.[66] As reward for this loyalty, Richard bestows upon the coat of arms of London: 'That Dagger which thy loyal Hand so well, Employ'd in the Deliverance of thy Country, [as] a glorious Ornament'. As a final statement that the City of London's proper place is as a faithful supporter of the nation's monarch, *Wat Tyler* ends with Richard II proclaiming, ''Till in the happy Years of *George's* Reign, Another Race shall grace our Isle again, Loyal as this, undaunted, and as free, Great, and not proud – yet proud of Liberty'.[67] Hanoverian audiences thus received a strong message constituting their own royal support as part of a long-standing and noble civic tradition.

Not all treatments of London life were as celebratory and patriotic as *Wat Tyler*, however. Londoners' conception of themselves as projected in fair theatre revolved just as much around the city's institutions and inhabitants. In a city whose growing population challenged over-taxed and poorly managed authorities in their efforts to ensure social order, city institutions and officials easily became fodder for satire. In this way, fair theatre retained the earlier tradition of 'festive misrule' within temporary play booths, which sometimes became occasions allowing Londoners to vent everyday frustrations.[68] City officials were especially good targets because their attempts to regulate fair amusements made them the adversaries of fairs. One play performed in 1728 at Lee, Harper, and Spiller's booth in Bartholomew Fair and later at Southwark Fair – *The Quaker's Opera* – poked fun at London's gaol-keepers, attorneys and other city officials.[69] A shortened ballad opera, and one of many imitations of Gay's *Beggar's Opera*, *The Quaker's Opera* responds to city attempts to regulate play-booth entertainment in its prologue, a dialogue between a player and a reform-minded Quaker. This Quaker's son is the playwright, and the player wonders why the Quaker father has allowed his son's play to be 'expos'd to the Prophane'. The Quaker's reasoning echoes city officials' opinions regarding dramatic entertainment. Though he argues that 'the Stage is a well-instituted thing, if not Corrupted', he goes on to say that it has been lately 'debas'd and revert[ed] from its Original Intention [of] exposing … Follies and Vice in an agreeable manner'. Instead of improving audiences, the Quaker argues, recent plays 'set odious and abominable Characters off in the most Ornamental Colours, and thereby incourage Lewdness and Immorality'.[70] Though the Quaker father believes that nothing good can come from dramatic performance, he is faced with reality: his son has left him and his religion and, despite his father's advice, become a playwright. A generational dispute and hope of a father/son reconciliation motivates the Quaker to consider the *actual* social effects of his son's play. He hopes to determine that despite his worries, his son's play will produce no harm. Here, the dramatist imbues his Quaker father with the understanding fair-goers and performers hoped their own *City* fathers would adopt. By observing his son's play, the Quaker wishes not only to indulge his boy, but also to recover him and 'keep him from greater Extravagancies'. Plays may have been full of scandalous remarks and actions, but those who produced, performed, and attended them no doubt thought they were the lesser of the many evils plaguing London. *The Quaker's Opera* poses this question: 'Are plays themselves actually dangerous, or can they be viewed, instead, as instruments keeping people from 'greater Extravagancies?' Thus, the play's narrator reveals a tension still extant between understandings of plays as damaging to social order and an older understanding of fair entertainment as a 'safety valve' necessary to relieve social pressures.

The play opens in Newgate, where Rust and Careful, the two goal-keepers, plan the best means of profiting from the prison's current most interesting inhabitant, the infamous criminal Shepard. Over the course of the play, Rust and Careful are visited by a drunken Quaker, a gentleman, and an Irishman, all of whom pay a fee to get a look at Shepard. The men are disappointed, however, when they find that Shepard has escaped before they are able to view him in his cell. The Quaker laments the certain danger England (and its commerce) will face now that Shepard has escaped. With this criminal on the loose, he cries 'Woe to the Shopkeepers' and dealers in Ware and he weeps for the sins of the Nation. Meanwhile, Shepard is the only character exhibiting industriousness, having escaped and met up with his den of thieves. Here, he resolves to use his time productively, explaining that while in prison he contemplated 'the lazy Life [he] led'. Now free, he exclaims, 'let me not be Idle – Idleness is the Road to the Gallows'. He even encounters a young man with so much ambition and 'Love of [Shepard's] great Actions' that he hopes to be apprenticed to him and learn the 'Mystery of Thieving'. *The Quaker's Opera* inverts the world of show, turning London's criminal system into the 'real' disorderly festival diverting people from commerce and religion while promoting a work ethic only among its criminals. Everyone from lawyers to religious reformers to constables is too concerned with his own self-interests to be effectual in his occupations; at the same time, criminals are industrious.

By presenting this elaborate droll, Lee, Harper, and Spiller questioned whether or not campaigns against idleness and immorality were focused on the right types of urban behaviour and whether or not male authorities' fears actually reflected social realities. The drama also questioned whether or not moral male authority understood or knew how to implement what was best for London. This play engages with and critiques discourses directed at restricting play-booth entertainment, revealing that it was easy to circumvent local regulation attempts. Though fair drolls sometimes offended and challenged London authorities' notions of what entailed a properly ordered commercial city, they remained a central aspect of London amusement, and therefore, London identity. Laughing at the city's inability to effectively deal with crime, drunkenness, and even fairs was one way to cope with the city's social problems.

Beyond representations and entertainments associated with the urban environment, notions of common local and national identity were often centred on an appreciation of the English land and seascape. Pastoral themes in early Stuart painting and literature had been invoked to 'reduce the distance between the urban and the rural', reminding England's landed elite, increasingly present in London, of the source of their authority in the countryside.[71] This pastoral impulse was present at a popular level in the later exhibitions of mechanized landscape paintings

at fairs. Idyllic portraits depicting the wonder and beauty of natural set-
tings celebrated places far from the urban clutter and disorder of London.
Pinchbeck's 'grand theatre of the muses' displayed in 1729 at Southwark
Fair contributed to a growing tradition of providing natural retreats to
Londoners within their urban environment. This movement was literally
manifest in pleasure resorts such as Vauxhall Gardens, opened in 1726 by
Jonathan Tyres.[72] Before these commercialized garden resorts, leisure-
seeking Londoners who could not actually leave the city imaginatively
inhabited the rural spaces depicted in mechanical pictures and musical
clocks. Accompanied by music composed by Handel, Corelli, and 'other
celebrated masters', viewers enjoyed their respite from the crowded,
dusty, and hot fair as they examined 'a landscape with a view of the sea,
terminating insensibly at a very great distance; with ships sailing plying
to windward and diminishing by degrees as they seem to go further from
the eye … till they disappear'. On the shore, spectators could see 'horse-
men, carts, chaises, etc. passing along the wheel turning round as tho on
the road, the men and horses altering their position to keep themselves
upright', and 'swans swimming, fishing and feathering themselves their
motions as natural as tho really alive'.[73] Mechanical pictures such as
Pinchbeck's allowed popular audiences to participate in a valorization
of natural settings found in the elite culture of aristocratic gardens or
landscape portraiture. They also provided any members of the gentry in
town a reminder of their homes in the country and reinforced the idea
even to those removed from the sea or countryside that England's natural resources and land were its real source of wealth.[74]

Fair exhibits both created and consolidated Londoners' notions of
metropolitan versus rural identity. Though mechanical figures and wax
replicas of living beings were common at fairs, the notion that 'common'
people would not understand them in their appropriate, Enlightenment
context provided middling people a means by which to define themselves against less-educated and less-worldly folk. In *The London Spy*,
Ned Ward's protagonists visit an exhibition of mechanical wax works,
advertised by a 'Comical Figure Gaping and Drumming', at the entrance
of a Bartholomew Fair attraction. Here, they admire the exhibition and
observe the responses of fair-goers who are less aware than they are
of the science behind mechanics and natural philosophy. Ward's satirical portrait of popular response to this figure reveals his and his audiences' belief that such objects were out of the realm of ordinary English
people's understanding. Though such figures were quite common at
fairs and most likely understood by ordinary viewers as replicas of life,
Ward's main characters reinforce middling and elite notions that such

figures represented new scientific advances not yet encountered by some Britons, particularly the more 'Ignorant Spectators' who 'crowded beneath' the display. He depicted these common folk as so amazed by the sight, and fooled by the representation that they cried out, 'Lord! do but see how he stares at us, and Gnashes his Teeth as if he could eat us for looking at him'.[75]

Ward's humorous presentation of popular response to an automaton is driven by his understanding of the appropriate response educated spectators should have while witnessing such a spectacle, and he educates his reader about the appropriate reaction to such exhibits. His narrative reveals conflicting notions regarding the usefulness and pleasure of man-made marvels such as automatons and wax figures. Ward presents a separation between learned response to life-like reproductions and popular, more visceral responses to these figures. Instead of sharing with a wider group of spectators one's physical and psychological response to the figure, Ward's protagonists have a more measured response. It is the 'naturalness', not the imagined horror of the spectacle, which induces the London spies to more closely view this exhibit. They enter the exhibit because they are impressed by the exact reproduction of a 'Wax-Baby' displayed outside the entrance. Once inside, they are 'astonish'd [by] the Liveliness of the Figures, who sat in such easie [sic] Postures'. Knowing full well that these were lifelike reproductions of people, and not willing to be swept up in an imaginative response to the figures, they focus instead on details. With a controlled manner, they remark upon the figure's hands, which are 'dispos'd with such a becoming freedom', and they comment that 'Life it self could not have appear'd less stiff, or the whole Frame more regular'. These two rational viewers notice, especially, the 'tenderness' of the figure's eyes which, to them, makes this a superior display knowing that reproducing lifelike and expressive eyes is quite difficult to master. Their delight in the waxworks, or 'Temple of Diana', as the booth proprietor calls it, is informed by their reasoned understanding of the skill it took to execute such a reproduction. Familiar with the scientific practice of such life-reproductions, they dispassionately evaluate the skill with which it is executed. This is not the case with a 'Country Carter in his Boots', who viewed the waxworks.[76]

The London spies watch as this man, who drove a hay cart for a living, hesitantly makes his way into the wax figure exhibit. At the door of the room, he 'peeps in, and seeing, as he thought, such a Number of Great Persons steps back and doffs his Hat'. Not able to distinguish between reality and representation, as the London spies so skilfully do, this man proclaims, "Ads-bleed … I want gooe in amang zo many vine

Vouk, not I; … Pray gim mau my Money agan, for I don't come here to be Laugh'd at', which is exactly what the booth's occupants proceed to do. [77] Not wanting to return this man's admission fee, the 'Mistress of the Show' attempts to convince the 'Bumpkin' that these were not living creatures. The humorous episode continues with the man at last entering the booth, only to ask the proprietor, 'They are woundy Silent. I pray you, Vorzooth, can they Speak?' At this comment, all of the 'Young Damsels' also present in the booth 'fell a Laughing, saying, You must Speak to 'em first, and then, perhaps, they'll Answer you'. The crowded booth continues to be entertained by the country-man's response, as he does proceed to speak to the figures and is frustrated by their silence as well as his fellow fair-goer's commentary. He is especially upset by a 'Notable pert Gentlewoman', who asks him, 'what would you think of that Lady you spoke to for a Bed-fellow?' to which he responded, without her makeup and fine clothing, she might look 'as Ugly as you do Vorzooth'. That this country man who is unable to understand this auto-mated world is nevertheless able to '[dash] the Lady out of Countenance, [whose] Blushes shew'd she had a modest Sense of her own Failings and Imperfections',[78] is interesting because it reveals the power masculin-ity bestowed upon a man of any economic background. Though Ward characterizes this noble woman as having a modest and socially accept-able response to the cart-man's come-back, it is interesting that the only authority he provides this otherwise powerless male figure comes from his ability to appeal to a larger gender hierarchy in which learning mat-ters less than sex.[79]

Ward portrays different classed and gendered responses to waxwork depictions of life. In the later eighteenth century, with the turn to 'sensi-bility' and its emphasis on emotion over reason, the goal of such displays may have been to produce particular emotions within the viewers.[80] In the late eighteenth century, the London spies would have had the curious reaction and might have been perceived as lacking in the appropriate feelings. The waxwork displays of the late-Stuart fairground could have been easily transformed into sublime experiences in the late eighteenth century.

Englishness and fair monstrosities

In the late seventeenth century, 'monsters' and other natural wonders were exhibited in the Strand (especially around Charing Cross) and in Fleet Street.[81] As the eighteenth century progressed, London entrepreneurs recognized the commercial value of public interest in natural philosophy.

Once only commonly exhibited at European courts or to members of England's Royal Society founded in 1662, businessmen in possession of curious people, natural wonders, and machines now displayed them to paying customers.[82] Coffee house and tavern owners attempted to attract good paying customers to their shops by procuring curiosities or contracting exhibits more wonderful than those of their competitors. In 1698, for example, a 'monster' was exhibited at Moncress's Coffeehouse near the Royal-Exchange where, for sixpence, a customer might view this creature who 'lately died there'. It was 'Humane upwards, and Bruit [sic] downwards, Wonderful to behold'.[83] At the Golden-Cross near Charing Cross a more costly fee (2s 6d) gained one entry to see 'Faemina, Mas, Marus, Mundi mirabile monstrum, An Hermaphrodite (Lately brought over from Angola)'. Only those with formal educations (and most likely, mostly men) could decipher what exactly a paying customer would see as the second half of the advertisement containing a 'scientific' description of this 'monster's' genitalia appeared only in Latin.[84] Realizing the profitability of featuring curiosities in one's place of business, a Charing Cross coffee house asked 'all persons who may have curiosities to be dispos'd of and for the conveniency of the curious and those of the most elegant Tasted', to consider selling any of their unwanted 'curiosities in art and nature (which are not cumbersome) viz. medals, antient coins, bustos, mechanical performances, pieces of antiquity, manuscripts, stones, minerals, fossils, insects, and other uncommon products'. This unusual 1736 advertisement attests to the continuing popularity and profitability of curious exhibitions well into the eighteenth century.[85]

Though there were opportunities in London to view living and deceased monsters, 'wonder's [sic] of nature' or 'great curiosities', throughout the year, common Londoners would not have found these sites very accessible. Their opportunity to marvel at nature's mysteries (at much lower prices) came at yearly fairs. Some exhibitions presented at fairs were likely the same exhibited in the slightly more exclusive venues of Strand and Fleet Street coffee houses and taverns. People who viewed the various curious sights of fairs learned about lives very different from their own. They encountered new fashions, were educated with representations of military victories, viewed animals, people, and plants brought to London through Britain's colonial trade network, and examined new inventions. The curious exhibits of fairs provided fair-goers with sights and sounds against which they might understand their own place in the world as British subjects and/or Londoners. These shows contributed to developing notions of race and consolidated gender systems and ideas about sexuality.

Natural marvels and strange people or animals promised to draw crowds away from the many other fair amusements. Some shopkeepers who worked in or around areas that became fairs for part of the year used this as an opportunity to acquaint customers with their product and hopefully promote their own trade. For example, in 1716, a Perfumer in Southwark, presented a 'Human Skeleton, or the Skeleton of a Man, which by a Mechanical Projection performs several very strange and surprising Actions, also Groans like a Dying Person and Smoaks [sic] a Pipe of Tobacco ...'.[86] In the late seventeenth century, an Irish 'Gyant-like Young-Man' was on display at a shop in Cow-Lane-End during Bartholomew Fair, and at Mrs. Croomes, at the Sign of the Shoe and Slap, the 'Wonder of Nature' awaited paying fair-goers.[87] This particular 'wonder' was a

> girl above Fifteen years of Age, born in Cheshire, and not much above eighteen inches long, having never a perfect Bone in any part of her, only the head, yet she hath all her senses to admiration; and Discourses, reads very well, sings, whistles, and all very pleasant to hear.[88]

Curious exhibits sponsored by shopkeepers were an effort to exploit the increased traffic of fairs and bring customers into their shops where they might promote their usual trade. Should customers not buy any goods, at least the shopkeeper had the shilling or so that customers paid to view the curiosity.

Shopkeepers wrote detailed advertisements and handbills in which they traced the lineage of the various specimens or people they exhibited. Shopkeepers and fair exhibitors who displayed such objects depended on their audience's awareness of what constituted a 'natural' marvel and they hoped spectators would share some interest in 'scientific' examination. In the late seventeenth century, a shopkeeper next to the Black Raven in West Smithfield exhibited 'A Changling Child' during Bartholomew Fair. This child was a 'Living Skeleton', unusual not only for its physical appearance, but because it was such a rare thing and obtained for view in London only due to a series of accidental encounters initiated by trade and worldwide connections. The child was 'Taken by a Venetian Galley, from a Turkish Vessel in the Archipelago'. This 'fairy child' was 'supposed to be born of Hungarian parents, but changed in the nursery, aged nine years and more, not exceeding a foot and a half high'. Its legs and arms were so small that 'they scarce exceed the bigness of a man's thumb'. This creature's face, which was 'no bigger than the palm of one's hand', was 'so grave and solid as if it were threescore years old'. Patrons were welcome to examine this natural wonder and promised that they might witness 'the whole anatomy of its body by setting it against the sun, or by holding candles behind it'. They were also warned that the creature never spoke, but only cried 'like a cat'. Though it was toothless, this was the 'most voracious and hungry creature in the world [and it] devours more victuals than the stoutest man in England'.[89]

Advertisers selling their exhibits of curious people and objects in print were aware of the diverse audiences such spectacles might attract. Wealthy collectors such as Sloane (and others) famously attended fair exhibits, and those who hosted or provided these exhibits may have hoped such patrons would purchase curious objects. Beyond hoping to make a windfall from showing objects or people in fairs, fair exhibitors hoped to attract and accommodate as many paying spectators as possible. One means by which they did this was to give their objects special meaning by embedding them in a wider world of commerce, adventure, and the 'exotic'. With London being a port city, late seventeenth- and early-eighteenth-century Londoners were no doubt aware of the many goods and people being produced and residing in England's already vast and expanding colonial world. Not only did goods pour into the capital city, its shops, and the homes of the wealthy (where they would be viewed not only by genteel families, but also by their visitors and domestic servants), but colonial themes were often also featured in print.[90] If a Londoner could not read, there were many visual reminders of England's wider world networks from the signs advertising shops and inns to oral accounts individuals may have heard from soldiers returning from sites of colonial contests, or maritime workers from the 'Atlantic maritime culture'.[91] Fair, coffee house, and tavern exhibits of 'monsters' and other curiosities contributed to people's understanding of England's wider colonial world, the people, plants, and objects that inhabited it, and their place in relation to England's subjects. Notions of the superiority of English religion as well as ideas about race and the superiority of whiteness were created, reinforced, and spread to a popular audience through fair exhibits. Newspapers or printed advertisements of such exhibits contributed to a growing mass culture of colonial and racial knowledge, as well.

Not convinced his 'prodigious Monster' (a man with one head and two bodies 'both Masculine') exhibited in Bartholomew Fair during the early eighteenth century would draw enough spectators for its deformity alone, a Mr. Parker elaborated his advertisement to include this 'monster's' heritage. What made this exhibit interesting went beyond its physical difference: in fact, its mystery was enhanced by its origins and family relations. Parker described how this 'curiosity' was 'brought over from the great Moguls Countrey by Sir Thomas Grantham', while accompanied by his brother 'a Priest of the Mahometan Religion'.[92] For 6d, or 1s for the 'best places', thrill-seekers would get two curiosities for the price of one – a prodigious Monster as well as his brother – and both Muslim. Seeing such an advertisement in print or paying to view it in person contributed to understandings of religions besides Christianity as different – in this case, being non-Christian was nearly as odd as being a two-bodied monster. Encountering a Muslim in the streets of London may have been even more unusual than encountering a monster, which is why the monster's 'brother' is featured so prominently in this advertisement.

Notions of difference consolidated and created by fair exhibits for a popular audience included ideas that being anything other than white, English, and Protestant was somewhat remarkable. English encounters with individuals of different religious persuasions and skin colour multiplied as colonial ventures, trade networks, and military conflicts with European states in other parts of the world increased. Scholars have begun to analyse how these worldwide encounters contributed to English understandings of race. During England's early period of colonial expansion, languages of race were pivotal to the creation of English and later British national identity. As England's interest in colonial trade and travel to Africa grew in the mid-sixteenth century, elite cultural products such as sonnets, plays, court masques, cameos, and portraits began to reflect a 'semantic shift' in the use of the binary opposition between fair and dark, especially in discussions of beauty.[93] These new understandings emerged in a nation increasingly aware of its geographically isolated position and unsure of its place in the world vis-à-vis other European and world powers. In this context, elites developed a 'race prejudice' that reassured them, minimized their sense of insecurity, and enhanced group cohesion.[94] English elites used their sixteenth-century encounters with Africa, for example, as one means to shape British identity not only as 'white' as opposed to black African bodies, but also as ordered around a particular 'civil' gender and familial order.[95] Late seventeenth- and early eighteenth-century fair exhibits illustrate how similar understandings of British identity defined by manners, gender, religion, and skin colour formed at a popular level.[96]

The foreign as commodity

A passage in Ned Ward's *The London Spy* reveals how popular ideas about race and gender coalesced at fairs. The two protagonists stop to watch an entertainment performed by a '*Negro* woman and *Irish* Woman'. One man from the country who is also in the audience finds this display amusing and somewhat shocking. Before the two women even begin their performance, the man is sent into fits of laughter by merely observing the black woman. The 'country' London spy asked his fellow rural-dweller what he found amusing, to which the man replied, 'I have oftentimes heard of the Devil upon two Sticks, but never zee it bevore in my Life … who can forbear Laughing to see the Devil going to Dance?'[97] This country character refers to a figure in popular lore. Ward refers to the character here, and it was later featured in the 1707 *Le Diable Boiteux*, written by Alain René Le Sage, a novel which was based on an earlier Spanish work. A 1708 version of this story purportedly performed at May Fair described the Devil upon two sticks as 'a very surprizing [sic] figure … resting upon two crutches with goats legs, a long sharp chin, a yellow and black complexion, a very flat Nose, and eyes that seem'd like two lighted coals'.[98] Ward's country man envisions the 'devil upon two sticks' similarly, and this view informs his perception of the black acrobat woman. Not only would the bumpkin's comparison of this woman to a demonic character in a popular legend reveal that the bumpkin believes the two shared physical characteristics, but as well, Ward's comparison casts the black woman as spiritually inferior. As 'the devil', she is no less than the manifest opposite of God.

While this woman represented 'the devil' and seemed an almost indescribable curiosity to at least one audience member, the Irish woman represented tangible barbarity. Her body was described in detail, giving her a completely uncivilized character and making her the epitome of impoliteness and masculinity. Her shoulders were 'of an *Atlas-Built*; her Buttocks as big as two Bushel-Loaves, and shak'd as she Danc'd like two Quaking Puddings'. To the London spies, the woman's lack of civility was evident to the audience during her 'grand finale'. Ready to demonstrate the 'utmost of her Excellencies', the 'poor creature' 'Cut a Caper as high as a Hog Trough, [when] she happen'd to strain her Twatling-strings, and let fly an unsavory Sound, as loud as a Note of the double Curtel'. Upon this unfortunate occurrence, one audience member from the country admonished the woman, yelling, 'Wounds, my Lady, … have a care you don no [sic] fall, for by the Mass you made the Rope give a woundy Crack'. The other men 'laughed; the Women they Blush'd; Madam *Lump* quitted the Rope with a shameful Expedition'.[99] Through the lens of their own understandings of proper gender and sexual order, the English 'mapped' ideas of difference onto the indigenous bodies of those they encountered in the world, from Africa to Ireland.[100] English value judgments of 'others' were themselves 'coloured' by gendered and sexualized belief systems.

Popular understandings of race are largely ignored in recent studies of race in early modern England, which are primarily focused on elite culture.[101] However, it is clear from late seventeenth- and eighteenth-century fair advertisements of monsters and other curiosities as well as literary and visual depictions of this industry that popular notions of difference were being negotiated during this period. Popular audiences encountered notions of race and difference at fair exhibitions, which reinforced notions of whiteness or gender and sexual order for people unable to physically encounter other regions of the world. Bringing the people and objects of colonial holdings and 'exotic' locales home and displaying them as curiosities contributed to popular conceptions of a hegemonic English position in relation to others, both in the world and within the British Isles.[102] The nature of fair exhibits featuring monsters or natural wonders culturally reinforced for popular audiences a relationship that divided the exhibit and viewer into a 'spectacle' and 'spectator', and emphasized the superiority of the paying customer.[103] Displayed in booths and rooms adjacent to exhibitions of automatons, waxworks, and machines, human and animal shows were presented to spectators as one of many unusual curious fair exhibits. They were pulled from their indigenous contexts and displayed not as humans, animals, or plants living within a viable society or ecosystem, but instead were featured alongside other curiosities as components in a living cabinet of curiosity in which Londoners could roam and process the order and nature of the wider world. Beyond making up a living cabinet of curiosity, however, such fair displays reinforced conceptions of the people and things of empire as commodities.

Fair exhibitors and shopkeepers presumed customers would have enough knowledge of the wider world to be intrigued by the possibility to witness living things (and people) from diverse world locales, but at the same time they educated people about these distant places. From the 'Mountains of Leamea' came two rattle snakes, one of which rattled so that one 'may hear him at a quarter of a mile almost'. An unnamed 'fine creature, of small size, taken in Mocca, that burrows under ground', was displayed in Bartholomew Fair, as were a 'Sea Snail' from the Coast of India, teeth from a dead rattlesnake, the 'horn of a flying buck', and a 'curious collection of Animals and Insects from all Parts of the World'.[104] Human specimens (both living and dead) were displayed alongside other 'Strange Rarities', a practice that undoubtedly reinforced the public's understanding of them as commodities divested of humanity.

In an effort to communicate the difference of their displays, exhibitors often compared their human displays to mythical figures familiar to

English people. During Queen Anne's reign those who visited the Harts-House in Pye Corner during Bartholomew Fair could view 'A Little Farey Woman' from Italy. This woman was 'but two foot two inches high, the shortest that ever was seen in England'. In this advertisement, the exhibitor disassociates his 'fairy' from his competitors, saying that his is in 'no ways Deform'd, as the other two Women are, that are carried about the Streets in Boxes from house to house ... this being Thirteen Inches shorter than either of them'.[105] While such exhibitors ignored the humanity of their displays in their advertisements, some scholars have argued this was one means by which a person who embodied some sort of difference could find a livelihood in early modern Europe.[106]

In some cases, fair exhibitions of interesting people consolidated early modern notions of race and difference at a popular level while evoking people's compassion for the person's humanity. This was particularly true of the 'tall Black, called the Indian-King', who was displayed as a curiosity at the Golden-Lyon Inn during one Bartholomew Fair. This man stood in front of Golden-Lyon customers wearing his 'Indian Garb', while customers heard details of his trials and tribulations, provided so that spectators understood how this man's life had been disrupted by world trade networks: '[he was] Betrayed on Board of an English Interloper, and Barbarously abused on Board of that Ship, by one Waters and his Men, and put in Irons; from thence [he was] carried to Jamaica and sold there for a Slave, and now redeem'd by a merchant in London; the like hath not been seen in England'. The irony of this passage, of course, is that the advertiser chastises the inhumanity with which this noble man was treated while forcing him to stand in 'Indian Garb' and charging people 3d to see him.[107] This particular display is interesting because it contributed on a popular level to an emerging British understanding of themselves as more humane in their treatment of 'others' than rival European nations were.

Besides displays of 'Indian noble men', fair-goers might find exhibits from closer to home. Though from the British Isles, these curiosities seemed just as foreign as those from around the world. Such exhibits informed Londoners and viewers from surrounding areas that there were recesses within England and its environs that were nearly as mysterious as the farthest reaches of the Earth. The short Cheshire girl, or 'wonder of nature' from near the Welsh border must have intrigued fair-goers not only because of her height, but also because of her origins within a vastly different culture.[108] Wonders from around Britain from the late seventeenth and early eighteenth centuries included the 'Wonderful Tall Essex Woman ... Seven foot high, and Proportionable [*sic*] to her

Height', a 'Woman Dwarf, but Three Foot and one Inch high, born in Sommersetshire', and Irish 'Gyant-like Young-Man', and 'a Tall English-man eight foot high, but seventeen years of Age'.[109] The exhibition of people from around the British Isles who were markedly different from the average person taught fair-goers about differences close to home.

Trouble in the cloisters

Though fairs communicated and consolidated notions of London or even British identity to fair-goers, these festivals were also often opportunities to contest dominant understandings of the orderly nation.[110] Popular understandings of the appropriate use of urban space drove an alterna-tive world to that of the mechanically driven clocks and automatons found in more open areas of fairs. Gaming and prostitution were noto-rious attractions commonly found in secluded corners or alleys. City officials regularly attempted to curtail gaming at fairs, but it nevertheless remained popular. One writer describes both the allure and danger of gambling at fairs. Inside a crowded Gaming-Room 'Rakes and Footmen', maybe even a Lord '*incognito*', all 'make a splendid show'.[111] Appearances were likely deceiving, however, and all was not splendid. This writer warned the unwise that in such rooms 'Country Youths, from trad-ing Shop releas'd, With sharping Gamesters have their Breeches eas'd, By yielding Stakes, o'er Thoughtless they prevail, To cheat, false Dice, and Bullying ne'er fail'. The losers of these games 'stamp and swear, Go home, and curse the Time they went to Fair; An Hour's Pleasure starves them all the Year'.[112] In this poem, the author echoes city officials' fears that gaming did not ruin Londoners with expendable funds – it was the young working men of London who were most susceptible to attractions such as gaming and sexual intrigue, and their moral destruction could potentially cost London the most. If distracted from their occupations and divested of their money, young men would not only become a drain on city institutions providing charity, but immersed in amusements such as gaming and drinking, they might become an unwieldy and socially disruptive force. City officials as well as social critics were well aware that containing youth and masculinity was essential to maintaining both social and commercial order in the city.[113]

Other perilous locations at fairs included music booths. Though they seemed innocent, they in fact attracted some of the city's most 'unsa-voury' folk. The author of *A Walk to Smithfield: or, a true description of the humours of Bartholomew Fair*, exercises his will when he encoun-ters the door of a music booth, which he refuses to enter. Conscious of his well-being as well as his reputation, he thinks twice before entering because 'Reformation of Manners had suppress'd them all but one', and so he 'declin'd going thither, least [he] should be thought a Debauch'd person'.[114] This writer refers, tongue in cheek, to reformation of manners societies' focus on these institutions, which Josiah Woodward referred to as '*Nursuries of Lewdness and Debauchery*', where 'some of both Sexes had shamelessly danced naked in these licentious Brothels', and that the disorder caused by such behaviour had caused 'above twenty Murders ... in a very little time'.[115] The London spies, on the other hand, heartily visited a music booth. While there, they heard music poorly performed, saw soldiers entranced by 'Scoundrel Strumpets', drunken madams 'rural sots', and dance-challenged sailors.[116] Already aware of the reputation of music booths prior to entering, the two label them 'Diabolical Academies, where ... all sorts of Wickedness [is] practic'd for the good Instruction of unwary youth, who are too apt to imbibe the Poisonous Draughts that flow from these pernicious Fountains, to which we often owe the Sorrows of our Riper Years'.[117] Though they know better, they enter the booth and what they witness there certainly meets their expectations.

Debauchery only continued at night, in the cloisters and dark recesses of fairs. As some customers enjoyed the thrills of the 'ups and downs' or 'whirligigs' located around the outside of fairs, others went in search of sexual pleasure.[118] In a nineteenth-century account of Bartholomew Fair, the author quotes from *The Observator* of 21 August 1703, which calls the cloisters of St. Bartholomew Hospital a

> market of lewdness [that does not] tend to any thing else but the ruin of bodies, souls, and estates of the young men and women of the City of London, who here met with all the temptations to [destruction.] The lotteries to ruin their estates ... and in the cloisters (those conscious scenes of polluted amours) in the evening they strike the bargain to finish their ruin. What strange medley of lewdness has that place not long since afforded? Lords and ladies, aldermen and their wives, 'squires and fiddlers, citizens and rope dancers, jack-puddings and lawyers, mistresses and maids, masters and apprentices! This is not an ark, like Noah's, beasts enter this ark, and such as have the Devil's livery on their backs.[119]

In the case of the London spies, participating in sexual acts or gambling was not something they described, but they did view and comment upon those who purchased such pleasures (and if they did participate, they certainly did not communicate this to their polite audience). These men visited the '*Bedlam* for Lovers' in the cloisters of St Bartholomew Hospital, where they viewed a 'Rendezvous of *Jilts*, *Whores*, and *Sharpers*'. The two protagonists and the surrounding crowd of men watched and laughed when one 'red-faced' gentleman approached a prostitute and 'claped his bare Hand in her Neck', saying, 'Dear Madam … you are as Cold as a Cricket in an Ice-house'. The woman looked at him and replied, 'If you please to clap your Fiery-Face to my Back-side, 'twill be the ready way to warm me'. Upon leaving this gentleman, she entered a 'Raffling-Shop, where some civil Gentlemen follw'd her, and to reward her Wit, Loaded her and her She-Friend … with Silver Nick-Nacks, and guarded her into a Coach from the Insolence of the Town *Cormorants*, who had a wonderful mind to be Snapping at so fair a Bait'.[120] Another writer also visited the cloister in Bartholomew Fair and found a 'lewd Matron at the Entrance', smiling at all of the 'spectators' who entered. Inside, the spectacle included 'shining *Nymphs*' who were 'deck'd in gay [though borrowed] Attire'. In dim light, these women's dresses may have seemed fine enough to command high sums of money, but this poet uncovers what he believes to be the reality behind their artifice, writing:

> Their thin-wrought Silks compleat a gawdy Shew,
> Unseen the Smock and Filthiness below

The writer continues his warning to unwary young men with a description of how patrons drunk on 'Cherry-Bounce and Brandy' gain entrance to 'fam'd *Pandora's Box*', only to find 'Transmissive Poyson flowing in his Veins, The joyless Swain retires with fiery Tail, Unfelt 'til Morning, he perceives his Ail'.[121] Literature, which satirized fair pleasures sternly, warned men of what was at stake when they ignored their better judgment and participated in activities writers labelled most morally dubious. To one author, a spectator would find more peace at Bedlam than at Bartholomew Fair. There, he heard no 'outcry' from 'Lunaticks', and people were 'Not half so mad … as in the Fair'.[122] In any case, at Bedlam at least one knew they were going to encounter 'lunatics' before entering.

Health, money, reputation – these were all endangered by the fair entertainments middling writers labelled least reputable. At the same time, descriptive narratives of fairs celebrated these less visible fair entertainments, and their descriptions most likely intrigued many more readers than they disgusted. Literature about fairs helps us understand what types of activities may have occurred in the dark reaches of fairs, but it also illustrates that this shady side of fair life was becoming immortalized in print as an intriguing, and particularly British, fair offering. This reputation was surely known by city officials seeking to regulate and limit fair activities and did not project their idea of a commercial and well-ordered city.

During the late seventeenth and early eighteenth centuries, London fair-goers enjoyed and consumed the often unpredictable culture of fairs as their activities were monitored and recorded by both literary satirists and city officials. Authorities and social critiques were fascinated by the culture of fairs because it could not be defined. From year to year, while some exhibitions and entertainments stayed the same, there were always new interpretations or versions of old entertainment. Crowds who sought unique attractions encouraged this novelty. On some levels, new attractions did not directly confront, and even supported local and national interests. Watching the performance of a musical clock, admiring a 'living' picture of a celebrated military victory, enjoying a droll supporting local and national pride, or even viewing a room full of wax works and automatons did not threaten civic order. As this chapter demonstrates, such activities disseminated patriotic views and new knowledge to a diverse audience, limited as it was by small admittance fees. Drolls had the potential to become a social threat because themes did not always support national or local issues. As in the *Quaker's Opera*, fair theatre was often an opportunity for common London citizens to humorously critique city institutions or civic decisions. City officials became concerned with theatrical entertainment at fairs and temporary play booths constructed away from London's professional theatres, especially as these venues increased in number, became more popular at fairs, and began to utilize the professional actors readily available in London.

Henry Morley's focus on Bartholomew Fair demonstrates how even in modern Britain, visual and aural culture centrally defined national identity. For Morley, the sights, sounds, and smells of Bartholomew Fair were foundational and unifying for more than Londoners – the festival represented qualities he found uniquely 'English', which he found central to a larger British identity. In the events of the historical fair, Morley claims, 'we [see] the humour of the nation blended with the riot of its mob', but by 1855 'the nation had outgrown it'.[123] In 1880, when Morley's book was published, the 'nation' was apparently ready to remember the fair as a foundational aspect of British culture. With the 'riot of the mob' no longer threatening, fair entertainment was safely contained and remembered within the pages of his book. Morley's attention to Bartholomew Fair as well as his contemporary Thomas Frost's who, in 1881, memorialized fairs and their exhibits in *The Old Showmen and the Old London Fairs*, reveal the importance of fair culture in consolidating and communicating notions of national identity and memory to popular audiences.[124] In the early eighteenth century, common understandings of local and national identity were consumed by fair patrons who viewed fair exhibits such as mechanical and musical clocks, 'moving' pictures, or fair theatre. By the nineteenth century, print culture communicated the uniqueness of infamous London festivals to a much wider audience, reinforcing their place in popular memory.

Prostitution, gaming, music booths, and drinking were all activities civic authorities may have tolerated at one time, but with London's population continuing to increase at a rapid rate, these activities seemed more potentially disruptive. City officials targeted these entertainments because they, more than any other activity, appeared to make male customers abandon their reason. Activities such as prostitution and gaming were linked to the overall experience of fairs through descriptive accounts of fairs. For better or worse, this linkage contributed to understandings of London as a unique locale. London fair-goers may have looked in amazement at Cheshire fairies and Irish giants, but while they were so occupied, the rest of England and the British Isles looked in disbelief at the culture of London fairs.

Notes

1 Nineteenth-century historians and folklorists commonly judged the progression of past societies and their degree of 'civilization' according to the recreations practiced. See Emma Griffin, *England's Revelry: A History of Popular Sports and Pastimes, 1660–1830* (Oxford: Oxford University Press, 2005), 3–4.

2 Morley, of course, lived in Victorian Britain, but he rarely refers to his nation as 'Britain'. For him, 'Englishness' equals 'Britishness', which reveals much about his hegemonic position.

3 Henry Morley, *Memoirs of Bartholomew Fair* (1880; reprint Detroit, MI: Singing Tree Press, 1968).

4 *Ibid.*, 390.

5 Social and topographical developments in Victorian London are elaborated in Peter Whitfield, *London: A Life in Maps* (London: British Library, 2006), 106–13.

6 See Griffin for a historiography regarding the treatment of popular recreations from the eighteenth through twentieth centuries.

7 Benedict Anderson focuses on how print-capitalism helped consolidate ideas of an 'imagined community' in *Imagined Communities, Reflections on the Origin and Spread of Nationalism* (New York: Verso, reprint, 1991 [1983]). Scholars consider the ways in which visual culture is also instrumental in creating and disseminating ideas of national belonging. See Joan Landes, *Visualizing the Nation: Gender, Representation, and Revolution in Eighteenth-Century France* (Ithaca, NY: Cornell University Press, 2001); Vanessa Schwartz, *Spectacular Realities: Early Mass Culture in Fin-De-Siècle Paris* (Berkeley, Los Angeles and London: University of California Press, 1998).

8 Kim Hall discusses the ways in which 'vernacular' printed images seen as central

to Benedict Anderson's notion of 'imagined communities' were at the same time involved in marking those who existed outside of that community. Some fair exhibitions and especially their description in periodical literature operated in the same way. See Kim F. Hall, 'Object into Object?: Some Thoughts on the Presence of Black Women in Early Modern Culture', in Peter Erickson and Clark Hulse, *Early Modern Visual Culture: Representation, Race, and Empire in Renaissance England* (Philadelphia: University of Pennsylvania Press, 2000), 172.

9 See Anderson, *Imagined Communities*. Also Kathleen Wilson, *The Island Race: Englishness, Empire and Gender in the Eighteenth Century* (London and New York: Routledge, 2003). Wilson reiterates just how important newspapers were to 'structuring national and political consciousness, binding ordinary men and women throughout the localities in particular ways to the processes of state and empire building', 32.

10 Though Morley never stated this, his perception is informed by his era's firm understanding of natural and racial taxonomies and his discomfort with the less-scientifically entrenched notions of difference in the late seventeenth and early eighteenth centuries. See Nicholas Hudson, 'From 'Nation' to 'Race': The Origin of Racial Classification in Eighteenth-Century Thought', *Eighteenth Century Studies*, 29 (1996), 247–64. Morley's notions also reflect the convergence in British imperialism between science, racial knowledge, and colonial practices. See Nancy Stepan, *The Idea of Race in Science: Great Britain, 1800–1960* (Basingstoke: Macmillan, 1982); Douglas A. Lorimer, 'Race, Science, and Culture: Historical Continuities and Discontinuities, 1850–1914', in Shearer West (ed.), *The Victorians and Race* (Aldershot: Scolar Press, 1996); Catherine Hall, *Civilising Subjects: Metropole and Colony in the English Imagination, 1830–1867* (Chicago: Chicago University Press, 2002); Philippa Levine, *Prostitution, Race and Politics: Policing Venereal Disease in the British Empire* (New York and London: Routledge, 2003).

11 Morley, *Memoirs*, 246.

12 *Ibid.*

13 Kathleen Wilson argues that '… the Georgian period [and I would argue, late Stuart] reveals the rhetorical strategies and practices through which ideas of nation and national belonging become systematically linked to ideas about ethnic difference … and to a racialised understanding of community – real and imagined – that grouped some people together, and irrevocably separated others', *The Island Race*, 13. These ideas are explored for France in William H. Schneider, *An Empire for the Masses: The French Popular Image of Africa, 1870–1900* (Westport, CT: Greenwood Press, 1982).

14 See Kim Hall, *Things of Darkness: Economies of Race and Gender in Early Modern England* (Ithaca, NY and London: Cornell University Press, 1995) for a discussion of elite early modern ideas about race and colonialism; for a discussion of how the colonial project was informed by discourses of domination inherent to Renaissance Bearbaiting, see Rebecca Ann Bach, 'Bearbaiting, Dominion, and Colonialism', in Joyce Green MacDonald (ed.), *Race, Ethnicity, and Power in the Renaissance* (Cranbury, NJ and London: Associated University Press, 1997).

15 Morley, *Memoirs*, 245.

16 Sybil Rosenfeld, *The Theatre of the London Fairs in the Eighteenth Century* (Cambridge: Cambridge University Press, 1960), 135.

17 David Kerr Cameron, *London's Pleasures, from Restoration to Regency* (Thrupp, Stroud: Sutton Publishing, 2001), 189.

18 Kathleen Wilson argues that Georgian culture was 'permeated' by empire at a number of levels including 'literature … gardening, philanthropy, fashion, religion, politics, and graphic and literary propaganda'. Wilson, 'The Good, the Bad, and the Impotent: Imperialism and the Politics of Identity in Georgian England', in Ann Bermingham and John Brewer (eds), *The Consumption of Culture, 1600–1800, Image, Object, Text* (London and New York: Routledge, 1995), 238.

19 Frances Terpak examines widening elite and popular exposure to 'science' in 'Free Time, Free Spirit: Popular Entertainments in Gainsborough's Era', *Huntington Library Quarterly* 70, no. 2, 2007. John Brewer demonstrates how 'high culture moved out of the narrow confines of the court and into diverse spaces in London', in *The Pleasures of the Imagination: English Culture in the Eighteenth Century* (Chicago: University of Chicago Press, 1997), 1.

20 Richard D. Altick, *The Shows of London* (Cambridge, MA: Belknap Press of Harvard University Press, 1978), 54.

21 At an elite level, scientific understanding helped formulate a 'cosmopolitan experience' among men and some women who participated in early modern scientific culture. Margaret Jacob, *Strangers Nowhere in the World: The Rise of Cosmopolitanism in Early Modern Europe* (Philadelphia: University of Pennsylvania Press, 2006), 43. Deborah Harkness demonstrates how the foundational labour, tools, and techniques for the practical application of science broadened in Elizabethan London and that common meeting places fostered the dissemination of knowledge. *The Jewel House: Elizabethan London and the Scientific Revolution* (New Haven, CT and London: Yale University Press, 2007). See also, Margaret Jacob, *The Cultural Meaning of the Scientific Revolution* (Philadelphia: Temple University Press, 1988).

22 Sir Hans Sloane was the 'first collector' in London. He began his collection while serving as the general physician for Jamaica's governor and assembled probably the most extensive collection of 'Animal, Vegetable and Mineral' curiosities in England. His vast collection was eventually acquired by the British Museum. See Altick, *Shows of London*, 15 and chapters 1 and 2. See also, Kay Dian Kriz, 'Curiosities, Commodities and Transplanted Bodies in Hans Sloane's "Natural History of Jamaica"'. *William and Mary Quarterly*, 3rd Series, Vol. 57, No. 1 (January 2000), 35–78.

23 *Daily Post*, 15 September 1725.

24 Marjorie Swann, *Curiosities and Texts: The Culture of Collecting in Early Modern England* (Philadelphia: University of Pennsylvania Press, 2001). Paula Findlen discusses how European collectors fashioned their own identities through their collections, in *Possessing Nature: Museums, Collecting, and Scientific Culture in Early Modern Italy* (Berkeley and Los Angeles: University of California Press, 1996), 295–7.

25 Harkness, *The Jewel House*, 124–30.

26 Barbara Maria Stafford, 'Presuming Images and Consuming Words: the Visualization of Knowledge from the Enlightenment to Post-Modernism', in John Brewer and Roy Porter (eds), *Consumption and the World of Goods* (London and New York: Routledge, 1993), 469.

27 See Mark Burnett, *Constructing 'Monsters' in Shakespearean Drama and Early Modern Culture* (New York: Palgrave Macmillan, 2002), 21. In this provocative study

of sixteenth- and early seventeenth-century monsters and drama, Burnett argues that a fascination with monsters spanned the court and fairground, establishing 'lines of communication' between the two.

28 *Bartholomew Fair: An Heroi-Comical Poem* (London, 1717).

29 *Ibid.*

30 Altick, *Shows of London*, 7. It is important to understand, however, that holy relics were tangible objects that supported a wider religious belief system than the curious objects collected and shown by wealthy men.

31 *Ibid.*, 8.

32 Paolo L. Rossi, 'Society, Culture and the Dissemination of Learning', in Stephen Pumfrey, Paolo L. Rossi and Maurice Slawinski, eds., *Science, Culture and Popular Belief in Renaissance Europe* (Manchester and New York: Manchester University Press, 1991), 164.

33 Altick, *Shows of London*, 8.; Paula Findlen outlines the ways in which the sociability of English scientific culture differed from that of the continent, in *Possessing Nature*, 146–50.

34 Altick, *Shows of London*, 9.

35 Lisa Jardine, *Ingenious Pursuits: Building the Scientific Revolution* (London: Little, Brown and Company, 1999), 144–57.

36 Roy Porter, *The Creation of the Modern World* (New York and London: W.W. Norton, 2000), 138–42.

37 *Ibid.*, 142.

38 Altick, *Shows of London*, 58–60.

39 *Daily Courant*, 23 September 1717 in Southwark Fair Scrapbook, London Borough of Southwark, Central Reference Library.

40 *Daily Courant*, 18 September 1716.

41 Ann Bermingham, *Landscape and Ideology: The English Rustic Tradition, 1740–1850* (Berkeley: University of California Press, 1986).

42 *Daily Post*, 6 September 1723.

43 Eveline Cruickshanks and Howard Erskine-Hill explore this plot in, *The Atterbury Plot* (New York: Palgrave, 2004).

44 *Daily Post*, 31 August 1728 and 12 September 1728.

45 John Brewer discusses the patriotic messages in publically displayed landscape paintings, which had reached the scale of dioramas, in late eighteenth-century Britain in 'Sensibility and the Urban Panorama', *Huntington Library Quarterly* 70, no. 2, 2007. Such themes existed, also, much earlier in the eighteenth-century.

46 Proceedings of the Old Bailey, 20 April 1737, Ref: t17370420–59.

47 *Daily Post*, Friday, 19 September 1729.

48 *Post Boy*, 24–7 August 1706.

49 *Ibid.* and Rosenfeld, *Theatre of London Fairs*, 18.

50 *Post Boy*, 24–7 August 1706.

51 No visual evidence of this presentation remains, but it was likely a type of mechanical landscape picture or may have been a large 'peep show'. These entertainments are described by Frances Terpak in 'Popular Entertainments'.

52 *An Historical Account of Bartholomew Fair: containing a view of its origin, and the purposes it was first instituted for, Together with a concise detail of the changes it hath*

undergone in its traffic, amusements, &c. &c. (London: John Arliss, 1810), 9. British Library, In BL 11644 c 55.

53 *Ibid.*

54 *Post Boy*, 24–7 August 1706.

55 See for example Rosenfeld, *Theatre of London Fairs*, 72. Newspaper accounts of royal visits to fair booths include those in *Post Boy*, 25–7 August 1719, *Daily Journal*, 26 August 1721, and *Daily Post*, 24 August 1724.

56 *Daily Post*, 31 August 1728 and 12 September 1728. Fawkes presented a moving picture of the City and Bay of Gibraltar. Both Morley and Rosenfeld contest the date of the fan, said to have been printed in 1721. The Siege of Gibraltar peep show dates the fan to 1728, or later. Rosenfeld believes the fan is probably based on a water colour in the British Museum most likely executed by Thomas Loggan in 1740.

57 *London Evening Post*, 21–3 September 1738.

58 Linda Colley discusses the construction of national identity in *Britons: Forging the Nation, 1707–1837* (New Haven, CT and London: Yale University Press, 1992). She argues that war was central to forming English conceptions of themselves in relation to European and non-Protestant others. The popular culture of fairs contributed to conceptions of Englishness in terms of the military strength of the nation.

59 *Daily Post*, 10 September 1730.

60 Christopher Baugh, 'Technology-Driven Entertainment and Spectacle', *Huntington Library Quarterly 70*, no. 2 (2007), Ann Bermingham (ed.), *Technologies of Illusion: The Art of Special Effects in Eighteenth-Century Britain*, 229–49.

61 Rosenfeld, *Theatre of the London Fairs*, 34.

62 *Wat Tyler and Jack Straw; or, the Mob Reformers. A dramatick entertainment As it is perform'd at Pikethman's and Giffard's Great Theatrical Booth in Bartholomew Fair.* (London, 1730).

63 *Ibid.*

64 *Ibid.*, 13–14.

65 *Ibid.*, 24.

66 *Ibid.*, 30–1.

67 *Ibid.*, 32.

68 See Chris Humphrey, *The Politics of Carnival: Festive Misrule in Medieval England* (Manchester and New York: Manchester University Press, 2001).

69 Emmet L. Avery (ed.), *The London Stage, 1660–1800* (Carbondale, IL: Southern Illinois University Press, 1960–1968), 985. This play was also performed at the Haymarket Theatre in November of the same year.

70 Thomas Walker, *The Quaker's opera. As it is perform'd at Lee's and Harper's great theatrical booth in Bartholomew-Fair. With the musick prefix'd to each song* (London, 1728).

71 Leah S. Marcus, 'Politics and Pastoral: Writing the Court on the Countryside', in Kevin Sharpe and Peter Lake (eds), *Culture and Politics in Early Stuart England* (Stanford, CA: Stanford University Press, 1993), 140.

72 Warwick Wroth, *The London Pleasure Gardens of the Eighteenth Century* (London: Macmillan, 1896; reprint, Hamden, CT: Archon Books, 1979).

73 *Daily Post*, 19 September 1729.

74 See Marcus, '"Politics and Pastoral"' and Bermingham, *Landscape and Ideology*.

75 Edward Ward, *The London Spy*, 4th edn (London: J. How, 1709), in Randolph Trumbach (ed.), *Marriage, Sex and the Family in England 1660–1800* (New York and London: Garland Publishing, 1985), 253.

76 *Ibid.*

77 *Ibid.*, 254.

78 *Ibid.*, 254–5.

79 The way in which popular culture reinforced gender hierarchy is explored in Susan Dwyer Amussen, 'The Gendering of Popular Culture in England', in Tim Harris (ed.), *Popular Culture in England, c. 1500– 1850* (New York: St. Martin's Press, 1995). Work on early modern English masculinity does little to explore the existence of a cross-class, masculine 'brotherhood'. Such an exploration would reveal the contexts in which late seventeenth- and early eighteenth-century gender hierarchy mattered more than class. Work addressing masculinity in early modern England includes Philip Carter, *Men and the Emergence of Polite Society, Britain, 1660–1800* (London: Longman, 2001); Tim Hitchcock and Michèle Cohen (eds), *English Masculinities, 1660–1800* (London and New York: Longman, 1999); Tim Hitchcock, *English Sexualities, 1700–1800* (New York: St. Martin's Press, 1997).

80 See Ann Bermingham (ed.), *Sensation and Sensibility: Viewing Gainsborough's Cottage Door* (London and New Haven, CT: Yale University Press, 2005).

81 Altick, *Shows of London*, 34–5.

82 Roy Porter, *Creation of Modern World*, 39 and 270; Richard Sorrenson, 'The State's Demand for Accurate Astronomical and Navigational Instruments in Eighteenth-Century Britain', in Ann Bermingham and John Brewer (eds), *The Consumption of Culture, 1600–1800: Image, Object, Text* (London and New York: Routledge, 1995), 264–5.

83 Book of Advertisements, British Library N. TAB 2026/25.

84 *Ibid.*

85 Bodleian Library, Oxford. John Johnson Collection, Playhouses, 3, misc.

86 *Daily Courant*, 10 September 1716.

87 Cornelius McGrath was a later well-known 'Irish Giant' born in the late 1730s. He was 6' 8' tall and in the 1750s was 'persuaded to exhibit himself as a show', in Bristol, London, Paris and 'most of the great cities in Europe'. *The Annual Register, or a view of the History, Politicks, and Literature, for the Year 1760* (London, 1775), 79.

88 *Book of Advertisements*, British Library, BL N TAB 2026 25.

89 Bartholomew Fair Scrapbook, MS 1514, Guildhall Library.

90 There are many recent studies which examine literature and drama about the colonies. See for example Walter Lim, *The Arts of Empire: The Poetics of Colonialism from Raleigh to Milton* (Newark, DE: University of Delaware Press; London: Associated University Presses, 1998); Rebecca Ann Bach, *Colonial Transformations: The Cultural Production of the New Atlantic World, 1580–1640* (New York: Palgrave, 2000); Heidi Hunter, *Colonial Women: Race and Culture in Stuart Drama* (Oxford and New York: Oxford University Press, 2001); Thomas Scanlan, *Colonial Writing and the New World, 1583–1671* (Cambridge and New York: Cambridge University Press, 1999); Bridget Orr, *Empire on the English Stage, 1660–1714* (Cambridge and New York: Cambridge University Press, 2001).

91 Peter Linebaugh, *The London Hanged: Crime and Civil Society in the Eighteenth*

Century (Cambridge: Cambridge University Press, 1992), 135. For information on visual culture, see Peter Erickson and Clark Hulse (eds), *Early Modern Visual Culture: Representation, Race, and Empire in Renaissance England* (Philadelphia: University of Pennsylvania Press, 2000); Beth Fowkes Tobin, *Picturing Imperial Power: Colonial Subjects in Eighteenth-Century British Painting* (Durham, NC and London: Duke University Press, 1999).

92 British Library, N TAB 2026/25.

93 Hall, *Things of Darkness.*

94 Peter Fryer, *Staying Power, The History of Black People in Britain* (London: Pluto Press, 1984), 133.

95 Hall, *Things of Darkness*, 124.

96 Here, I am borrowing Wilson's definition of the eighteenth-century understanding of 'race', 11.

97 Ward, *London Spy*, 241.

98 *The Devil upon two sticks: or, the town until'd: with the comical humours of Don Stulto, and Siegnior Jingo: as it is acted in Pinkeman's both in May-Fair.* London, 1708. In Eighteenth Century Collections Online. Gale Group. http://galenet.galegroup. com/servlet/ECCO.

99 Ward, *London Spy*, 241.

100 Kathleen Brown, 'Native American and Early Modern Concepts of Race', in Martin Daunton and Rick Halpern (eds), *Empire and Others: British Encounters with Indigenous Peoples, 1600–1850* (Philadelphia: University of Pennsylvania Press, 1999), 80–4.

101 See Hall, *Things of Darkness* and Tobin, *Picturing Imperial Power*, for example.

102 For an intriguing analysis of fears of anything 'foreign' and of 'otherness' found in canonical works of British literature, see Rajani Sudan, *Fair Exotics: Xenophobic Subjects in English Literature, 1720–1850* (Philadelphia, PA: University of Pennsylvania Press, 2002).

103 For an examination of the spectator/spectacle relationship, see Peter Stallybrass and Allon White, *The Politics and Poetics of Transgression* (Ithaca, NY: Cornell University Press, 1986); See, also, Kristina Straub, who is particularly interested in the ways in which spectatorship is gendered on the eighteenth-century English stage, *Sexual Suspects: Eighteenth-Century Players and Sexual Ideology* (Princeton, NJ: Princeton University Press, 1992).

104 BL N. TAB 2026/25.

105 *Ibid.*

106 Burnett, *Constructing 'Monsters'*, 53.

107 BL N. TAB 2026/25.

108 MS 1514, Guildhall Library.

109 Book of Advertisements, British Library N. TAB. 2026/25.

110 In this sense, fairs maintained aspects of the carnivalesque and provided common people a means to subvert authority. They provided people with yearly occasions to vent their discontent, and if properly used as 'safety valves' helped relieve pressure and maintain order during regular times of the year. Natalie Davis, *Society and Culture in Early Modern France* (Stanford, CA: Stanford University Press, 1975); Peter Burke, *Popular Culture in Early Modern Europe* (Brookfield, VT: Ashgate, reprint

1994 [1978]); Emmanuel LeRoy Ladurie, *Carnival in Romans*, trans. Mary Feeney (New York: G. Braziller, 1979); Chris Humphrey, *The Politics of Carnival: Festive Misrule in Medieval England* (Manchester and New York: Manchester University Press, 2001).

111 *Bartholomew-Fair: An Heroi-Comical Poem*, 25–6.

112 *Ibid.*

113 J.M. Beattie, *Policing and Punishment in London, 1660–1750* (Oxford: Oxford University Press, 2001), 55–6.

114 *A Walk to Smithfield: or, a true description of the humours of Bartholomew Fair*, 4.

115 Josiah Woodward, *An Account of the Rise and Progress of the Religious Societies in the City of London, & etc. And of the Endeavours for Reformation of Manners Which have been made therein* (London, 1698), 79.

116 Ward, *London Spy*, 260–8.

117 *Ibid.*, 255.

118 *Ibid.*, 264. The two protagonists describe 'Flying-Coaches' full of children outside Bartholomew Fair. Morley also describes some of these entertainments, 309 and 351.

119 In BL 11644 c 55, *An Historical Account of Bartholomew Fair*, 11–12.

120 Ward, *London Spy*, 265–6.

121 *Bartholomew-Fair: An Heroi-Comical Poem*, 28–9.

122 *Ibid.*, 32–3.

123 Morley, *Memoir*, 390.

124 Thomas Frost, *The Old Showmen and the Old London Fairs* (1881; reprint, Ann Arbor, MI: Gryphon Books, 1971).

Conclusion

Festive spaces in cities are often sites at which urban identities and social or gender hierarchies are contested, but are also often reinforced. In eighteenth-century London, conflicting views of the best uses for London's streets were frequently opposed, and the resulting debates reveal contemporary understandings of metropolitan living, social order, and gender hierarchies. From the late seventeenth century, London's infrastructure was being 'modernized', or rebuilt, re-planned, and cleaned. This 'cleaning campaign' usually tied to the development of polite commerce and modernization, extended beyond transforming city streets. London inhabitants were also targeted as city officials attempted to reform customary types of public amusement and re-configure gendered and social hierarchies for the shifting urban environment. Eighteenth-century fairgrounds are rich sites for historical analysis. Debates about them reveal that concerns about morality and gender order were central to the organization of urban space in the long eighteenth century.

As London's built environment became increasingly controlled, featuring paved, well-lit streets, new buildings for living and conducting commerce, and a skyline dotted with church buildings built according to polite taste – its population did not conform neatly into re-configured urban streets. Though the weight of state and local authorities was on the side of regulation, efforts to abolish or limit fairs encountered concerted and repeated resistance. Urban reform efforts in eighteenth-century London always involved conflict and negotiation with the city's inhabitants. These occurred between various groups, including established and emerging elites, performers and audiences, working men and women and merchants and consumers. From the level of the everyday, we see that Enlightenment notions of industriousness, leisure, politeness, and social and gender order did not easily take root in the urban environment – rather, modernity emerged gradually and was never total.

Reform-minded officials informed by notions of polite masculinity concerned themselves with making London's spaces suitable for men's commerce. In most cases, however, what motivated attempted regulation of fairs were fears (real or exaggerated) related to maintaining order in a rapidly growing city. Urban authorities who hoped to create a mannered city attempted repeatedly to restrict the types of fair activities to only those that promoted their own understanding of 'commerce'. The public resisted regulations and throughout the early eighteenth century there was an upsurge in unlicensed fairs and public amusements.

While city fathers did not recognize these amusements as true 'commerce', fairs remained popular, and this industry of sociability, games, drinking, eating, spectacles, and dramatic entertainment provided work for labouring men and women and amused Londoners from all social backgrounds.

Debates over the place of festivity and usefulness of fairs in eighteenth-century London reveal how concerns about morality and gender order were vital in ordering eighteenth-century London, but discourses about politeness and festivity can obscure the realities of what fairs offered Londoners in terms of culture and employment. Existing fair records complicate our understandings of gender and work in interesting ways, and provide us one means of looking behind literary and visual depictions of men and women at fairs. Literary depictions of women working at fairs often mislead our understanding of the everyday working lives of women. While late seventeenth- and eighteenth-century city officials and social critics developed new ideas about how urban streets should be used and considered the city appropriate only for controlled, polite, and masculine commerce, fairs continued as a workspace for women. Pamphlet literature criticized women on 'show' at fairs – but for every new idea about what was appropriate work for women in London, women who made a living at fairs found ways around those new ideas. Women reshaped themselves and their labour, or just carried on in the face of gendered understandings of urban workspace.

Examining women's work at fairs complicates our understandings of gendered work spheres. First, historical records from fairs demonstrate that women worked in managerial positions often considered 'male' – especially women working as play-booth managers. More importantly, examining women's work at fairs reveals that women were instrumental in the creation of commercialized leisure. Play-booth manager Hannah Lee's contemporaries, from urban authorities to moral reformers, did not consider fair amusement commerce. Their equation defined work opposed to entertainment and placed women's work at fairs outside the bounds of what was considered true labour. If we fail to consider women's work at fairs an important type of labour, we reinforce notions held by London's patriarchs who held specific notions of what constituted mannered and masculine commerce. In fact, providing and supporting amusement has been a lucrative source of women's work, as well as men's. From Hannah Lee to Madam Tussaud, women have been active as entertainment entrepreneurs.[1] Successful female actresses and singers were also powerfully involved in shaping the eighteenth- and nineteenth-century entertainment industries. As performers and patrons of seasonal and commercialized amusement, women found a niche in a growing industry. This industry should be understood as one in which both men and women had permanent occupations, and when examined more closely as legitimate labour, upsets our notions of gendered work spheres.

Men and women resisted fair regulation not only because they were a vital location for summertime commerce, but also because they were important spaces in which ordinary Londoners could become active participants in local and national cultures. Fair-goers consumed versions of the same entertainment as Londoners who could afford to see some of the same actors perform in theatres. While watching fair theatre, audiences heard debates about and criticisms of life in their city and larger nation. Fair-goers also had opportunities to view fair exhibits featuring the science of machinery and waxworks, and many of these displays provided Londoners a forum for celebrating national victories or leaders, and educated diverse audiences about the cities, people, and topography of England and the growing British empire. Examining more closely the culture of fairs reveals how popular audiences participated in the creation of national and local identities. Identities performed and consolidated at fairs were not only gendered, but based on notions of class and race, as well. These early fair displays helped create a style of pseudo-educational entertainment that emerged later in two popular types of nineteenth- and twentieth-century exhibitions – circus-style 'side shows' and informative exhibitions found in venues such as world's fairs and expositions.

By the middle of the eighteenth century, as fairs were increasingly becoming known as dangerous locations, class-specific amusements featuring some of the same entertainments of fairs – music, dancing, food, and sociability – emerged as alternative, more controlled venues for this type of entertainment, especially after 1752 when this type of entertainment became officially licensed.[2] Such venues included Sadler's Wells, which had begun as a spa in the late seventeenth century, but by 1697 spa water stopped flowing and entertainment was the primary attraction.[3] Entertainment there included theatre, rope dancing, and even an occasional sermon.[4] In 1742, the proprietor of Sadler's Wells, Francis Forcer, was targeted by the Court of Aldermen for 'acting pantomimes and other entertainments', though his shows continued to be advertised in London newspapers.[5]

The circus also had its origins in this period and has connections to fair entertainment. Philip Astley, often considered the founder of the modern circus in London, began providing public entertainment in his riding school in 1768. As a former horse-breaker and 'rough-rider' who served under the King of Prussia, Astley turned his expertise as a horseman into a commercial venture. By 1769, his riding school featured horsemanship and dancing dogs in a permanent structure near Westminster Bridge. In 1776, he was advertising entertainments similar to those presented at fairs including 'tumbling and rope-vaulting' as well as a 'Grand Temple of Minerva'.[6]

The eighteenth-century campaign against fairs reveals that the purpose of London fairs had shifted from providing marketing opportunities to providing entertainment. As urban reformers struggled to conform fairs to their earlier commercial purpose, fair-style entertainment proved to be a profitable business on its own. Those who recognized the potential to harness and profit from outdoor, summertime entertainment borrowed aspects of the seasonal pleasures of fairs and transformed them according to polite tastes and gendered understandings of what was appropriate for mixed crowds. For a time during the eighteenth century, fairs and pleasure gardens coexisted as night-time summer entertainment available to Londoners. On one early September day in 1749, during the time of Southwark Fair, the *General Advertiser* included announcements for shows and entertainment at the New Wells, Ranelagh House, the 'Assembly Room at the Whiteheart', and a theatrical entertainment at Lee, Yeates, and Warner's Great Tiled Booth in Southwark Fair.[7] The mid-eighteenth century was a transitional period in which many types of outdoor entertainment flourished.

Jonathan Tyers, proprietor of Vauxhall Gardens, was among the first to recognize the commercial opportunity of creating a permanent seasonal location at which paying customers could enjoy outdoor evening entertainment. Tyers negotiated between the traditional experience of urban festivity and newer understandings of polite conduct. Sanitized and confined to particular areas of the metropolis, night-time urban festivity remained in London. Tyres may have recognized how an air of illicit sexuality contributed to the popularity of his commercial venture when he opened Spring 'Vauxhall' Gardens in 1726 on the site of gardens already associated with elite sexual intrigue. However, he also understood something about politeness, particularly gendered notions of appropriate entertainment venues for both men and women. Tyers realized the importance of controlling the environment in which he held his festivities, and so he used landscaping and architecture to create a 'safe' venue for evening entertainment. His gardens featured entertainment familiar at fairs, such as music performances, eating, and people-watching, but these activities took place in well-lit walks, open spaces, and a common semi-circular seating arrangement in which all boxes opened onto the public and an elevated bandstand.[8] Crowds at Vauxhall were not described as the jumbled mixtures of people found at fairs. Though crowds at pleasure gardens could sometimes become unruly, their potential for rowdiness was not necessarily the reason one attended.

Vauxhall Gardens provided a controlled venue for anyone interested in assuming polite clothes and persona and exhibiting themselves to contemporaries, which was not always possible at fairs, as the Duke of Montrose's cook discovered.[9] Hired guards patrolled the surrounding grounds, helping to ensure patrons' safe night-time journeys to and from the location, and an admission fee charged at the gate filtered out some of the most disorderly types who often frequented fairs. Tyers provided controlled areas for intrigue in the midst of his polite retreat, including the dark 'Lover's' or 'Druid's' walk.[10] The location of his commercialized fair in an area associated with aristocratic intrigue may have appealed to both London's elite as well as middling customers interested in pursuing these pleasures themselves. Such a location imbued the entertainment with sexual danger similar to that of London's fairs, though Vauxhall's illicit spaces were contained in areas separate from the central meeting ground intended for socializing.

Tyers harnessed the night-time thrill of unknown and unpredictable encounters in a polite package, borrowing much from the entertainment of London's fairs. His controlled fair included variations of their entertainment, with such spectacles as an illuminated painting of a mill and stream – similar to the mechanical paintings shown at fairs.[11] Vauxhall itself seems to be a three-dimensional mechanical painting because its success hinged on customers' willing acceptance of its artifice. Patrons enjoyed walking along tree-lined, aristocratic garden paths as they strolled beneath arches and past obelisks constructed from painted canvas and boards, the same materials used to construct fair booths. Similar to Bartholomew Fair, Vauxhall was known for its pork, though Tyers's version was delicately offered to customers by polite, male servers who expertly carved paper-thin slices. Vauxhall's entertainments were intended to attract polite middling customers hoping to set themselves apart from labouring people. Consuming paper-thin ham served by polite carvers instead of thick slices trimmed by greasy servers from visibly cooking pigs was one method by which discriminating consumers adopted new eating customs at pleasure gardens.[12] Not only were patrons more polite at pleasure gardens, but workers as well adopted more mannered appearances and behaviours.

It is not possible to determine whether or not customers expected a certain degree of danger and recklessness within the polite garden walks, but some unpredictability continued at pleasure gardens. On Vauxhall's opening night, attended by over 400 people, a pickpocket was apprehended for stealing fifty guineas.[13] Uncontained young men were a problem at pleasure gardens, just as they had been at fairs, and were known to riot in Vauxhall's dark walks, forcing Tyers to fence them off in 1763. His barricade was torn up by rioting men the following year, and Tyers never again replaced them. Such rioting customers demonstrate how popular resistance continued to determine the practice of festivity even at commercialized venues. Another perceived problem always present at pleasure gardens were prostitutes, who were known to frequent the dark walks. Even crowds continued to be a spectacle at and outside of pleasure gardens, and were frequently described in everything from newspaper accounts to novels.[14] Despite guards hired to accompany people across dark fields adjacent to pleasure gardens, crime remained a problem in these areas. In 1760, for example, a 'young gentleman and lady' on their way home from Vauxhall were, '… attacked by two Foot pads in St. George's-Fields, and robbed of their Watches, and about four Pounds in Money'.[15] To any pickpockets, prostitutes, or other opportunists who gained entrance to Vauxhall Gardens and other similar types of pleasure resorts, or merely laid in wait outside these venues, the spoils were great. Their presence contributed to the general fair-like atmosphere of these amusements.

Venues that commercialized and regulated fair-style entertainment responded to a demand for such entertainment within the context of an increasingly accepted idea that festivity in London should be contained to particular areas. Proprietors made efforts to control the classes of people who could frequent these locations by charging admission fees or hiring police.[16] Though more of these orderly venues for night-time festivity appeared in London by the mid-eighteenth century, wary justices maintained their suspicion of the entertainments offered there and the type of morality they encouraged. While some pleasure gardens maintained the appearance that boundaries existed between polite, paying customers inside garden walls and the type of riotous behaviour found at urban fairs, this was not something they could guarantee. Apparently, the Middlesex justices were not convinced initially that walled-off entertainment occurring in commercial venues was much different than the amusement offered at fairs. In April 1750, justices ordered that the constables in the area surrounding Ranelagh House make inquiries into activities happening at that supposedly polite establishment. The justices had evidence that 'Gamesters and disorderly Persons' attended a masquerade ball held on 25 April 1750. These people reportedly frequented events at Ranelagh House, where they were responsible for defrauding people of their money, and 'diverse other disorders'.[17] In response to the disorders happening at Ranelagh, the justices formed a committee to investigate assemblies at the pleasure gardens and provided that committee with the authority to summon Justices of the Peace to attend events at the garden should another 'Jubilee Masquerade Ball' be held.[18] In fact, it seems as if this order was followed. The court paid Thomas Wilkinson £3.14 s.6d. to print in 'Several Publick News Papers The Orders of Sessions for Suppressing unlawfull Fairs, Advertisements against the Jubilee Masquerade Ball at Ranelagh House in Chelsea, and for Several other Matters'.[19] Further, in 1750 and 1751, justices ordered payment to the Deputy Cryer to the Court for the purpose of posting orders against fairs and Sabbath breakers and also for 'attending several times at Ranelagh House at Chelsea' and serving summons at Sadler's Wells in Clerkenwell (a music house and pleasure garden catering to a middling audience).[20] The officer of the court attended masquerades in an effort to 'discover what offences were there committed and to bring the offenders to Justice'.[21]

By the 1750s, commercialized amusement joined fairs as another option for festive Londoners. Festivity offered in commercial establishments proved easier to regulate and the Middlesex Justices achieved some level of success regulating the more confined entertainments of pleasure gardens. The few years spent overseeing Ranelagh House are overshadowed by the decades urban authorities spent attempting to regulate London's fairs. Rowdy or not, pleasure gardens, with their admission fees, would not have been likely to attract crowds of young working men and they did not seep into urban spaces dedicated to commerce in the way that fairs did.

Despite efforts to control pleasure gardens, there was always the possibility that entertainment in these venues could become dangerous. Cuper's Gardens was so notoriously unruly that it was targeted by the 1752 Licensing Act created to oversee London's burgeoning industry of commercialized leisure.[22] Operated by a woman, Mrs. Evans, Cuper's Gardens reminds us that women remained active in providing entertainment to Londoners, but Evans shared the same fate as Hannah Lee, becoming the first person to have her business shut down due to new legislation. Similarly to Lee, Evans found a way to evade legal regulation – even without a licence, Cuper's Gardens continued to operate for some years and remained popular.

City officials' new understandings of appropriate urban amusement conflicted with popular practice, both in the traditional settings of fairs and in the commercialized venues of pleasure gardens. Contests over the use of urban space for amusement reveal how ideas about gender, sexuality, and leisure were not merely implemented from above, but formulated through conflicts between imagined notions of mannered urbanity and the everyday use of city streets. Through conflicts over appropriate urban amusement, both ordinary people and city officials co-constructed new boundaries circumscribing appropriate use of urban space. Traditional amusements still had appeal, but once commercialized, charters were not an issue. Pleasure gardens were the entertainment entrepreneur's way around charters for public amusements, though official regulation eventually caught up with the passage of the Licensing Act. With investment, and a licence, festivals continued for weeks during the summer and at other times of the year – surpassing even Bartholomew Fair's late seventeenth-century 21-day tenure. Wrapped in polite trappings, and removed from the backyard of apprentices, Londoners retained opportunities to partake in public amusement. At licensed pleasure gardens, they continued to imagine that 'evil disposed persons' lurked in dark walks, and they occasionally became unruly themselves. Impropriety and danger could not be regulated out of London amusement, but they could be contained within garden hedgerows at the outskirts of the city.

While pleasure gardens maintained some features of popular fair shows and provided a polite space for regular, night-time festivity, the function of fairs as places of national and local identity formation have obvious connections to nineteenth- and twentieth-century exhibitions at expositions and World's Fairs. Without the earlier negotiations over what were appropriate spaces for urban festivals and proper gendered or classed behaviour at these locations, fairs might not have evolved into these later, more sanitized and 'industrious' versions.[23] The 1851 Great Exhibition is the ultimate realization of a polite and productive fair. It showcased the latest technological achievements of the Victorians, displayed in an impressive Crystal Palace. Industrial wonders from around the British world came together and were displayed next to European exhibitions, providing audiences opportunities to compare themselves and British technology to that of their rivals. Iron, glass, innovation, commerce, and industriousness were on display – the 'industry and ingenuity of all nations'.[24] At last, two years after the demise of Bartholomew Fair, here was a fair that might have pleased London's eighteenth-century officials. Rather than interrupting commerce, this festival was meant to be a 'stimulus to British industry and trade'.[25] Against such an exhibition, Bartholomew Fair certainly seemed 'infantile', as Henry Morley suggested. Yet, without the eighteenth-century controversy over fairs and their place in London, the idea for this Victorian fair might not have emerged. Through the eighteenth-century negotiation over how to best use urban space, fairgrounds were circumscribed by newer, polite ideas that they should be moral and confined. Exhibitions at eighteenth-century fairs had demonstrated how creatively packaged messages, new ideas, and national values could be popularly consumed. Once confined, as festive spaces had been with their commercialization in venues such as pleasure gardens, it became possible to populate fairgrounds with 'safe' exhibitions. Thus sterilized, fairs became a tool through which it was possible to showcase and promote elite and national values.

Notes

1 See Pamela Pilbeam, *Madame Tussaud and the History of Waxworks* (London and New York: Hambledon and London, 2003).

2 Bob Harris, *Politics and the Nation: Britain in the Mid-Eighteenth Century* (Oxford: Oxford University Press, 2002), 303.

3 Dennis Arundell, *The Story of Sadler's Wells, 1683–1964* (London: Hamish Hamilton, 1965), 4–5.

4 *Ibid.*, 5–11.

5 Rep. 146, 265, 15 June 1742 and 288, 29 June 1742. Advertisements continue to appear for the New Wells in the *Universal London Morning Advertiser*, 8–10 August 1743 and *General Advertiser* 24 August 1749. Francis Forcer died in 1743 and Sadler's Wells was taken over by John Warren. The venue went into decline for a few years. See Arundell, 15.

6 Ruth Manning-Sanders, *The English Circus* (London: Northumberland Press, 1952), 33–5.

7 *Ibid.*

8 David Coke, *The Muses' Bower Vauxhall Gardens, 1728–1786* (Sudbury: Gainsborough's House, 1978); Warwick Wroth, *The London Pleasure Gardens of the Eighteenth Century* (London: Macmillan, 1896; reprint, Hamden, CT: Archon Books, 1979).

9 See Chapter 3.

10 *A Sketch of the Spring-Garden, Vaux-Hall* (London, 1750).

11 Frances Terpak discusses Vauxhall Gardens' illuminated transparencies in, 'Free Time, Free Spirit: Popular Entertainments in Gainsborough's Era', *Huntington Library Quarterly* 70, no. 2 (June 2007).

12 *Ibid.* See also Warwick Wroth. Miles Ogborn discusses Vauxhall as a 'landscape of commodified consumption' in *Spaces of Modernity: London's Geographies, 1680–1780* (New York: Guilford Press, 1998), 122.

13 Wroth, *London Pleasure Gardens*, 288.

14 See for example Tobias Smollet, *Humphrey Clinker* (London, 1771; reprint London:

Penguin Classics, 1985) and Fanny Burney, *Evelina* (London, 1778; reprint, New York: Penguin, 1992).

15 *London Evening Post*, 22–4 July, 1760.

16 Admission fees for London-area pleasure gardens varied – at Ranelagh it cost 3 shillings on nights when fireworks were displayed or half a guinea to 2 guineas for masquerades. Vauxhall and Cuper's Gardens were typically a shilling per night, but this varied depending on the entertainment offered. Food and drink, of course, were extra. See Wroth, *London Pleasure Gardens*.

17 Middlesex Sessions of the Peace, SM/GO 26 April 1750.

18 *Ibid.*

19 Middlesex Sessions of the Peace, SM/GO 12 July 1750.

20 Middlesex Sessions of the Peace, SM/PS 13 September 1750. Sadler's Wells featured many of the same amusements as fairs, including rope dancing and tumbling. See Wroth, *London Pleasure Gardens*, 48.

21 Middlesex Sessions of the Peace, SM/PS 6 May 1751.

22 Licences for Places of Public Entertainment, Surrey Record Office, QS 2/2/1 v. 7, 8 October 1751.

23 See Anne Wohlcke, 'Policing Masculine Festivity at London's Early Modern Fairs', in T.J. Boisseau and Abigail M. Markwyn (eds), *Gendering the Fair: Histories of Women and Gender at World's Fairs* (Urbana, IL: University of Illinois Press, 2010).

24 Jeffrey A. Auerbach, *The Great Exhibition of 1851, A Nation on Display* (New Haven, CT: Yale University Press, 1999), 91.

25 *Ibid.*

Bibliography

Manuscripts

Bodleian Library, Oxford
John Johnson Collection

Bridewell and Bethlem Archives
Bridewell and Bethlem, Minutes of the Court of Governors

British Library
Book of Advertisements, British Library N. TAB 2026/25
Burney Collection

Guildhall Library
Bartholomew Fair Scrapbook, MS 1514, Guildhall Library
Diary of Stephen Monteage, MS 205
Receipts and Expenditures at Bartholomew Fair, MS 3465
Smithfield Court Book Proceedings in Court of Piepowder, 1790–1854. MS 95

Highclere Castle Archive
Pie Powder Court Rolls, St. Bartholomew Fair

London Borough of Southwark, Central Reference Library
Southwark Fair Scrapbook

London Metropolitan Archives
Middlesex Sessions of the Peace
Repertories of the Court of Aldermen
Journals of the Court of Common Council
Journals of the City Lands Committee

The National Archives
Lease Book, Earl of Warwick

Newspapers
Aplebee's Original Weekly Journal
British Journal or The Censor
British Journal, or The Traveller
Country Journal or The Craftsman
Daily Advertiser
Daily Courant
Daily Journal

Daily Post
English Post with News Foreign and Domestick
Evening Post
Flying Post or the Postmaster
Fog's Weekly Journal
General Advertiser
General Evening Post
Lloyd's Evening Post and British Chronicle
London Daily Post and General Advertiser
The Observator
Old Whig or the Consistent Protestant
Original Weekly Journal
The Post Boy
The Post Man
Post Man and The Historical Account
Read's Weekly Journal or British Gazetteer
St. James Chronicle or the British Evening Post
Universal London Morning Advertiser
The Universal Spectator and Weekly Journal
Weekly Journal or British Gazetteer
Weekly Journal or Saturday's Post
Weekly Miscellany
Weekly Packet

Ordinary of Newgate Prison
Ordinary's Accounts: Biographies of Executed Convicts. *London Lives* Online, Reference: OA17030811030811o001.

Proceedings of the Old Bailey

Surrey Records Office
Licences for Places of Public Entertainment, QS 2/2/1

Printed sources

Addison, William. *English Fairs and Markets*. London: B.T. Batsford, 1953.
Alexander, David. *Retailing in England During the Industrial Revolution*. London: Athlone, 1970.
Altick, Richard D. *The Shows of London*. Cambridge, MA: Belknap Press of Harvard University Press, 1978.
Amussen, Susan Dwyer. 'The Gendering of Popular Culture in England'. In *Popular Culture in England, c. 1500– 1850*, Tim Harris (ed.). New York: St. Martin's Press, 1995.

——. *An Ordered Society: Gender and Class in Early Modern England.* New York: Columbia University Press, 1988.

Anderson, Benedict. *Imagined Communities, Reflections on the Origin and Spread of Nationalism.* 1983. Reprint New York: Verso, 1991.

Anderson, Norman. *Ferris Wheels: An Illustrated History.* Bowling Green, OH: Bowling Green State University Press, 1992.

The Annual Register, or a view of the History, Politicks, and Literature, for the Year 1760. London, 1775.

Archer, Ian. 'Material Londoners?' In *Material London ca. 1600,* Lena Cowen (ed.). Philadelphia: University of Pennsylvania Press, 2000.

——. *The Pursuit of Stability: Social Relations in Elizabethan London.* Cambridge: Cambridge University Press, 1991.

Arnold, Dana (ed.). *The Metropolis and Its Image: Constructing Identities for London, c. 1750–1950.* Philadelphia: University of Pennsylvania Press, 2001.

Arundell, Dennis. *The Story of Sadler's Wells, 1683–1964.* London: Hamish Hamilton, 1965.

The Atheneum; or, Spirit of the English Magazines. Vol. XIII, April to October. Boston: Munroe and Francis, 1825.

Auerbach, Jeffery. *The Great Exhibition of 1851, A Nation on Display.* New Haven, CT: Yale University Press, 1999.

Authentick memoirs relating to the lives and adventures of the most eminent gamesters and sharpers, from the Restoration of King Charles. London, 1744.

Avery, Emmet L. (ed.). *The London Stage, 1660–1800.* Carbondale, IL: Southern Illinois University Press, 1960–1968.

Bach, Rebecca Ann. 'Bearbaiting, Dominion, and Colonialism'. In *Race, Ethnicity, and Power in the Renaissance,* Joyce MacDonald (ed.). Cranbury, NJ and London: Associated University Press, 1997.

——. *Colonial Transformations: The Cultural Production of the New Atlantic World, 1580–1640.* New York: Palgrave, 2000.

Bailey, Amanda and Roze Hentschell (eds). *Masculinity and the Metropolis of Vice, 1550–1650.* New York: Palgrave Macmillan, 2010.

Ballaster, Rosalind, et. al. *Women's Worlds: Ideology, Femininity and the Woman's Magazine.* Houndmills: Macmillan, 1991.

Bancks, John. *Miscellaneous works, in verse and prose, of John Bancks.* London, 1738. Reprinted in Eighteenth Century Collections Online, Gale Group.

Barker-Benefield, G.J. *Culture of Sensibility: Sex and Society in Eighteenth-Century Britain.* Chicago: University of Chicago Press, 1992.

Barker, Hannah and Elaine Chalus. *Gender in Eighteenth-Century England: Roles, Representations and Responsibilities.* London: Longman, 1997.

Bartholomew Fair: An Heroi-Comical Poem. London, 1717.

Bartholomew Fair: or, A Ramble to Smithfield. A Poem in Imitation of Milton. London, 1729.

Bartholomew Faire, or Variety of Fancies. London: Richard Harper, 1641.

Baugh, Christopher. 'Technology-Driven Entertainment and Spectacle'.

Huntington Library Quarterly 70, no. 2 (2007): Ann Bermingham (ed.), *Technologies of Illusion: The Art of Special Effects in Eighteenth-Century Britain*, 229-49.

Beattie, J.M. 'The Criminality of Women in Eighteenth-Century England'. *Journal of Social History* 8 (1975): 80-116.

——. *Policing and Punishment in London, 1660-1750: Urban Crime and the Limits of Terror*. Oxford: Oxford University Press, 2001.

Beier, A.L. *Masterless Men: The Vagrancy Problem in England, 1560-1640*. London and New York: Methuen, 1985.

Beier, A.L. and Roger Finlay. 'Introduction, The Significance of the Metropolis'. In *The Making of the Metropolis, London, 1500-1700*, Beier and Finlay (eds). London and New York: Longman, 1985.

Ben-Amos, Ilana Krausman. *Adolescence and Youth in Early Modern England*. New Haven, CT and London: Yale University Press, 1994.

Bermingham, Ann. *Landscape and Ideology: The English Rustic Tradition, 1740-1850*. Berkeley: University of California Press, 1986.

—— (ed.). *Sensation and Sensibility: Viewing Gainsborough's Cottage Door*. London and New Haven, CT: Yale University Press, 2005.

Berry, Helen. *Gender, Society and Print Culture in Late-Stuart England: The Cultural World of the Athenian Mercury*. Burlington, VT: Ashgate, 2003.

Black, Jeremy. *Eighteenth-Century Britain, 1688-1783*. Basingstoke and New York: Palgrave, 2001.

Boisseau, T.J. and Abigail M. Markwyn. *Gendering the Fair: Histories of Women and Gender at World's Fairs*. Urbana, IL: University of Illinois Press, 2010.

Bond, Donald F. (ed.). *The Spectator*. Oxford: Clarendon Press, 1965.

Borsay, Peter. *The English Urban Renaissance: Culture and Society in the Provincial Town, 1660-1770*. Oxford: Oxford University Press, 1989.

——. 'The Rise of the Promenade: The Social and Cultural Use of Space in the English Provincial Town c. 1660-1800'. *Journal for Eighteenth Century Studies* (Fall 1986): 125-40.

Bray, Thomas. *For God, or for Satan: Being a Sermon Preach'd at St. Mary le Bow, Before the Societies for Reformation of Manners, December 27, 1708*. London, 1709.

Brewer, John. *The Pleasures of the Imagination: English Culture in the Eighteenth Century*. Chicago: University of Chicago Press, 1997.

——. 'Sensibility and the Urban Panorama'. *Huntington Library Quarterly* 70, no. 2 (2007): Ann Bermingham (ed.), *Technologies of Illusion: The Art of Special Effects in Eighteenth-Century Britain*. 229-49.

—— and Roy Porter (eds). *Consumption and the World of Goods*. London and New York: Routledge, 1993.

Broich, Ulrich. *The Eighteenth-Century Mock-Heroic Poem*. Trans. David Henry Wilson. Cambridge: University of Cambridge Press, 1990.

Brown, Kathleen. 'Native American and Early Modern Concepts of Race'. In *Empire and Others British Encounters with Indigenous Peoples, 1600-1850*,

Martin Daunton and Rick Halpern (eds). Philadelphia: University of Pennsylvania Press, 1999.

Burke, Peter. *Popular Culture in Early Modern Europe*. Reprint, Brookfield, VT: Ashgate, 1994 [1978].

Burling, William J. *Summer Theatre in London, 1661–1820 and the Rise of the Haymarket Theatre*. London: Associated University Press, 2000.

Burnett, Mark. *Constructing 'Monsters' in Shakespearean Drama and Early Modern Culture*. New York: Palgrave Macmillan, 2002.

Burney, Fanny. *Evelina*. London, 1778. Reprint, New York: Penguin, 1992.

Butler, Lilly. *A Sermon Preached before The Right Honourable The Lord Mayor and Aldermen and Citizens of London at St. Lawrence Jewry On the Feast of St. Michael, 1696*. London: Brabazon Aylmer, 1696.

Cameron, David Kerr. *London's Pleasures, from Restoration to Regency*. Thrupp, Stroud: Sutton Publishing, 2001.

Carter, Philip. *Men and the Emergence of Polite Society, Britain, 1660–1800*. London: Longman, 2001.

Castle, Terry. *Masquerade and Civilization: The Carnivalesque in Eighteenth-Century English Culture and Fiction*. Stanford, CA: Stanford University Press, 1986.

Charles, Lindsey and Lorna Duffin. *Women and Work in Pre-Industrial England*. London, Sydney and Dover, NH: Croom Helm, 1985.

Clark, Alice. *Working Life of Women in the Seventeenth Century*. London: G. Routledge & Sons; New York: E.P. Dutton & Co., 1919. Reprint, New York, A.M. Kelley, 1968.

Clark, Anna. *The Struggle for the Breeches: Gender and the Making of the British Working Class*. Berkeley: University of California Press, 1995.

The Cloyster in Bartholomew Fair; or, The Town Mistress Disguis'd. A Poem. London: A. Banks, 1707.

Cockayne, Emily. *Hubbub: Filth, Noise and Stench in England, 1600–1770*. New Haven, CT: Yale University Press, 2007.

Coffey, John. *Persecution and Toleration in Protestant England, 1558–1689*. Harlow: Pearson Education, 2000.

Cohen, Michèle. 'Manliness, Effeminacy and the French: Gender and the Construction of National Character in Eighteenth-Century England', in Hitchcock and Cohen, *English Masculinities, 1660–1800*. London and New York: Longman, 1999.

Coke, David. *The Muses' Bower Vauxhall Gardens, 1728–1786*. Sudbury, Suffolk: Gainsborough's House, 1978.

Colley, Linda. *Britons: Forging the Nation, 1707–1837*. New Haven, CT and London: Yale University Press, 1992.

The compleat English secretary, and newest academy of complements. Containing the true art of indicting letters, suitable to the capacity of youth and age ... To which is added. 1. The art of good breeding and behaviour, ... 6. The comical humours of the jovial London gossips, ... With a collection of the newest play-house songs. London, 1714.

Cooke, Arthur L. 'Addison's Aristocratic Wife', *PMLA* 72, no. 3 (June 1957).

Corfield, P.J. 'Walking the Streets: The Urban Odyssey in Eighteenth-Century England'. *Journal of Urban History* 16, no. 2 (February 1990): 132–74.

Crawford, Patricia. *Women and Religion in England, 1500–1720.* London and New York: Routledge, 1993.

Cressy, David. *Bonfires and Bells: National Memory and the Protestant Calendar in Elizabethan and Stuart England.* Berkeley: University of California Press, 1989.

Crouch, Kimberly. 'The Public Life of Actresses: Prostitutes or Ladies?' In *Gender in Eighteenth-Century England: Roles, Representations and Responsibilities,* Martin Daunton and Rick Halpern (eds). London and New York: Longman, 1997.

Cruickshanks, Eveline and Jeremy Black (eds). *The Jacobite Challenge.* Edinburgh: J. Donald; Atlantic Highlands, NJ: Humanities Press, 1988.

Cruickshanks, Eveline and Howard Erskine-Hill. *The Atterbury Plot.* New York: Palgrave, 2004.

The Curiosity: or, the Gentleman and Lady's General Library. York: 1738.

Dabhoiwala, Faramerz. *The Origins of Sex: A History of the First Sexual Revolution.* Oxford: Oxford University Press, 2012.

——. 'The Pattern of Sexual Immorality in Seventeenth and Eighteenth-Century London', in Mark S.R. Jenner and Paul Griffiths (eds), *Londinopolis: Essays in the Cultural and Social History of Early Modern London,* Manchester: Manchester University Press, 2000.

——. 'Summary Justice in Early Modern London.' *English Historical Review* (June 2006): 796–822.

Davidoff, Leonore and Catherine Hall. *Family Fortunes: Men and Women of the English Middle Class 1780–1850.* London: Hutchinson Education, 1987.

Davis, Dorothy. *Fairs, Shops and Supermarkets: A History of English Shopping.* Toronto: University of Toronto Press, 1966.

Davis, Natalie. *Society and Culture in Early Modern France.* Stanford, CA: Stanford University Press, 1975.

Davis, Tracy. *Actresses as Working Women: Their Social Identity in Victorian Culture.* London and New York: Routledge, 1991.

Davison, Lee, Tim Hitchcock, Tim Keirn, and Robert Brink Shoemaker (eds). *Stilling the Grumbling Hive The Response to Social and Economic Problems in England, 1689–1750.* New York: St. Martin's Press, 1992.

De Certeau, Michel. *The Practice of Everyday Life.* Trans. Steven Rendall. Berkeley and Los Angeles: University of California Press, 1984.

Devereaux, Simon and Paul Griffiths. *Penal Practice and Culture, 1500–1900: Punishing the English.* New York: Palgrave Macmillan, 2004.

The Devil upon two sticks: or, the town until'd: with the comical humours of Don Stulto, and Siegnior Jingo: as it is acted in Pinkeman's both in May-Fair.

London, 1708. In Eighteenth Century Collections Online. Gale Group. http://galenet.galegroup.com/servlet/ECCO.

Dugaw, Dianne. *Warrior Women and Popular Balladry, 1650–1850*. Cambridge: University of Cambridge Press, 1989.

Earle, Peter. 'The Female Labour Market in London in the Late Seventeenth and Early Eighteenth Centuries'. *Economic History Review*, New Series, 42, no. 3 (August 1989): 328–53.

——. *The Making of the English Middle Class, Business, Society and Family Life in London, 1660–1730*. Berkeley and Los Angeles: University of California Press, 1989.

——. *A City Full of People: Men and Women of London, 1650–1750*. London: Methuen, 1994.

Ellis, Joyce M. *The Georgian Town, 1680–1840*. New York: Palgrave, 2001.

An Entire New Collection of Humourous Songs, Never Exhibited in any Joyous Company Whatever. London, 1750.

Erickson, Amy Louise. 'Married Women's Occupations in Eighteenth-Century London', *Continuity and Change*, 23, no. 2 (August 2008): 267–307.

Erickson, Peter and Clark Hulse (eds). *Early Modern Visual Culture: Representation, Race, and Empire in Renaissance England*. Philadelphia: University of Pennsylvania Press, 2000.

Findlen, Paula. *Possessing Nature: Museums, Collecting, and Scientific Culture in Early Modern Italy*. Berkeley and Los Angeles: University of California Press, 1994.

Finlay, R. *Population and Metropolis: The Demography of London, 1580–1639*. Cambridge: Cambridge University Press, 1981.

Finlay, R. and B. Shearer. 'Population Growth and Suburban Expansion'. In *London 1500–1700: The Making of the Metropolis*, A.L. Beier and R. Finlay (eds). London and New York: Longman, 1986.

Flather, Amanda. *Gender and Space in Early Modern England*. London: The Royal Historical Society/Boydell Press, 2007.

Fleming, Robert the Younger. *The Divine Government*. London, 1699.

Fletcher, Anthony. *Gender, Sex and Subordination in England, 1500–1800*. New Haven, CT: Yale, 1999.

Fort, Bernadette and Angela Rosenthal (eds). *The Other Hogarth, Aesthetics of Difference*. Princeton and Oxford: Princeton University Press, 2001.

Fritz, Paul Samuel. *The English Ministers and Jacobitism between the Rebellions of 1715 and 1745*. Toronto and Buffalo: University of Toronto Press, 1975.

Froide, Amy M. *Never Married: Singlewomen in Early Modern England*. Oxford: Oxford University Press, 2005.

Frost, Thomas. *The Old Showmen and the Old London Fairs*. 1881. Reprint, Ann Arbor, MI, Gryphon Books, 1971.

Fryer, Peter. *Staying Power, The History of Black People in Britain*. London: Pluto Press, 1984.

Glassey, Lionel K.J. *Politics and the Appointment of Justices of the Peace, 1675–1720*. Oxford: Oxford University Press, 1979.

Gordon, Andrew. 'Performing London: The Map and the City in Ceremony'. In *Literature, Mapping, and the Politics of Space in Early Modern Britain*, Gordon and Klein (eds). Cambridge: Cambridge University Press, 2001.

Gordon, Andrew and Bernhard Klein (eds). *Literature, Mapping, and the Politics of Space in Early Modern Britain*. Cambridge: Cambridge University Press, 2001.

Gowing, Laura. '"The Freedom of the Streets": Women and Social Space, 1560–1640'. In *Londinopolis: Essays in the Cultural and Social History of Early Modern London*, Paul Griffiths and Mark S.R. Jenner (eds). Manchester: Manchester University Press, 2000.

Gregg, Stephen H. '"A Truly Christian Hero": Religion, Effeminacy, and Nation in the Writings of the Societies for the Reformation of Manners'. *Eighteenth-Century Life* 25, no. 1 (2001): 17–28.

Griffin, Emma. *England's Revelry: A History of Popular Sports and Pastimes, 1660–1830*. Oxford: Oxford University Press, 2005.

Griffiths, Paul. *Lost Londons: Change, Crime, and Control in the Capital City, 1550–1660*. Cambridge: Cambridge University Press, 2008.

——. *Youth and Authority: Formative Experiences in England, 1560–1640*. Oxford: Clarendon Press, 1996.

Griffiths, Paul, Adam Fox, and Steve Hindle (eds). *The Experience of Authority in Early Modern England*. New York: St. Martin's Press, 1996.

Hall, Catherine. *Civilising Subjects: Metropole and Colony in the English Imagination, 1830–1867*. Chicago: University of Chicago Press, 2002.

—— (ed.). *White, Male and Middle Class: Explorations in Feminism and History*. Oxford: Oxford University Press, 1992.

Hall, Kim F. 'Object into Object?: Some Thoughts on the Presence of Black Women in Early Modern Culture'. In Peter Erickson and Clark Hulse, *Early Modern Visual Culture: Representation, Race, and Empire in Renaissance England*. Philadelphia: University of Pennsylvania Press, 2000.

——. *Things of Darkness: Economies of Race and Gender in Early Modern England*. Ithaca, NY and London: Cornell University Press, 1995.

Harding, Vanessa. 'Recent Perspectives on Early Modern London', *Historical Journal* 47, no. 2 (2004): 435–50.

Hare, Arnold and David Thomas. *Theatre in Europe: A Documentary History, Restoration and Georgian England, 1660–1788*. Cambridge: Cambridge University Press, 1989.

Harkness, Deborah. *The Jewel House: Elizabethan London and the Scientific Revolution*. New Haven, CT and London: Yale University Press, 2007.

—— and Jean E. Howard. 'Introduction: The Great World of Early Modern London'. *Huntington Library Quarterly* 71, no. 1 (March 2008).

Harris, Andrew T. *Policing the City: Crime and Legal Authority in London, 1780–1840*. Columbus, OH: Ohio State University Press, 2004.

Harris, Bob. *Politics and the Nation: Britain in the Mid-Eighteenth Century.* Oxford: Oxford University Press, 2002.

Hascard, Gregory. *A Sermon Preached Before the Right Honourable the Lord Mayor Sir James Smith.* London: William Crook, 1685.

Henderson, Tony. *Disorderly Women in Eighteenth-Century London: Prostitution and Control in the Metropolis, 1730–1830.* London and New York: Longman, 1999.

Highfill, Philip H., Kalman A. Burnim, and Edward A. Langhans. *A Biographical Dictionary of Actors, Actresses, Musicians, Dancers, Managers, and Other Stage Personnel in London, 1660–1800.* 10 vols. Carbondale, IL: Southern Illinois University Press, 1973–93.

Hill, Bridget. *Women, Work, and Sexual Politics in Eighteenth-Century England.* Oxford and New York: Basil Blackwell, 1989.

——. *Servants: English Domestics in the Eighteenth Century.* Oxford: Clarendon Press, 1996.

Hinkle, William G. *A History of Bridewell Prison, 1553–1700.* Lampeter, UK: Mellen Press, 2006.

An Historical Account of Bartholomew Fair: containing a view of its origin, and the purposes it was first instituted for, Together with a concise detail of the changes it hath undergone in its traffic, amusements, &c. &c. London: John Arliss, No. 87 Bartholomew Close, 1810.

Hitchcock, Tim. *Down and Out in Eighteenth Century London.* London: Hambledon Continum, 2007.

——. *English Sexualities, 1700–1800.* New York: St. Martin's Press, 1997.

Hitchcock, Tim and Michèle Cohen (eds). *English Masculinities, 1660–1800.* London and New York: Longman, 1999.

Hoppit, Julian. *A Land of Liberty? England, 1689–1727.* Oxford: Clarendon Press, 2000.

Howard, Jean E. *Theatre of a City: The Places of London Comedy, 1598–1642.* Philadelphia: University of Pennsylvania Press, 2007.

Hudson, Nicholas. 'From "Nation" to "Race": The Origin of Racial Classification in Eighteenth-Century Thought'. *Eighteenth Century Studies* 29 (1996): 247–64.

Hufton, Olwen. *The Prospect Before Her, A History of Women in Western Europe, 1500–1800.* New York: Alfred A. Knopf, 1996.

Hugh, Douglas. *Jacobite Spy Wars: Moles, Rogues and Treachery.* Thrupp, Stroud: Sutton Publishing, 1999.

Humphrey, Chris. *The Politics of Carnival: Festive Misrule in Medieval England.* Manchester and New York: Manchester University Press, 2001.

Hunt, Alan. *Governing Morals, A Social History of Moral Regulation.* Cambridge and New York: Cambridge University Press, 1999.

Hunt, Margaret R. *The Middling Sort: Commerce, Gender, and the Family in England, 1680–1780.* Berkeley and Los Angeles: University of California Press, 1996.

Hunter, Heidi. *Colonial Women: Race and Culture in Stuart Drama*. Oxford and New York: Oxford University Press, 2001.

Ingram, Martin. 'Ridings, Rough Music and the "Reform of Popular Culture" In Early Modern England'. *Past and Present* 105, no. 1 (1984): 79–113.

Jacob, Margaret. *The Cultural Meaning of the Scientific Revolution*. Philadelphia: Temple University Press, 1988.

——. *Strangers Nowhere in the World: The Rise of Cosmopolitanism in Early Modern Europe*. Philadelphia: University of Pennsylvania Press, 2006.

Jardine, Lisa. *Ingenious Pursuits: Building the Scientific Revolution*. London: Little, Brown and Company, 1999.

Jenner, Mark S.R. and Paul Griffiths (eds), *Londinopolis: Essays in the Cultural and Social History of Early Modern London*, Manchester: Manchester University Press, 2000.

Johnson, E.D.H. *Paintings of the British Social Scene from Hogarth to Sickert*. London: Weidenfeld & Nicolson, 1986.

Johnson, Samuel. *Lives of the Most Eminent English Poets*. New York: Derby and Jackson, 1857.

Jones, Vivien (ed.). *Women in the Eighteenth Century: Constructions of Femininity*. London and New York: Routledge, 1990.

——. *Women and Literature in Britain, 1700–1800*. Cambridge and New York: Cambridge University Press, 2000.

Jonson, Ben. *Bartholomew Fair*. ed. Suzanne Gossett. Manchester: Manchester University Press, 2001.

Jordan, Constance. *Renaissance Feminism: Literary Texts and Political Models*. Ithaca, NY and London: Cornell University Press, 1990.

Kellett, J.R. 'The Breakdown of Gild and Corporation Control over the Handicraft and Retail Trade in London'. *Economic History Review*, New Series, 10, no. 3 (1958): 381–94.

Kiaer, Christina. 'Professional Femininity in Hogarth's *Strolling Actresses Dressing in a Barn*'. In *The Other Hogarth: Aesthetics of Difference*, Bernadette Fort and Angela Rosenthal (eds). Princeton, NJ and Oxford: Princeton University Press, 2001.

Klein, Lawrence. *Shaftesbury and the Culture of Politeness: Moral Discourse and Cultural Politics in Early Eighteenth-Century England*. Cambridge: Cambridge University Press, 1994.

——. 'Gender, Conversation and the Public Sphere in Early Eighteenth-Century England'. In *Textuality and Sexuality: Reading Theories and Practices*, J. Still and M. Worton (eds). Manchester: Manchester University Press, 1993.

Kriz, Kay Dian. 'Curiosities, Commodities and Transplanted Bodies in Hans Sloane's "Natural History of Jamaica"'. *William and Mary Quarterly*, Third Series, 57, no. 1 (January 2000): 35–78.

Kyle, Chris R. 'Remapping London'. *Huntington Library Quarterly* 71, no. 1 (March 2008): 243–53.

Lake, Peter. 'From Troynouvant to Heliogabulus's Rome and Back: "Order" and its Others in the London of John Stow'. In *Imagining Early Modern London: Perceptions and Portrayals of the City from Stow to Strype 1598–1720*. J.F. Merritt (ed.). Cambridge: Cambridge University Press, 2001.

Landau, Norma, 'The Trading Justices Trade'. In *Law, Crime and English Society, 1660–1830*, Norma Landau (ed.). Cambridge: Cambridge University Press, 2002.

Landes, Joan. *Visualizing the Nation: Gender, Representation, and Revolution in Eighteenth-Century France*. Ithaca, NY: Cornell University Press, 2001.

Langford, Paul. *A Polite and Commercial People: England 1727–1783*. Oxford: Clarendon Press, 1989.

Laqueur, Thomas. *Making Sex: The Body and Gender from the Greeks to Freud*. Cambridge, MA: Harvard University Press, 1990.

Latham, Robert and William Matthews (eds). *The Diary of Samuel Pepys*, Vol. IX, *1668–1669*. Berkeley: University of California Press, 1976.

Leach, Neil (ed.). *The Hieroglyphics of Space: Reading and Experiencing the Modern Metropolis*. London and New York: Routledge, 2002.

Lemire, Beverly. *The Business of Everyday Life: Gender, Practice and Social Politics in England, c. 1600–1900*. Manchester and New York: Manchester University Press, 2005.

LeRoy Ladurie, Emmanuel. *Carnival in Romans*. Trans. Mary Feeney. New York: G. Braziller, 1979.

Levine, Philippa. *Prostitution, Race and Politics: Policing Venereal Disease in the British Empire*. New York and London: Routledge, 2003.

Liesenfeld, Vincent J. *The Licensing Act of 1737*. Madison: University of Wisconsin Press, 1984.

Lim, Walter. *The Arts of Empire: The Poetics of Colonialism from Raleigh to Milton*. Newark, DE: University of Delaware Press; London: Associated University Presses, 1998.

Linebaugh, Peter. *The London Hanged: Crime and Civil Society in the Eighteenth Century*. Cambridge: Cambridge University Press, 1992.

Lorimer, Douglas A. 'Race, Science, and Culture: Historical Continuities and Discontinuities, 1850–1914'. In *The Victorians and Race*, Shearer West (ed.). Aldershot: Scolar Press, 1996.

Lowry, Beverly. *Her Dream of Dreams: The Rise and Triumph of Madam C.J. Walker*. New York: Alfred A. Knopf: Random House, 2003.

Lynford, Thomas. *A Sermon Preached before the Right Honourable The Lord Mayor and Court of Aldermen of the City of London, at Guild-Hall Chappel. February the 24th 1688/9*. London: Walter Kettilby, 1689.

Mack, Phyllis. *Visionary Women: Ecstatic Prophecy in Seventeenth-Century England*. Berkeley: University of California Press, 1992.

Malcolmson, Robert W. *Popular Recreations in English Society, 1700–1850*. Cambridge: Cambridge University Press, 1973.

Manley, Lawrence. 'Why Did London Inns Function as Theatres?' *Huntington Library Quarterly* 71, no. 1 (March 2008).

Manning-Sanders, Ruth. *The English Circus*. London: Northumberland Press, 1952.

Marcus, Leah S. 'Politics and Pastoral: Writing the Court on the Countryside'. In *Culture and Politics in Early Stuart England*, Kevin Sharpe and Peter Lake (eds). Stanford, CA: Stanford University Press, 1993.

Margary, Harry, Lympne Castle, Kent, in association with Guildhall Library, London, *The A to Z of Georgian London*. Ashford, Kent and London: Headley Brothers, Invicta Press, 1981.

McIntosh, Marjorie Keniston. *Controlling Misbehavior in England, 1370–1600*. Cambridge: Cambridge University Press, 1998.

McKellar, Elizabeth. *The Birth of Modern London, The Development and Design of the City, 1660–1720*. Manchester and New York: Manchester University Press, 1999.

McKendrick, Neil, John Brewer and J.H. Plumb (eds). *The Birth of a Consumer Society: The Commercialization of Eighteenth-Century England*. London: Europa Publications, 1982.

Meldrum, Tim. *Domestic Service and Gender, 1660–1750: Life and Work in the London Household*. Harlow: Pearson Education, 2000.

Merritt, J.F. (ed.). *Imagining Early Modern London: Perceptions and Portrayals of the City from Stow to Strype 1598–1720*. Cambridge: Cambridge University Press, 2001.

Misson, Henri. M. *Misson's Memoirs and Observations in his Travels over England. With Some Account of Scotland and Ireland. Dispos'd in alphabetical order. Written originally in French*. London, 1719.

Monod, Paul Kléber. *Jacobitism and the English People, 1688–1788*. Cambridge and New York: Cambridge University Press, 1989.

Morley, Henry. *Memoirs of Bartholomew Fair*. London: Chatto and Windus, 1880. Reprint, Detroit, MI: Singing Tree Press, 1968.

Munro, Ian. *The Figure of the Crowd in Early Modern London: The City and its Double*. New York: Palgrave Macmillan, 2005.

A New View of London, or an ample account of that city, in two volumes, or eight sections. Vol. 2, London, 1708.

Newman, Karen. *Cultural Capitals: Early Modern London and Paris*. Princeton, NJ:Princeton University Press, 2007.

Ogborn, Miles. *Spaces of Modernity, London's Geographies, 1680–1780*. New York: Guilford Press, 1998.

Orlin, Lena. *Private Matters and Public Culture in Post-Reformation England*. Ithaca, NY: Cornell University Press, 1994.

Orlin, Lena Cowen (ed.). *Material London ca. 1600*. Philadelphia: University of Pennsylvania Press, 2000.

Orr, Bridget. *Empire on the English Stage, 1660–1714*. Cambridge and New York: Cambridge University Press, 2001.

Parratt, Catriona M. *'More Than Mere Amusement': Working-Class Women's Leisure in England, 1750–1914.* Boston: Northeastern University Press, 2001.

A Peep at Bartholomew Fair; Containing an interesting account of the amusements and diversion of that famous metropolitan carnival. London: R. MacDonald, 1837.

Peters, Christine. *Women in Early Modern Britain, 1450–1640.* Houndmills, Basingstoke: Palgrave Macmillan, 2004.

Philalethes. 'A view of the times, their principles and practices'. In *The Rehearsals*, Vol. 3. London, 1708–09.

Pilbeam, Pamela M. *Madame Tussaud and the History of Waxworks.* London and New York: Hambledon and London, 2003.

Pinchbeck, Ivy. *Women Workers and The Industrial Revolution, 1750–1850.* New York: Augustus M. Kelley Publishers, 1930. Reprint, New York: A.M. Kelley, 1969.

Plumb, J.H. *The Growth of Political Stability in England, 1875–1725.* Baltimore, MD: Penguin, 1969.

Pocock, J.G.A. *Virtue, Commerce and History.* Cambridge and New York: Cambridge University Press, 1985.

Porter, Roy. *London: A Social History.* Cambridge, MA: Harvard University Press, 1994.

——. *The Creation of the Modern World.* New York and London: W.W. Norton, 2000.

Prior, Mary. 'Women and the Urban Economy, Oxford 1500–1800'. In *Women in English Society 1500–1800*, Mary Prior (ed.). London and New York: Methuen, 1985.

Proceedings on the King's Commissions of the Peace, Oyer and Terminer, and goal [sic] delivery for the city of London; and also the goal [sic] delivery for the county of Middlesex, ... in the mayoralty of the Right Honble Henry Marshall, Esq; Lord-Mayor (London, 1744–45).

Rabin, Dana. 'Drunkenness and Responsibility for Crime in the Eighteenth Century'. *Journal of British Studies* 44, no. 3 (July 2005).

Reasons for Suppressing the Yearly Fair in Brookfield, Westminster; Commonly Called May-Fair. London, 1709.

Reasons Formerly Published for the Punctual Limiting of Bartholomew Fair. London, 1711.

Rendell, Jane. 'The Pursuit of Pleasure: London Rambling'. In *The Hieroglyphics of Space Reading and Experiencing the Modern Metropolis*, Neil Leach (ed.). London and New York: Routledge, 2002.

Reynolds, Elaine A. *Before the Bobbies: The Night Watch and Police Reform in Metropolitan London, 1720–1830.* Stanford: Stanford University Press, 1998.

Roberts, Michael. '"Words they are Women, and Deeds they are Men": Images of Work and Gender in Early Modern England'. In *Women and Work in Pre-Industrial England*, Lindsey Charles and Lorna Duffin (eds). London, Sydney and Dover, NH: Croom Helm, 1985.

Roger in Amaze: Or The Country-mans Ramble Through Bartholomew Fair. London, 1705.

Rogers, Katharine. *Feminism in Eighteenth-Century England.* Urbana, IL: University of Illinois Press, 1982.

Roper, Lyndal. *The Holy Household: Women and Morals in Reformation Augsburg.* Oxford: Oxford University Press, 1989.

Rosenfeld, Sybil. *The Theatre of the London Fairs in the Eighteenth Century.* Cambridge: Cambridge University Press, 1960.

Rossi, Paolo L. 'Society, Culture and the Dissemination of Learning'. In *Science, Culture and Popular Belief in Renaissance Europe,* Stephen Pumfrey, Paolo L. Rossi and Maurice Slawinski (eds). Manchester and New York: Manchester University Press, 1991.

Rule, John. 'Employment and Authority: Masters and Men in Eighteenth-Century Manufacturing'. In *The Experience of Authority in Early Modern England,* Paul Griffiths, Adam Fox and Steve Hindle (eds). New York: St. Martin's Press, 1996.

Rupp, Gordon. *Religion in England, 1688–1791.* Oxford: Clarendon Press, 1986.

Saville, George, *Marquis of Halifax. Miscellanies. By the Right Honourable, George Saville, Marquis of Halifax.* Glasgow, 1751.

Scanlan, Thomas. *Colonial Writing and the New World, 1583–1671.* Cambridge and New York: Cambridge University Press, 1999.

Schneider, William H. *An Empire for the Masses: The French Popular Image of Africa, 1870–1900.* Westport, CT: Greenwood Press, 1982.

Schwartz, Vanessa. *Spectacular Realities: Early Mass Culture in Fin-De-Siècle Paris.* Berkeley, Los Angeles and London: University of California Press, 1998.

Shevelow, Kathryn. *Women and Print Culture: The Construction of Femininity in the Early Periodical.* London and New York: Routledge, 1989.

Shoemaker, Robert. 'Gendered Spaces: Patterns of Mobility and Perceptions of London's Geography, 1660–1750'. In *Imagining Early Modern London: Perceptions and Portrayals of the City from Stow to Strype, 1598–1720.* J.F. Merritt (ed.). Cambridge: Cambridge University Press, 2000.

——. *Gender in English Society, 1650–1850: The Emergence of Separate Spheres?* London and New York: Longman, 1998.

——. *The London Mob: Violence and Disorder in an Eighteenth Century City.* London and New York: Hambledon and London, 2004.

——. *Prosecution and Punishment: Petty Crime and the Law in London and Rural Middlesex, c. 1660–1725.* Cambridge: Cambridge University Press, 1991.

——. 'Reforming the City: The Reformation of Manners Campaign in London, 1690–1738.' In *Stilling the Grumbling Hive: The Response to Social and Economic Problems in England, 1689–1750,* Lee Davison, Tim Hitchcock, Tim Keirn, and Robert Shoemaker (eds). New York: St. Martin's Press, 1992.

——.'Streets of Shame? The Crowd and Public Punishments in London, 1700–1820'. In *Penal Practice and Culture, 1500–1900: Punishing the English*, Simon Devereaux and Paul Griffiths (eds). New York: Palgrave Macmillan, 2004.

A Sketch of the Spring-Garden, Vaux-Hall. London, 1750.

Smollet, Tobias. *Humphrey Clinker*. London, 1771. Reprint, London: Penguin Classics, 1985.

Society for Reformation, *Proposals for a National Reformation of Manners*. London: John Dunton, 1694.

Sorrenson, Richard. 'The State's Demand for Accurate Astronomical and Navigational Instruments in Eighteenth-Century Britain'. In *The Consumption of Culture, 1600–1800: Image, Object, Text*, Ann Bermingham and John Brewer (eds). London and New York: Routledge, 1995.

Spufford, Margaret. *The Great Reclothing of Rural England: Petty Chapmen and Their Wares in the Seventeenth Century*. London: Hambledon Press, 1984.

Spurr, John. '"Virtue, Religion and Government": the Anglican Uses of Providence'. In *The Politics of Religion in Restoration England*, Tim Harris, Paul Seaward and Mark Goldie (eds). Oxford: Basil Blackwell, 1990.

——. 'The Church, the Societies and the Moral Revolution of 1688', in John Walsh, Colin Haydon, and Stephen Taylor (eds), *The Church of England c.1689–c.1833: From Toleration to Tractarianism* (Cambridge: Cambridge University Press, 1993).

Stafford, Barbara Maria. 'Presuming Images and Consuming Words: The Visualization of Knowledge from the Enlightenment to Post-Modernism'. In *Consumption and the World of Goods*, John Brewer and Roy Porter (eds). London and New York: Routledge, 1993.

Stallybrass, Peter and Allon White, *The Politics and Poetics of Transgression*. Ithaca, NY: Cornell University Press, 1986.

Steedman, Carolyn. *Master and Servant: Love and Labour in the English Industrial Age*. Cambridge: Cambridge University Press, 2007.

Steele, Richard. *The Spectator*, no. 383 (20 May 1712), ed. Donald F. Bond. *The Spectator*. Oxford: Clarendon Press, 1965.

Stepan, Nancy. *The Idea of Race in Science: Great Britain, 1800–1960*. Basingstoke: Macmillan, 1982.

Stow, John. *A Survey of London*. 1598. Reprint edn, Henry Morley, LLD (ed.), Phoenix Mill, Thrupp and Stroud: Sutton Publishing, 1999.

Strange, Carolyn (ed.). *Qualities of Mercy: Justice, Punishment, and Discretion*. Vancouver: University of British Columbia Press, 1996.

Straub, Kristina. *Sexual Suspects: Eighteenth-Century Players and Sexual Ideology*. Princeton, NJ: Princeton University Press, 1992.

Sudan, Rajani. *Fair Exotics Xenophobic Subjects in English Literature, 1720–1850*. Philadelphia, PA: University of Pennsylvania Press, 2002.

Summerson, John. *Architecture in Britain 1530–1830*. Penguin, 1953; reprint New Haven, CT and London: Yale University Press, 1993.

Swann, Marjorie. *Curiosities and Texts: The Culture of Collecting in Early Modern England*. Philadelphia: University of Pennsylvania Press, 2001.

Tague, Ingrid. *Women of Quality: Accepting and Contesting Ideals of Femininity in England, 1690–1760*. Rochester, NY: Boydell Press, 2002.

Terpak, Frances. 'Free Time, Free Spirit: Popular Entertainments in Gainsborough's Era'. *Huntington Library Quarterly* 70, no. 2 (June 2007): iv.

Thomas, David (ed.). *Theatre in Europe: a Documentary History – Restoration and Georgian England, 1660–1788*. Cambridge: Cambridge University Press, 1989.

Thomas, Keith. *Religion and the Decline of Magic*. Oxford and New York: Oxford University Press, 1971. Reprint Weidenfeld & Nicolson, 1997.

Thompson, E.P. 'Eighteenth-Century Crime, Popular Movements and Social Control'. *Bulletin for the Study of Labour History* 25 (1972): 9–11.

Tobin, Beth Fowkes. *Picturing Imperial Power: Colonial Subjects in Eighteenth-Century British Painting*. Durham, NC and London: Duke University Press, 1999.

Todd, Janet. *The Sign of Angellica: Women, Writing and Fiction, 1660–1800*. London: Virago, 1989.

Troyer, Howard William. *Ned Ward of Grub Street: A Study of Sub-Literary London in the Eighteenth Century*. London: Frank Cass, 1968.

Trumbach, Randolph. *Sex and the Gender Revolution*, Vol. 1: *Heterosexuality and the Third Gender in Enlightenment London*. Chicago: University of Chicago Press, 1998.

Underdown, David. 'The Taming of the Scold: The Enforcement of Patriarchal Authority in Early Modern England', in Anthony Fletcher, *Order and Disorder in England*. Cambridge: Cambridge University Press, 1985.

Valenze, Deborah. *The First Industrial Woman*. New York and Oxford: Oxford University Press, 1995.

Vickery, Amanda. 'Golden Age to Separate Spheres? A Review of the Categories and Chronology of English Women's History'. *Historical Journal* 36, no. 2 (1993): 383–414.

Voiture, Mons. *Familiar and Courtly Letters to persons of honour and quality by Mons. Voiture*. London, 1700.

A Walk to Smith-field: or, A True Discription [sic] of the Humours of Bartholomew-Fair, with the many comical Intrigues and Frolicks that are acted in every particular Booth in the Fair, by Persons of all Ages and Sexes, from the Court Gallant to the Countrey Clown. London: 1701.

Walker, Thomas. *The Quaker's opera. As it is perform'd at Lee's and Harper's great theatrical booth in Bartholomew-Fair. With the musick prefix'd to each song*. London, 1728.

Wall, Cynthia. *The Literary and Cultural Spaces of Restoration London*. Cambridge and New York: Cambridge University Press, 1998.

Wallis, Patrick, Cliff Webb and Chris Minns. *Leaving Home and Entering Service:*

The Age of Apprenticeship in Early Modern London. LSE Economic History Working Paper, *No. 125/09.* London School of Economics, October, 2009.

Ward, Edward. *The London Spy,* 4th edn. London: J. How, 1709. In Randolph Trumbach (ed.). *Marriage, Sex and the Family in England 1660–1800.* New York and London: Garland Publishing, 1985.

Ward, Joseph P. *Metropolitan Communities: Trade Guilds, Identity, and Change in Early Modern London.* Stanford, CA: Stanford University Press, 1997.

——. *The Politics of Carnival: Festive Misrule in Medieval England.*Manchester and New York: Manchester University Press, 2001.

Wat Tyler and Jack Straw; or, the Mob Reformers. A dramatick entertainment As it is perform'd at Pikethman's and Giffard's Great Theatrical Booth in Bartholomew Fair. London, 1730.

Webb, E.A. *The Records of St. Bartholomew's Priory and of the Church and Parish of St. Bartholomew the Great, West Smithfield.* Vol. II. Oxford University Press, 1921.

Weil, Rachel. *Political Passions: Gender, The Family and Political Argument in England, 1680–1714.* Manchester: Manchester University Press, 1999.

Wheatley, Henry. *Hogarth's London.* London: Constable and Company, 1909.

Whitfield, Peter, *London: A Life in Maps.* London: British Library, 2006.

Wiesner, Merry. 'Having Her Own Smoke: Employment and Independence in Germany, 1400–1750'. In *Singlewomen In the European Past, 1250–1800,* Judith M. Bennett and Amy M. Froide (eds). Philadelphia: University of Pennsylvania Press, 1999.

——. *Women and Gender in Early Modern Europe.* Cambridge and New York: Cambridge University Press, 2000 [1993].

——. *Working Women in Renaissance Germany.* New Brunswick, NJ: Princeton University Press, 1986.

Wilson, Kathleen. *The Island Race: Englishness, Empire and Gender in the Eighteenth Century.* London and New York: Routledge, 2003.

——. 'Citizenship, Empire and Modernity in the English Provinces, *c.*1720–1790'. *Eighteenth-Century Studies* 29, no. 1 (1995): 69–96.

——. 'The Good, the Bad, and the Impotent: Imperialism and the Politics of Identity in Georgian England'. In *The Consumption of Culture, 1600–1800, Image, Object, Text,* Ann Bermingham and John Brewer (eds). London and New York: Routledge, 1995.

Wiltenburg, Joy. *Disorderly Women and Female Power in the Street Literature of Early Modern England and Germany.* Charlottesville and London: University of Virginia Press, 1992.

Wohlcke, Anne. 'The Fair Sex: Working Women at London's Fairs, 1698–1732'. *Journal of Interdisciplinary Feminist Thought* 1, Issue 1, 2005: 1–34.

——. 'Policing Masculine Festivity at London's Early Modern Fairs', in T.J. Boisseau and Abigail M. Markwyn (eds), *Gendering the Fair: Histories of Women and Gender at World's Fairs* (Urbana, IL: University of Illinois Press, 2010).

Wood, Andy. *Riot, Rebellion and Popular Politics in Early Modern England.* New York: Palgrave, 2002.

Woodward, Josiah. *An Account of the Rise and Progress of the Religious Societies in the City of London, & etc. And of the Endeavours for Reformation of Manners Which have been made therein.* London, 1698.

Wrigley, E.A. 'Urban Growth and Agricultural Change: England and the Continent in the Early Modern Period'. In *Population and Economy*, R.I. Rothberg and T.K. Rabb (eds). Cambridge: Cambridge University Press, 1986.

Wroth, Warwick. *The London Pleasure Gardens of the Eighteenth Century.* London: Macmillan, 1896. Reprint, Hamden, CT: Archon Books, 1979.

Wunder, Heide. *He is the Sun, She is the Moon: Women in Early Modern Germany.* Trans. Thomas Dunlap. Cambridge, MA: Harvard University Press, 1998.

Index

CPSIA information can be obtained
at www.ICGtesting.com
Printed in the USA
JSHW030822130121
10887JS00001B/128